WORLD EXPLORER

ASIA AND THE PACIFIC

Prentice
Hall

Needham, Massachusetts
Upper Saddle River, New Jersey
Glenview, Illinois

Program Consultants

Heidi Hayes Jacobs

Heidi Hayes Jacobs has served as an educational consultant to more than 1,000 schools across the nation and abroad. Dr. Jacobs served as an adjunct professor in the Department of Curriculum on Teaching at Teachers College, Columbia University. She has written a best-selling book and numerous articles on curriculum reform. She completed her undergraduate studies at the University of Utah in her hometown of Salt Lake City. She received an M.A. from the University of Massachusetts, Amherst, and completed her doctoral work at Columbia University's Teachers College in 1981.

The backbone of Dr. Jacobs' experience comes from her years as a teacher of high school, middle school, and elementary school students. As an educational consultant, she works with K–12 schools and districts on curriculum reform and strategic planning.

Brenda Randolph

Brenda Randolph is the former Director of the Outreach Resource Center at the African Studies Program at Howard University, Washington, D.C. She is the Founder and Director of Africa Access, a bibliographic service on Africa for schools. She received her B.A. in history with high honors from North Carolina Central University, Durham, and her M.A. in African studies with honors from Howard University. She completed further graduate studies at the University of Maryland, College Park, where she was awarded a Graduate Fellowship.

Brenda Randolph has published numerous articles in professional journals and bulletins. She currently serves as library media specialist in Montgomery County Public Schools, Maryland.

Michal L. LeVasseur

Michal LeVasseur is an educational consultant in the field of geography. She is an adjunct professor of geography at the University of Alabama, Birmingham, and serves with the Alabama Geographic Alliance. Her undergraduate and graduate work is in the fields of anthropology (B.A.), geography (M.A.), and science education (Ph.D.).

Dr. LeVasseur's specialization has moved increasingly into the area of geography education. In 1996, she served as Director of the National Geographic Society's Summer Geography Workshop. As an educational consultant, she has worked with the National Geographic Society as well as with schools to develop programs and curricula for geography.

Special Program Consultant
Yvonne S. Gentzler, Ph.D.
Iowa State University
College of Family and Consumer Sciences
Ames, Iowa

ISBN 0-13-062986-3

1 2 3 4 5 6 7 8 9 10   06 05 04 03 02

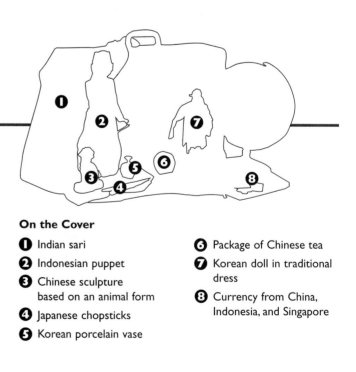

On the Cover

❶ Indian sari

❷ Indonesian puppet

❸ Chinese sculpture based on an animal form

❹ Japanese chopsticks

❺ Korean porcelain vase

❻ Package of Chinese tea

❼ Korean doll in traditional dress

❽ Currency from China, Indonesia, and Singapore

Content Consultants for the World Explorer Program

Africa
Barbara Brown
African Studies Center
Boston University
Boston, Massachusetts

Ancient World
Maud Gleason
Department of Classics
Stanford University
Stanford, California

East Asia
Leslie Swartz
Vice President for Program
    Development and Harvard East
    Asian Outreach Program at The
    Children's Museum, Boston
Boston, Massachusetts

Latin America
Daniel Mugan
Center for Latin American Studies
University of Florida
Gainesville, Florida

Middle East
Elizabeth Barlow
Center for Middle Eastern and
    North African Studies
University of Michigan
Ann Arbor, Michigan

North Africa
Laurence Michalak
Center for Middle East Studies
University of California
Berkeley, California

Religion
Michael Sells
Department of Religion
Haverford College
Haverford, Pennsylvania

**Russia, Eastern Europe,
Central Asia**
Janet Vaillant
Davis Center for Russian Studies
Harvard University
Cambridge, Massachusetts

South Asia
Robert Young
Department of History
West Chester University
West Chester, Pennsylvania

Western Europe
Ruth Mitchell-Pitts
Center for West European Studies
University of North Carolina
Chapel Hill, North Carolina

Teacher Advisory Board

Jerome Balin
Lincoln Junior High School
Naperville, Illinois

Elizabeth Barrett
Tates Creek Middle School
Lexington, Kentucky

Tricia Creasey
Brown Middle School
Thomasville, North Carolina

Patricia H. Guillory
Fulton County Schools
Atlanta, Georgia

Stephanie Hawkins
Oklahoma City Public Schools
Oklahoma City, Oklahoma

Fred Hitz
Wilson Middle School
Muncie, Indiana

Kristi Karis
West Ottawa Public Schools
Holland, Michigan

Peggy Lehman
Carmel Junior High/Carmel-Clay
    Schools
Carmel, Indiana

Peggy McCarthy
Beulah School
Beulah, Colorado

Cindy McCurdy
Hefner Middle School
Oklahoma City, Oklahoma

Deborah J. Miller
Detroit Public Schools
Detroit, Michigan

Lawrence Peglow
Pittsburgh Public Schools
Pittsburgh, Pennsylvania

Paula Rardin
Riverview Gardens Schools
St. Louis, Missouri

Kent E. Riley
Perry Meridian Middle School
Indianapolis, Indiana

Christy Sarver
Brown Middle School
Thomasville, North Carolina

Lyn Shiver
Northwestern Middle School
Alpharetta, Georgia

Mark Stahl
Longfellow Middle School
Norman, Oklahoma

TABLE OF CONTENTS

ASIA AND THE PACIFIC 1

O F S P E C I A L I N T E R E S T

Maps and charts providing a closer look at countries and regions

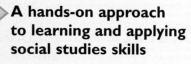

A hands-on approach to learning and applying social studies skills

ACTIVITY SHOP

Step-by-step activities for exploring important topics in Asia and the Pacific

Literature selections by Asian authors

CITIZEN HEROES

Profiles of people who made a difference in their country

Detailed drawings show how the use of technology makes a country unique

Map and statistics for every nation in Asia and the Pacific

A view of a country through the eyes of a student artist

MAPS

CHARTS, GRAPHS, AND TABLES

READ ACTIVELY

How can I get the most out of my social studies book? How does my reading relate to my world? Answering questions like these means that you are an active reader, an involved reader. As an active reader, you are in charge of the reading situation!

The following strategies tell how to think and read as an active reader. You don't need to use all of these strategies all the time. Feel free to choose the ones that work best in each reading situation. You might use several at a time, or you might go back and forth among them. They can be used in any order.

Give yourself a purpose

The sections in this book begin with a list called "Questions to Explore." These questions focus on key ideas presented in the section. They give you a purpose for reading. You can create your own purpose by asking questions like these: How does the topic relate to my life? How might I use what I learn at school or at home?

Preview

To preview a reading selection, first read its title. Then look at the pictures and read the captions. Also read any headings in the selection. Then ask yourself: What is the reading selection about? What do the pictures and headings tell about the selection?

Reach into your background

What do you already know about the topic of the selection? How can you use what you know to help you understand what you are going to read?

Ask questions

Suppose you are reading about the continent of South America. Some questions you might ask are: Where is South America? What countries are found there? Why are some of the countries large and others small? Asking questions like these can help you gather evidence and gain knowledge.

Predict

As you read, make a prediction about what will happen and why. Or predict how one fact might affect another fact. Suppose you are reading about South America's climate. You might make a prediction about how the climate affects where people live. You can change your mind as you gain new information.

Connect

Connect your reading to your own life. Are the people discussed in the selection like you or someone you know? What would you do in similar situations? Connect your reading to something you have already read. Suppose you have already read about the ancient Greeks. Now you are reading about the ancient Romans. How are they alike? How are they different?

Visualize

What would places, people, and events look like in a movie or a picture? As you read about India, you could visualize the country's heavy rains. What do they look like? How do they sound? As you read about geography, you could visualize a volcanic eruption.

Assess yourself

What did you find out? Were your predictions on target? Did you find answers to your questions?

Follow up

Show what you know. Use what you have learned to do a project. When you do projects, you continue to learn.

Respond

Talk about what you have read. What did you think? Share your ideas with your classmates.

ASIA AND THE PACIFIC

Asia and the Pacific islands form a region of extremes, with some of the driest deserts, longest rivers, and highest mountains in the world. In the Pacific east of the Asian continent are chains of islands, peninsulas, and the only continent that is also a country—Australia.

GUIDING QUESTIONS

The readings and activities in this book will help you discover answers to these Guiding Questions.

1 GEOGRAPHY What are the main physical features of Asia and the Pacific?

2 HISTORY How have ancient civilizations of Asia and the Pacific influenced the world today?

3 CULTURE What are the main characteristics of the cultures of Asia and the Pacific?

4 GOVERNMENT What types of government exist in Asia and the Pacific today?

5 ECONOMICS How do the people of this region make a living?

PROJECT PREVIEW

You can also discover answers to the Guiding Questions by working on creative projects. You can find several project possibilities on pages 188–189 at the back of this book.

1 What are the main physical features of Asia and the Pacific?

2 How have ancient civilizations of Asia and the Pacific influenced the world today?

3 What are the main characteristics of the cultures of Asia and the Pacific?

4 What types of government exist in Asia and the Pacific today?

5 How do the people of this region make a living?

A journal can be your personal book of discovery. As you explore Asia and the Pacific, you can use your journal to keep track of the things you learn and do. You can also record your thoughts about your journey. For your first entry, write your thoughts on where in Asia or the Pacific you would like to go and what you would want to see there.

EXPLORER'S • JOURNAL

Asia and the Pacific

Learning about Asia and the Pacific means being an explorer and a geographer. No explorer would start out without first checking some facts. Begin by exploring the maps of Asia and the Pacific on the following pages.

Relative Location

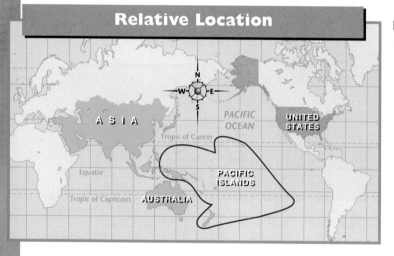

LOCATION

1. Explore the Locations of Asia and the Pacific Islands Look at the map at left. The land that is colored green is the land you will be reading about in this book. This area includes Asia, Australia, and the Pacific islands. What ocean lies between Asia and the Pacific islands and the United States? If you lived on the west coast of the United States, in which direction would you travel to reach Asia?

PLACE

2. Explore Asia's Size How large is Asia's mainland compared to the continental United States? Use a ruler to measure the greatest distance across Asia's mainland from north to south. Next, measure the greatest distance across Asia's mainland from east to west. Now make the same measurements for the United States. About how many times longer is Asia's mainland from north to south than the United States? About how many times wider is Asia's mainland from east to west?

Relative Size

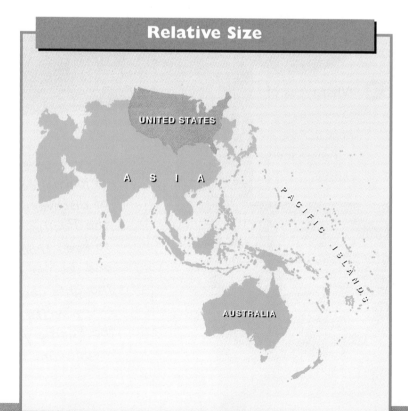

PLACE

3. Explore Countries in Asia Asia is the largest continent on the Earth. The map below shows countries in Asia. Which Asian country on the map do you think is the biggest? Asia also includes many countries that are located on islands. Find three island countries on the map below. What are their names? Asia extends far to the west and east. One country in the western part of Asia is Saudi Arabia. Name three countries that are near Saudi Arabia.

The continent of Asia also includes part of the country of Russia. Russia is such a big country that it is a part of two continents—Europe and Asia. Notice the location of Russia on the map below. Most of Russia lies in Asia. Most Russians, however, live in the European part of Russia. For this reason, geographers often include Russia in discussions of Europe, rather than in discussions of Asia.

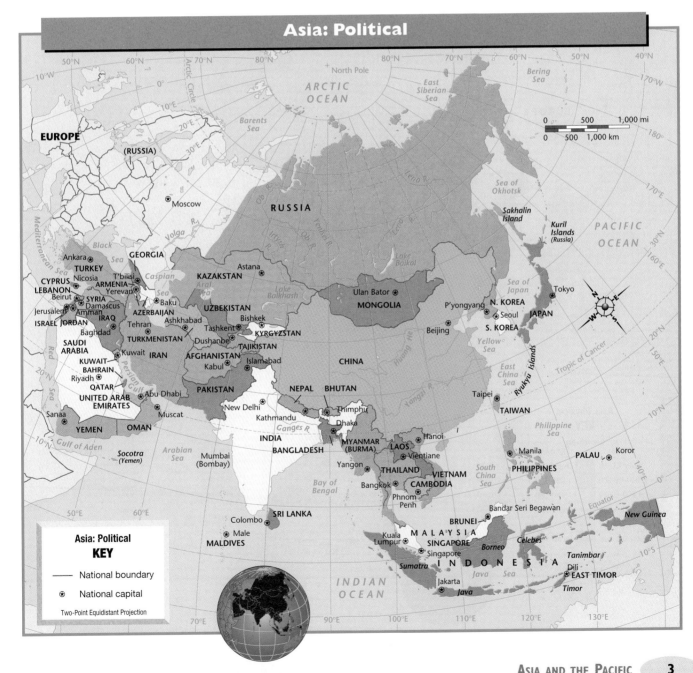

Asia: Political

Asia: Political
KEY

—— National boundary

⊛ National capital

Two-Point Equidistant Projection

PLACE

4. Identify Asia's Highest and Lowest Points

Asia is a continent of towering mountains, high plateaus, and low-lying plains. Use the elevation key to identify the highest and lowest areas on the map. What elevation do coastal areas usually have? The lowest and highest areas in Asia are also marked on the map. Where is each area located?

LOCATION

5. Find Water Bodies and Peninsulas in Asia

Asia is a region surrounded by bodies of water. Use the map below to locate and name the bodies of water from the eastern side of Asia to the western side. Asia also has several major peninsulas. A peninsula is an area of land almost completely surrounded by water. Asia's major peninsulas are labeled on the map below. What are their names?

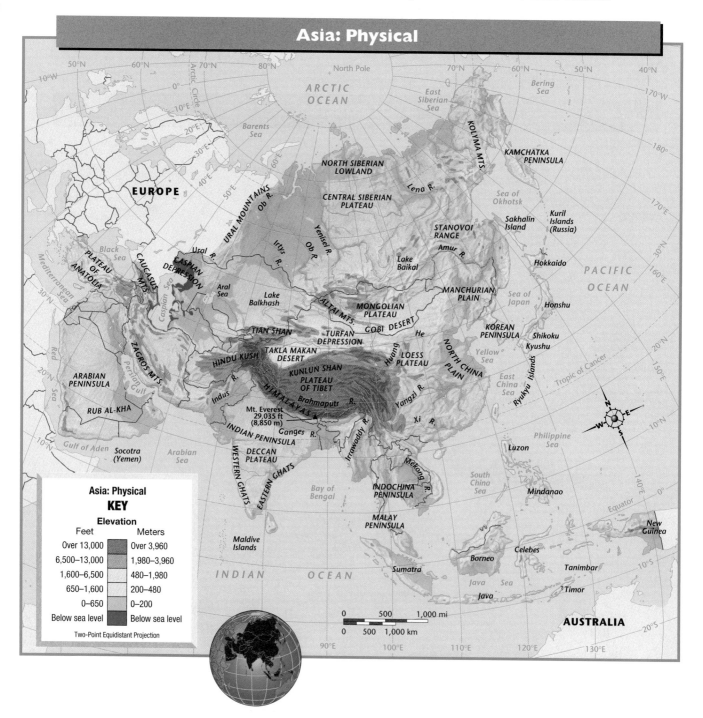

Asia: Physical

Asia: Physical
KEY
Elevation

Feet	Meters
Over 13,000	Over 3,960
6,500–13,000	1,980–3,960
1,600–6,500	480–1,980
650–1,600	200–480
0–650	0–200
Below sea level	Below sea level

Two-Point Equidistant Projection

INTERACTION

6. Follow the Asian Monsoons With Geo Cleo

Monsoons are great winds that blow across Southeast Asia and India every winter and summer. Winter monsoons blow dry air across the land and push clouds away from land toward the oceans. Summer monsoons blow clouds and moist air across the land, creating great rains. The map below shows the land use and monsoons in Asia. Use the map to trace Geo Cleo's trip across Asia.

A. My first stop is in a country that is on a peninsula. To its south is the Indian Ocean. The Bay of Bengal borders its east coast. What's the name of this country? What is the land used for in most of this country?

B. I just arrived in a large country with a long eastern coast. Nomadic herding takes place in the western half of the country. Wet monsoons blow from the south, affecting its southeastern coast. In what country am I?

C. Find the area on the map called Southeast Asia. Much of this area has a tropical wet climate. What kind of monsoon affects this area most? What two types of farming take place in this area?

GEO CLEO

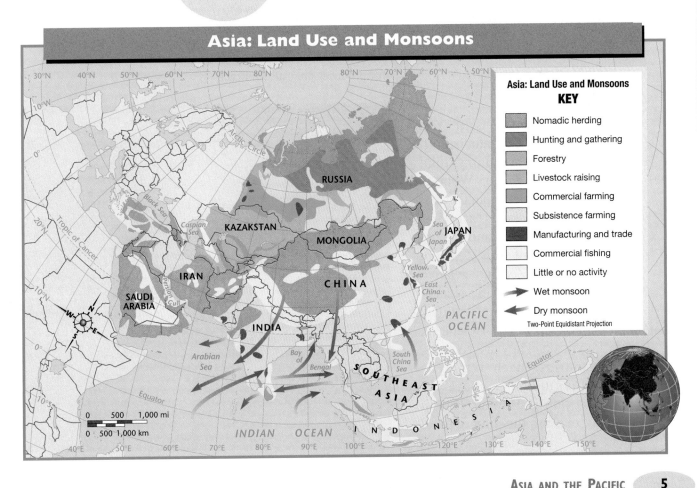

Asia: Land Use and Monsoons

Asia: Land Use and Monsoons
KEY

- Nomadic herding
- Hunting and gathering
- Forestry
- Livestock raising
- Commercial farming
- Subsistence farming
- Manufacturing and trade
- Commercial fishing
- Little or no activity
- → Wet monsoon
- ← Dry monsoon

Two-Point Equidistant Projection

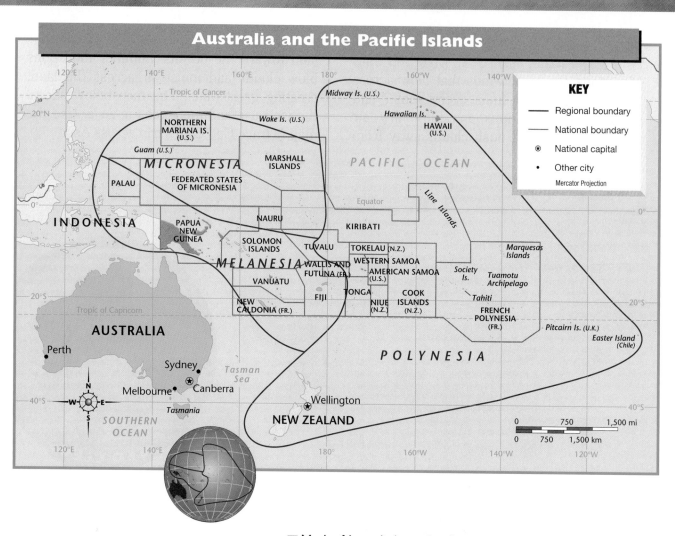

Australia and the Pacific Islands

KEY

—— Regional boundary

—— National boundary

⊛ National capital

• Other city

Mercator Projection

120°E   140°E   160°E   180°   160°W   140°W

Tropic of Cancer

Midway Is. (U.S.)

20°N

Wake Is. (U.S.)

Hawaiian Is.

HAWAII (U.S.)

NORTHERN MARIANA IS. (U.S.)

Guam (U.S.)

MICRONESIA

MARSHALL ISLANDS

PACIFIC OCEAN

PALAU

FEDERATED STATES OF MICRONESIA

0°

Equator

Line Islands

0°

INDONESIA

NAURU

KIRIBATI

PAPUA NEW GUINEA

SOLOMON ISLANDS

TUVALU

TOKELAU (N.Z.)

Marquesas Islands

MELANESIA

WALLIS AND FUTUNA (FR.)

WESTERN SAMOA

AMERICAN SAMOA (U.S.)

Society Is.

Tuamotu Archipelago

VANUATU

20°S

Tropic of Capricorn

NEW CALDONIA (FR.)

FIJI

TONGA

NIUE (N.Z.)

COOK ISLANDS (N.Z.)

FRENCH POLYNESIA (FR.)

Tahiti

Pitcairn Is. (U.K.)

Easter Island (Chile)

20°S

AUSTRALIA

Perth

Sydney

Tasman Sea

POLYNESIA

Melbourne

Canberra

40°S

Tasmania

Wellington

40°S

SOUTHERN OCEAN

NEW ZEALAND

0   750   1,500 mi

0   750   1,500 km

120°E   140°E   180°   160°W   140°W   120°W

▼ Much of Australia has a dry climate that produces dramatic landscape.

PLACE

7. Explore Australia and the Pacific Islands Australia is both a continent and a country. Find it on the map above. What is Australia's national capital? Most of the Pacific islands are tiny. Two of the larger islands make up the country of New Zealand. Where is New Zealand relative to Australia? The Pacific islands are divided into three groups. They are Micronesia, Melanesia, and Polynesia. They are regions, not countries. Each region is shown on the map above. In which region is Hawaii? Hawaii is also one of the fifty United States.

8. Trace the Ring of Fire Many active volcanoes surround the Pacific Ocean. Use the map to name countries with several volcanoes. Now trace these strings of volcanoes with your finger. Why do you think this region is called the Ring of Fire?

9. Examine Pacific Fault Lines Fault lines are breaks in the Earth's crust. Beneath the Earth's crust lies hot, liquid rock. Find the fault lines on the map and trace them with your finger. Where do you find volcanoes in relation to fault lines? During earthquakes, the Earth's crust briefly opens, and sometimes liquid rock, or lava, escapes. What might this have to do with volcanoes?

The Ring of Fire

120°E 150°E 180° 150°W 120°W 90°W

RUSSIA

ALASKA (U.S.)

60°N

CANADA

CHINA

JAPAN

UNITED STATES

30°N

TAIWAN

PHILIPPINES

MEXICO

Tropic of Cancer

COLOMBIA

PACIFIC OCEAN

Equator

INDONESIA

PAPUA NEW GUINEA

ECUADOR

PERU

AUSTRALIA

Tropic of Capricorn

BOLIVIA

30°S

CHILE

NEW ZEALAND

ARGENTINA

KEY

—— Major fault line

▲ Active volcano

Mercator Projection

0   1,000   2,000 mi
0   1,000   2,000 km

150°E 180° 150°W 120°W 90°W

EAST ASIA

Physical Geography

PICTURE ACTIVITIES

Sometime during their lives, most Japanese people climb Mount Fuji (FOO jee), a 12,388-foot (3,776-m) volcano that has not erupted since 1707. It takes between five and nine hours to travel the steep trails and reach the top. Clearly, people feel they have a connection to this mountain. To help you understand how physical geography affects the lives of the people of Japan and the rest of East Asia, do the following activities.

Make predictions
Use evidence from the picture to make some predictions about the physical geography of East Asia.

Study the picture
What thoughts do you suppose the Japanese people have about Mount Fuji? Use the picture and these lines written by an emperor in the A.D. 600s to provide clues.

"Lo! There towers the lofty
    peak of Fuji.
The clouds of heaven dare
    not cross it,
Nor the birds of the air
    soar above it.
It baffles the tongue, it
    cannot be named,
It is a god mysterious."

Land and Water

BEFORE YOU READ

Reach Into Your Background
Landforms are important no matter where you live. Make a list of all the physical features in your region that you can think of. Include mountains, hills, valleys, rivers, lakes, streams, oceans, islands, and forests. Be sure to include even those you have never seen. Which of these physical features attract visitors? Why?

Questions to Explore
1. What are the main physical features of East Asia?
2. How does physical geography affect where people live in East Asia?

Key Terms
plateau
desert
fertile
loess
archipelago
peninsula
population density

Key Places
Mount Everest
Himalaya Mountains
Yangzi
Huang He

▼ Rising 29,035 feet (8,850 m)—about five and a half miles—Mount Everest towers over a group of climbers marching across a snowfield.

It was 6:00 P.M. on September 24, 1975, when British climbers Doug Scott and Dougal Haston reached the summit of Mount Everest, on the border of China and Nepal. Their feelings of triumph and joy were mixed with concern. It would soon be night, and they would never make it back to their camp before dark. They would have to spend the night in a quickly built snow cave near the summit. But what they saw made them forget their concerns.

Looking toward the Plateau (pla toh) of Tibet, a huge highland region in southern China, they saw a vast range of small hills. Actually, these hills were mountains—some of which rose to 24,000 feet (7,315 m). They seemed so small next to Everest! Beyond those "hills," Everest cast a huge purple shadow some 200 miles (322 km) across Tibet. "The view was so staggering," Scott said, that it held them "in awe."

East Asia's Landforms

East Asia is a huge region of breathtaking landforms like Mount Everest. A single nation, China, takes up most of its land. In fact, China is the world's third-largest country in land area after Russia and Canada. Mountains, highlands, and **plateaus,** or raised areas of level land, make up much of

9

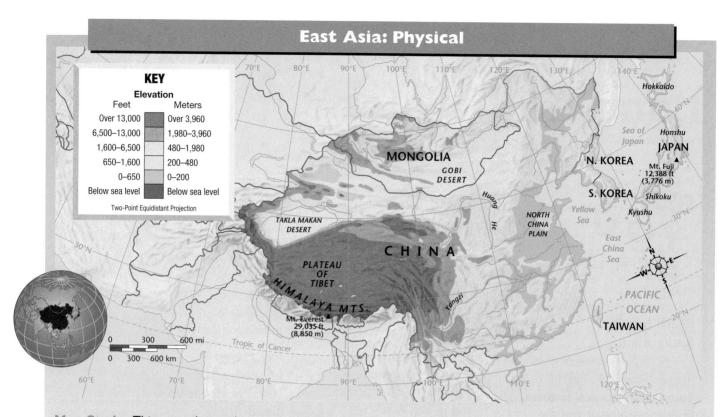

KEY
Elevation

Feet		Meters
Over 13,000		Over 3,960
6,500–13,000		1,980–3,960
1,600–6,500		480–1,980
650–1,600		200–480
0–650		0–200
Below sea level		Below sea level

Two-Point Equidistant Projection

Map Study This map shows the variety of East Asia's landforms. The Himalaya Mountains, whose name means "Snowy Range," border the Plateau of Tibet. Much of this plateau is flat, but its elevation is high. Many rivers of East Asia and other regions of Asia begin in this area. **Place** How can you tell just by looking at the map that China's greatest rivers, the Huang He and the Yangzi, flow toward the east?

READ ACTIVELY

Visualize Look at the physical map of East Asia. Visualize the landforms that you would see if you visited the region.

its landscape. The other countries of this region—Mongolia, North Korea, South Korea, Taiwan, and Japan—are mountainous like China. But they lack its wide plains and plateaus. In Japan and the Koreas, narrow plains are found mainly along coasts and rivers.

Powerful natural forces created the rugged landscape of East Asia. About 50 million years ago, a huge piece of a continent collided with Asia. It formed the land we now call India, located southwest of China. The collision caused the Earth's surface to fold and buckle, forming the Himalaya Mountains and other mountain ranges in China, as well as the Plateau of Tibet.

To the east, natural forces also shaped the islands of Japan. Earthquakes forced some parts of the country to rise and others to sink. Erupting volcanoes piled up masses of lava and ash, forming new mountains. Today, in many parts of East Asia, earthquakes and volcanoes are still changing the landscape.

A Land of Extremes China is a land of extremes. It is home to the oldest civilization on the Earth. With more than one billion people, it also has the most people of any nation in the world.

Mountains and deserts take up over two thirds of China. A **desert** is a dry region of extreme temperatures and little vegetation. As you can see from the map on the previous page, western and southwestern China are home to some of the highest mountains anywhere. The Himalaya Mountains contain Mount Everest and other mountains nearly as tall. Part of the Himalayan range is located in the area of China called Tibet. A high plateau surrounded by mountains covers much of Tibet. China's most important rivers, the Yangzi (YAHNG zuh) and the Huang He (hwahng hay), begin in this region and flow east.

The Yangzi flows 3,915 miles (6,300 km) to the East China Sea. It is the only river in East Asia that is deep enough for cargo ships to sail on. More than 400 million people live along the banks of the Huang He. It runs through one of the most fertile regions of China, the wide North China Plain. **Fertile** lands contain substances that plants need in order to grow well. The North China Plain is covered with deposits of **loess** (LOH es), a brownish yellow fertile soil.

Japan: An Island Country Japan is an **archipelago** (ar kuh PEL uh goh), or group of islands, in the western Pacific Ocean. It has four major islands and over 3,000 smaller ones. Every major Japanese city is located on the coast. As the map below shows, most of Japan's people live in coastal areas. Nearly 80 percent of the country is mountainous.

China's Deserts The Takla Makan Desert in western China is one of the world's driest deserts. Raindrops that fall here may evaporate before they touch the ground. Another Chinese desert, the Gobi, is almost twice the size of Texas. Temperatures in the Gobi can range from -40°F (-40°C) in January to 113°F (45°C) in July. In the Badain Jaran Desert, the sands make a singing sound even when there is no wind.

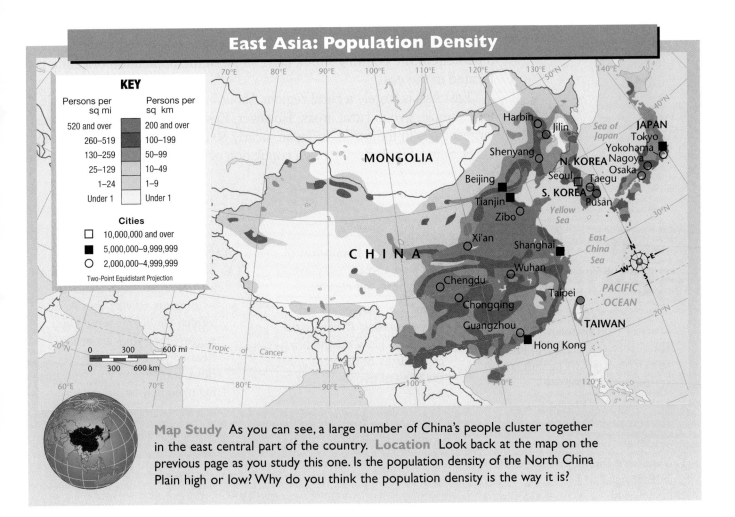

East Asia: Population Density

KEY

Persons per sq mi / Persons per sq km
- 520 and over / 200 and over
- 260–519 / 100–199
- 130–259 / 50–99
- 25–129 / 10–49
- 1–24 / 1–9
- Under 1 / Under 1

Cities
- ☐ 10,000,000 and over
- ■ 5,000,000–9,999,999
- ○ 2,000,000–4,999,999

Two-Point Equidistant Projection

0 300 600 mi
0 300 600 km

Map Study As you can see, a large number of China's people cluster together in the east central part of the country. **Location** Look back at the map on the previous page as you study this one. Is the population density of the North China Plain high or low? Why do you think the population density is the way it is?

▲ Shanghai, located near the mouth of the Yangzi, is China's leading port. With a population of over 12 million people, it is the largest city in China.

The Koreas: "Land of Golden Embroidery" Rocky peaks, narrow canyons, and rushing streams make Korea a land of great beauty. Sunlight reflecting off the water, some people say, turns the landscape into a "land of golden embroidery."

Korea occupies a **peninsula,** which is a piece of land nearly surrounded by water. The Korean peninsula stretches out into the Yellow Sea and the Sea of Japan. It is one of the world's most mountainous regions. More than 70 percent of the land consists of steep and rocky slopes. Compared with the mountains of China and Japan, however, these ranges are not very high. Since the end of World War II, in 1945, Korea has been divided into two separate countries, North Korea and South Korea.

Geography and Population

As you can see on the map on the previous page, the population of East Asia is not spread evenly across the land. Few people live in the deserts, highlands, and mountains. Yet, almost 1.5 billion people make their homes in this region. This means that people crowd into the lowland and coastal areas, where it is easier to live and grow food. These parts of East Asia have a very high **population density,** or average number of people living in a square mile (or square km).

In East Asia, level ground must be shared by cities, farms, and industries. Almost half the population of Japan is crowded on less than 3 percent of the country's total land. Most of the population of China is located in the east.

East Asia is largely a rural region. About 70 percent of China's people, for example, live in rural areas. However, East Asia also has some of the largest cities in the world. In Japan, nearly 80 percent of the people live in cities. Seoul, South Korea, has a population of about 10 million.

SECTION 1 REVIEW

1. **Define** (a) plateau, (b) desert, (c) fertile, (d) loess, (e) archipelago, (f) peninsula, (g) population density.

2. **Identify** (a) Mount Everest, (b) Himalaya Mountains, (c) Yangzi, (d) Huang He.

3. What are the major landforms in East Asia?

4. Why isn't the population of East Asia spread more evenly throughout the region?

Critical Thinking

5. **Recognizing Cause and Effect** How do the physical features of the area affect the lives of people in East Asia?

Activity

6. **Writing to Learn** You are a travel agent with a client who wants to visit East Asia. Which landforms would you suggest that your client visit? Record your recommendations and explain your reasons for making them.

Climate and Vegetation

BEFORE YOU READ

Reach Into Your Background

How would you describe the climate where you live? How does it affect what you do, wear, and eat? Make a list of five ways in which the climate affects what you do and how you do it.

Questions to Explore

1. What are the major climates and vegetation regions of East Asia?

2. How do climate and vegetation affect people's lives in East Asia?

Key Terms
monsoon
typhoon
deciduous

Key Place
North China Plain

Y ou and your family are visiting Japan in the middle of February. All of you are trying to decide where to go for a long weekend. Your brother wants to go north to the island of Hokkaido (hoh KY doh), where the skiing is perfect. Your parents, though, have had enough of winter. They would like to go to the island of Kyushu (kyoo shoo). The water there may be warm enough for swimming. What would you prefer, sun or snow?

East Asia's Climates

Even though Japan is much smaller in area than the United States, it has similar extremes of weather. People who live in the United States would have the same choices for a February weekend. They could enjoy winter sports in New England, the Midwest, or the Rocky Mountains. Or they might lie on the beach in Florida or California. In fact, much of East Asia, like the United States, has a variety of climates.

East Asia's Climate Regions Look at the climate map on the next page. What climates do you find in the eastern part of this region? A large part of eastern China has a humid subtropical climate—hot summers and cool winters with plenty of rain. To the north is an area of warm summers and cold winters. Because South Korea and Japan are almost

▼ Because it is surrounded by water, Japan has a mild climate. In this picture, people enjoy a walk through a park in Kyoto on a pleasant fall day.

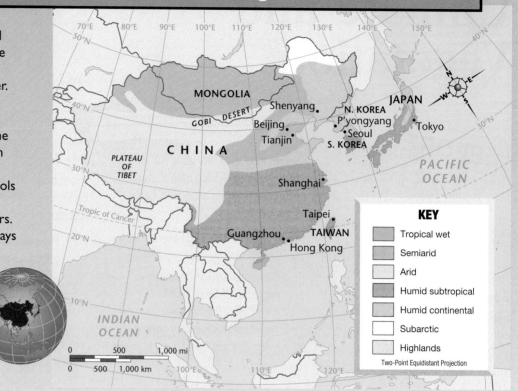

Map Study In Japan and Korea, the nearness of the ocean moderates the climate, or makes it milder. Water warms and cools more slowly than land. In summer, the ocean and the air over it are cooler than inland areas of the same latitude. This ocean air cools lands close to water. In winter, the opposite occurs. The air over the ocean stays warmer and so do places close to water. **Place** How do the climates of Hong Kong and Tokyo show the moderating effect of water?

KEY

	Tropical wet
	Semiarid
	Arid
	Humid subtropical
	Humid continental
	Subarctic
	Highlands

Two-Point Equidistant Projection

Divine Winds Typhoons twice saved Japan from invaders. In 1274, Kublai Khan, a great leader of China's Mongol people, sent a fleet of warships to Japan. The Mongols got only as far as the island of Kyushu. A typhoon frightened them back to China. When Kublai Khan tried again in 1281, a typhoon destroyed his huge fleet. The Japanese called this typhoon *kamikaze,* or "divine wind."

completely surrounded by water, summers are a bit cooler and winters are a bit warmer than in other places at the same latitude.

In contrast, the northern interior of China is very dry. Here, temperatures can range from very hot to very cold. To the south, the Plateau of Tibet has a cool, dry, highland climate. Look at the map to learn more about the climates of East Asia.

Storms in Asia Monsoons strongly affect the climates of East Asia. **Monsoons** are winds that blow across the region at certain times of the year. In summer, Pacific Ocean winds blow west toward the Asian continent. They bring rainfall that starts in June as a drizzle. The Japanese call this the "plum rain" because it begins just as the plums begin to ripen on the trees. The winds cause hot, humid weather and heavier rain in July.

In winter, the winds blow toward the east. The ones that begin in the interior of northern Asia are icy cold and very dry. In parts of China, they produce dust storms that can sometimes last for days. Where they cross warm ocean waters, such as those of the South China Sea, these monsoons pick up moisture. Later, they drop it as rain or snow.

East Asia has hurricanes like those that sometimes strike the southern coastline of the United States during August and September. These violent storms, which develop over the Pacific Ocean, are called **typhoons.** Whirling typhoon winds blow at a speed of 75 miles an hour or more. The winds and heavy rains they bring can cause major damage.

The Influences of Climate

In East Asia, climate influences everything from the natural vegetation, which is shown on the map below, to agriculture. Climate affects what people grow, how often they can plant, and how easily they can harvest their fields.

Vegetation   Much of the plant life in East Asia is strong enough to stand seasonal differences in temperature and rainfall. Bamboo, for example, grows unbelievably fast during the wet season in southern China and Japan. Yet it can also survive dry spells by storing food in its huge root system. Shrubs and many small flowering plants in the deserts of China spring up rapidly after summer rains. Then they disappear when dry weather returns. **Deciduous** (dih SIJ oo wus), or leaf-shedding, trees also change with the weather. Maples, birches, and other trees turn the hillsides of Korea and Japan gold, orange, and red once summer gives way to fall.

The Life of the People   Climate greatly affects life in East Asia. The region around the Huang He, or Yellow River, in China is a good example. The river gets its name from the brownish yellow loess that is blown by the desert winds. The river picks up the loess and deposits it to the east on the North China Plain. The loess covers a huge 125,000 square mile (32,375,000 hectare) area around the river. This plain is one of the best farming areas in China.

▲ Parts of Japan experience snowy winters, as shown in this scene by a Japanese artist.

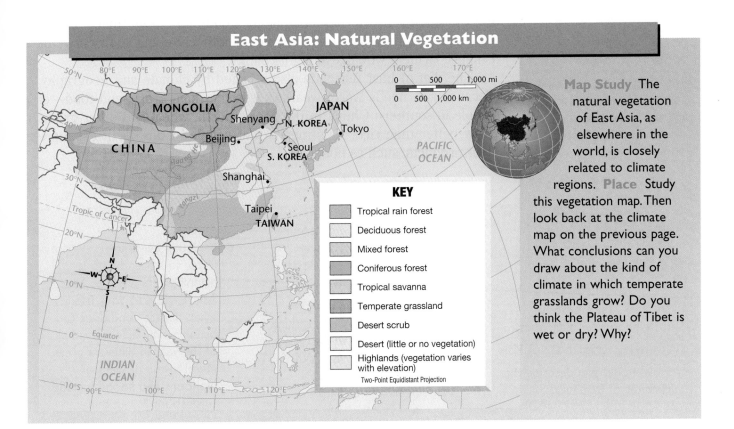

East Asia: Natural Vegetation

KEY

- Tropical rain forest
- Deciduous forest
- Mixed forest
- Coniferous forest
- Tropical savanna
- Temperate grassland
- Desert scrub
- Desert (little or no vegetation)
- Highlands (vegetation varies with elevation)

Two-Point Equidistant Projection

Map Study The natural vegetation of East Asia, as elsewhere in the world, is closely related to climate regions. **Place** Study this vegetation map. Then look back at the climate map on the previous page. What conclusions can you draw about the kind of climate in which temperate grasslands grow? Do you think the Plateau of Tibet is wet or dry? Why?

A River in Flood

Like the Huang He, the Yangzi, China's other great river, sometimes floods. In July 1996 and again in 1998, intense rains caused the Yangzi to overflow, flooding cities and farmland along its banks. The 1998 flood was the worst in 44 years, killing 4,100 people and causing about $30 billion in damages. Here, three workers visit their store in the downtown area of the city of Wuhan. Their only way to get there is by rowboat.

Critical Thinking How might a river like the Yangzi be a blessing and a curse for the people living along its banks?

Connect What foods are affected by climate or seasons in your region?

Unfortunately, the Huang He also floods. Today, a system of dams helps control the waters. But the river can still overflow its banks during the monsoons. In the past, damaging floods gave the Huang He its nickname, "China's Sorrow." The river is both a blessing and a curse for Chinese farmers who live along its banks.

The diet of East Asians is also affected by climate and geography. Because rice needs warm weather, it is the main crop—and food—of people in southern China. In the cooler north, wheat and other grains grow better than rice. This means that people in the north eat more flour products, such as noodles.

SECTION 2 REVIEW

1. **Define** (a) monsoon, (b) typhoon, (c) deciduous.

2. **Identify** North China Plain.

3. How would you describe the climates of East Asia?

4. How does climate determine what vegetation grows in different parts of East Asia?

Critical Thinking

5. **Identifying Central Issues** Where do you think a farmer moving to East Asia would choose to live? Why? Consider the effects of landforms and climate.

Activity

6. **Writing to Learn** Write a letter to a friend who is planning a long trip to East Asia. Explain to your friend what climate conditions can occur during different times of the year in different areas. Mention the dangers of typhoons and floods. Include suggestions for clothing.

Natural Resources

BEFORE YOU READ

Reach Into Your Background
Think about all of the different products you use in a day, from the alarm clock that wakes you in the morning to the plate that holds your evening snack. What natural resources were needed to make these items? Does a country have to have natural resources in order to manufacture things?

Questions to Explore
1. What are East Asia's major natural resources?

2. How can East Asia produce enough food to feed its large population?

Key Terms
import
developing country
developed country
export
hydroelectricity
aquaculture
terrace
double-cropping

On some days, oil workers in China's Takla Makan Desert regions battle stinging sand and blowing pebbles. On other days, extreme temperatures may freeze or burn their skin. Trucks sink in the sand as they collect the oil. But no matter how terrible the conditions are, the oil drilling never stops. Scientists estimate that 74 billion barrels of oil may lie beneath the Takla Makan. This amount is three times the oil reserves of the United States. If this estimate is correct, China will have enough oil to fuel its economy. If not, China will have to import oil, or buy it from other countries. This will reduce its industrial development.

▼ Hot, glowing metal rolls from a machine in this iron and steel plant in Wuhan, China. Iron ore and coal, the resources used to make iron and steel, are found not far from the city.

Using East Asia's Resources

Oil is an important natural resource. But it is just one of many found in East Asia. Although East Asia's lands and waters are filled with natural resources, some are too difficult or too expensive to obtain. The resource map on the next page will help you understand this region's natural resources.

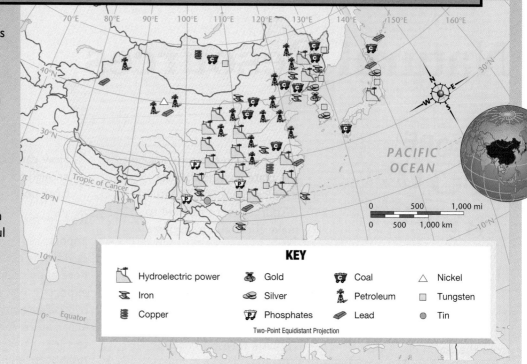

East Asia: Natural Resources

Map Study East Asia has valuable sources of energy, such as coal, oil, and hydroelectric power. Other resources found in the region are the raw materials for manufactured goods. **Place** What do the sites of hydroelectric power have in common? Why? Why are oil deposits located in eastern China more useful than those located in the west?

KEY

Hydroelectric power	Gold	Coal	△ Nickel
Iron	Silver	Petroleum	Tungsten
Copper	Phosphates	Lead	Tin

Two-Point Equidistant Projection

Predict What is the difference between a developing country and a developed country?

Minerals The two Koreas have limited mineral resources. Coal and iron, which are used in manufacturing, are plentiful in North Korea. But there is little coal or iron in South Korea, where much more manufacturing takes place. The only minerals that are in large supply in the South are tungsten and graphite. Tungsten is used in electronics. Graphite is a soft mineral used in pencils.

If South Korea could share North Korea's coal and iron, both countries would benefit. But the two do not share resources, since they do not get along. North Korea is a **developing country**—one that has low industrial production and little modern technology. South Korea is a **developed country**—one with many industries and a well-developed economy. Because of its limited resources, South Korea must import the iron, crude oil, and chemicals it needs for its industries from other countries. Nevertheless, it has become one of East Asia's richest economies. It **exports** many manufactured goods, or sells them to other nations.

Japan is a modern industrial society. Yet Japan—like South Korea—has few mineral resources. It imports vast quantities of minerals. Japan is the world's largest importer of coal, natural gas, and oil. It also imports about 95 percent of the iron ore, tin, and copper that its major industries need.

Unlike its East Asian neighbors, China has a large supply of natural resources. For more than 2,000 years, the Chinese have mined copper, tin, and iron. And along with its huge oil reserves, China has one of the world's largest supplies of coal. However, China does not have everything it needs and must import some raw materials.

Forests   Parts of East Asia have large forests. However, the nations of this region, like those in other parts of the world, have not treated their forests carefully. In the past, people gave little thought to replacing the trees that they cut down. Farmers needing to heat their homes cut wood without concern. Programs that plant new trees in all four countries may someday allow East Asia to meet its own needs for wood. At present, some countries must still import wood.

Waters   The rugged mountains and heavy rainfall of East Asia are perfect for developing water power. Using the power of East Asia's swiftly flowing rivers is important to the region's industrial development. However, building dams to collect water is costly. It is even more costly to build power plants that produce **hydroelectricity.** These plants use the power of running water to generate electricity.

The Pacific Ocean is an important resource for food in East Asia. In areas where cold and warm currents meet, tiny plants thrive. They attract a variety of fish. Some people in East Asia catch fish using poles and nets. Some even train birds called cormorants to help them fish. But fishing is also a big business. Huge boats owned by corporations catch large numbers of fish and shellfish.

East Asians also practice **aquaculture,** or sea farming. In shallow bays throughout the area, people raise fish in huge cages. Artificial reefs provide beds for shrimp and oysters. The lakes and rivers of China are also important sources of food. In fact, almost twice as many freshwater fish are caught in China as in any other country in the world.

LINKS TO SCIENCE

Saving Forests Forests once covered two thirds of South Korea. By the early 1970s, many were gone. Then the nation began its forestry program. Workers now plant new trees. They develop new kinds that can fight off diseases and pests. The program limits the number of trees that can be cut. Now, many more trees are growing in South Korea. The trees keep soil from being washed away by rain and floods.

◀▼ The Japanese raise oysters not only for food, but also for pearls. Here, a worker plants a tiny "seed" of shell inside an oyster (left). The oyster will cover it with layers of shiny material from its body to form the pearl. Only 1 out of 20 oysters will make a pearl (below).

Fertile Lands: A Valuable Resource

In order to feed its large population, East Asia needs to farm every bit of available land. With so many mountains and plateaus, only a small percentage of the land can be cultivated. Only 10 percent of China, 11 percent of Japan, and 14 percent of North Korea can be farmed. South Korea's 19 percent is about equal to the percentage of land farmed in the United States.

Land that in other countries would not be used is used with great care in East Asia. In China, Japan, and parts of Korea, farmers cut ledges called **terraces** into steep hillsides to gain a few precious yards of soil for crops. In China, farmers often plant one type of crop between the rows of another in order to grow more food. Farmers even use the sides of roads and railways lines for planting.

Where climate and soil allow it, farmers practice **double-cropping,** growing two crops on the same land in a single year. In some parts of the south, farmers are even able to grow three crops in a year. In southern Japan, rice seeds are sowed in small fields. When the seedlings are about a foot high, they are replanted in a larger field after wheat has been harvested.

In order to get the most out of their land, the farmers of East Asia have made their local conditions work for them. For example, in northern Japan, farmers raise a special rice that ripens fast. Farmers can harvest it in early fall before the severe winter begins.

▼ ▶ Terraces increase the amount of land available for farming. Fields of rice cover these terraces in China (below). Women (right) harvest tea grown on sloping hillsides in Japan.

Farming in North Korea

Like this young woman tending rice, about one third of all workers in North Korea earn their living by farming. Better seeds and more irrigation have improved farming in this country. However, a lack of good farmland and several years of poor harvests have led to food shortages.

In Japan, as in other crowded parts of Asia, cattle and other types of livestock are rare. Crops take up far less space than animals, and farmers can get more food from each acre of land by planting.

East Asian farmers will continue finding better ways to farm. They are trying to find new crops with larger yields. They also are looking for better fertilizers and better ways of managing farms. Only then will they be able to keep feeding East Asia's growing population.

SECTION 3 REVIEW

1. **Define** (a) import, (b) developing country, (c) developed country, (d) export, (e) hydroelectricity, (f) aquaculture, (g) terrace, (h) double-cropping.

2. What are some of East Asia's most important mineral resources?

3. In what ways are the waters of East Asia an important resource for the people?

4. How have the farmers of East Asia made the best use of their land?

Critical Thinking

5. **Drawing Conclusions** (a) How might natural resources help a nation to become a developed country? (b) How could a nation become developed without many natural resources?

Activity

6. **Writing to Learn** Choose one way that East Asians increase their food supply, such as double-cropping or aquaculture. Research your topic. Then write a five-minute speech to explain the process to your classmates.

Reading Actively

Steve dropped his books on the table. "I just can't seem to get this," he told his sister Lena.

Lena picked up one of her brother's books and looked at it. "What's wrong, Steve? This book is about volcanoes. I thought you were interested in volcanoes."

"I am, but there are no *real* volcanoes in that book. It's just a bunch of words on the page. It all seems to fly right out of my brain!" said Steve.

"I know what you mean," said Lena. "But if you read actively, it sticks a lot better."

Get Ready

Reading actively means using certain strategies to get the most from your reading. Four important reading strategies are described in the Try It Out section on the next page. By reading actively you will enjoy your reading more. You will also learn more. Reading actively can also help you remember what you read. This is important, because much of the information you will learn in your lifetime will probably come from reading.

What do I already know about volcanoes?

What can I learn from this reading?

Try It Out

Here are some strategies you can use to read actively.

A. Ask questions. Constantly ask yourself questions as you read. "Why is this information important?" "What made this happen?"

B. Predict. As you read, try to predict what you will read about next. This can help you focus on the topic. After you have read that part, think about whether your predictions matched what you read.

C. Connect. Try to make connections between what you are reading and other things you know or have read and seen. Put yourself in the picture. How would it feel to be part of what you are reading?

D. Visualize. Create pictures in your mind as you read. Think about what you would see if you were actually in the place you are reading about. Add your other senses. What would things sound and smell like?

Apply the Skill

The selection in the next column describes one of the world's most dramatic geographic features. Use the four reading strategies. To do this, get a blank sheet of paper and turn it sideways. Write the four strategies as headings across the top. List ideas under each heading as you read.

Try to apply the four strategies of reading actively every time you read. As you apply them, they will become a natural part of your reading. Then you will be a better reader.

The Ring of Fire

When a volcano starts to erupt, smoke and ash pour from the top. Then comes a huge explosion of hot liquid rock, which pours down the side of the mountain. This amazing event does not happen very often, but it happens in some parts of the world more than others.

The Ring of Fire is a narrow band of volcanoes that almost encircles the Pacific Ocean. It stretches through Japan, the Philippines, the Pacific islands, and New Zealand. It includes the western edge of South America, the middle of Central America, and a mountain range in the western United States.

Most of the world's volcanoes are in the Ring of Fire. So are the ones that are most likely to erupt. Scientists say there are about 540 active volcanoes on the Earth. Most of them are part of the Ring of Fire.

▶ A volcano erupts in the Kilauea crater of Hawaii Volcanoes National Park.

Review and Activities

Reviewing Main Ideas

1. Name three physical features of East Asia.

2. Where do the majority of East Asians live? Why?

3. Name and describe the type of climate found in most of East Asia.

4. How does East Asia's climate affect its natural vegetation?

5. How do both climate and vegetation affect the lives of people in East Asia?

6. What are five natural resources found in East Asia?

7. How do the natural resources of China compare to those of Japan in terms of number and variety?

8. What is the difference between importing and exporting?

Reviewing Key Terms

Use each key term below in a sentence that shows the meaning of the term.

1. plateau
2. desert
3. loess
4. archipelago
5. peninsula
6. population density
7. monsoon
8. typhoon
9. deciduous
10. developing country
11. developed country
12. hydroelectricity
13. aquaculture
14. terrace
15. double-cropping

Critical Thinking

1. **Cause and Effect** How might Japan's lack of natural resources affect its economy?

2. **Drawing Conclusions** About two thirds of China's land is covered by mountains and deserts. What conclusion about China's farmland can you draw from this?

3. **Drawing Conclusions** The Yangzi is the only river in East Asia that is deep enough for cargo ships to sail on. How might this affect the population density of the lands surrounding the river? Of East Asia?

Graphic Organizer

Copy the diagram onto a sheet of paper. Then fill it in so that it compares and contrasts the natural resources of China and Japan.

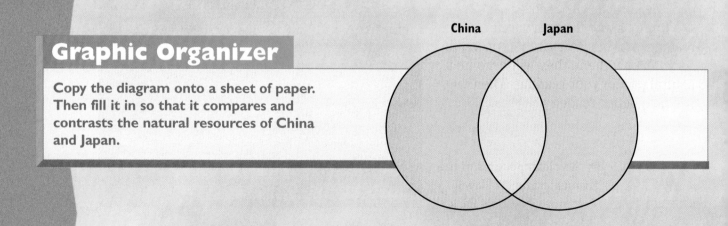

China   Japan

Map Activity

East Asia

For each place listed below, write the letter from the map that shows its location.

1. Mount Fuji

2. Mount Everest

3. North China Plain

4. Himalaya Mountains

5. Yangzi

6. Huang He

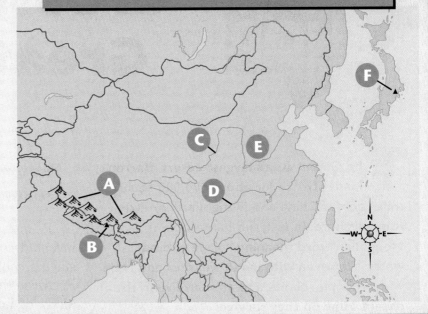

Writing Activity

Writing a Pamphlet

China's Huang He has created rich soil for the surrounding lands. This makes these lands the best agricultural areas in China. However, China's monsoon season causes the river to overflow frequently. Do some research to find out how people protect fields from flood damage. Write a pamphlet that contains suggestions for the farmers who live along the banks of the Huang He to protect their crops.

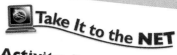

Take It to the NET

Activity Research the volcanoes found in Japan. Write a science news article on the volcano you find most interesting. For help in completing this activity, visit www.phschool.com.

Chapter 1 Self-Test To review what you have learned, take the Chapter 1 Self-Test and get instant feedback on your answers. Go to www.phschool.com to take the test.

Skills Review

Turn to the Skills Activity.

Review the four strategies for reading actively. Make notes as you ask questions, predict, connect, and visualize while reading this section. Explain how these strategies helped you read better.

How Am I Doing?

Answer these questions to help you check your progress.

1. Can I identify the main geographic features of East Asia?

2. Do I understand how climate has affected the vegetation and population of East Asia?

3. Can I identify the most important natural resources in East Asia?

4. What information from this chapter can I include in my journal?

ACTIVITY SHOP

Crossing the Great Gobi

The Gobi is Asia's largest desert. Barren lands stretch for about 500,000 square miles across China and Mongolia. Very little rain falls here. In fact, the name *Gobi* is a Mongolian word meaning "place without water." Yet even with harsh weather and little water, people, plants, and animals live in the desert. How do they survive?

Purpose

In this activity, you will plan a trip through the Gobi to study desert survival. As you learn more about life in the desert, you will plan for your own survival as well. Look in your library for books on deserts, their vegetation and animal life, books on East Asia, and books on the Gobi in particular.

Investigate Desert Life

People who live in desert climates have invented special ways of preserving water and staying cool during the day and warm at night. Research the people who live in the Gobi. What kinds of houses do they build? How do they dress? What advice might they give someone not used to desert life? Write a list of ways that people live in the desert. Draw pictures to illustrate your list.

Chart Your Trip

How many days' worth of supplies should you pack for your trek? Come up with an estimate and justify your answer. First, find and trace a map of the Gobi. Draw a dotted line on the map to chart the path of your trip. Now, use the map scale to determine how many miles you are planning to travel. To decide how many miles to travel each day, answer these questions. Write your answers on a sheet of paper.

- How many hours a day will you need for rest and for your research? How many hours are left for travel?
- How many miles an hour do you think your truck can cross the desert sand?
- What might slow you down? How much time will you plan for emergencies?

Links to Other Subjects

Studying desert peoples .... **Science, Art**

Calculating travel rates and distances .... **Math**

Researching desert health hazards ..... **Health**

Writing a travel journal ...... **Language Arts**

Drawing a desert plant
or an animal .... **Art, Science**

Protect Your Health

Desert travel can be hazardous to your health. Some dangers include heatstroke, sunburn, and dehydration. What are the symptoms of each? How can you avoid or treat each condition? Research these questions. Then write a fact sheet on health tips for desert travel.

Keep a Travel Journal

Research the Gobi's animals, plants, people, land, and weather. Then use the information you found to write a journal about your desert travel. Describe what you think it feels like to spend nights and days in the desert. What discoveries, setbacks, or dangers might you encounter? Give details using all your senses—sight, sound, smell, taste, touch.

Draw a Desert Plant or an Animal

Desert species have traits that help them survive. Research one animal or plant species that lives in the Gobi. What helps it survive in the dry desert? Draw a picture of this plant or animal. Include captions to point out special features adapted to desert life.

ANALYSIS AND CONCLUSION

Write a summary describing what you learned about the Gobi while planning your trip. Be sure to answer the following questions in your summary.

1. What steps would you take to be sure of your own survival in the desert? Why are these steps important?

2. How are people, animals, and plants that live in the Gobi able to survive the desert climate?

3. What are some reasons people might want to visit the desert in spite of its dangers?

CHAPTER 2

EAST ASIA

Cultures and History

PICTURE ACTIVITIES

Perhaps because East Asian cultures are among the oldest in the world, the people of East Asia cherish their past. To help you understand how the past and present mix in East Asia, look at this picture of a boat with the city of Hong Kong in the background. Do the following activities.

Study the picture
Identify what is old and what is new in the picture. Would you rather explore the old or the new? Why?

Make up a title
Write a short title for the picture that expresses the contrasts between the old and new things you see.

Historic Traditions

Reach Into Your Background

Each day, you come into contact with many cultures that may be different from your own. Make a list of the foods, words, clothing, entertainers, sports, and types of music from other countries that you enjoy.

Questions to Explore

1. What are some of ancient East Asia's major achievements?

2. How did Chinese culture influence the rest of East Asia?

Key Terms

civilization
irrigate
emperor
dynasty

migration
clan
cultural diffusion
communist

Key People and Places

Confucius
Commodore Matthew Perry
Great Wall of China
Middle Kingdom

O ver two thousand years ago, one of the most important thinkers of ancient times gave this advice to his pupils:

> "L et the ruler be a ruler and the subject a subject.
>
> . . .
>
> A youth, when at home, should act with respect to his parents, and, abroad, be respectful to his elders. He should be earnest and truthful. He should overflow in love to all, and cultivate the friendship of the good.
>
> . . .
>
> When you have faults, do not fear to abandon them."

These words are from the teachings of Confucius (kun FYOO shus), who lived in China about 500 B.C. He taught that everyone has duties and responsibilities. If a person acts correctly, the result will be peace and harmony. Confucius' ideas helped China's government run smoothly for years and Chinese culture to last for centuries.

▼ Chinese people all over the world still admire Confucius. This statue of Confucius stands in the Chinatown section of New York City.

29

East Asia's Achievements

Regions of Asia and Africa produced civilizations earlier than China's. A **civilization** has cities, a central government, workers who do specialized jobs, and social classes. Of the world's early civilizations, only China's has survived. This makes it the oldest continuous civilization in the world. Korea and Japan are not as old. But they, too, have long, important histories.

The Glory That Was China   For much of its history, China had little to do with the rest of the world. The Great Wall of China was begun in the 600s B.C. as many small walls between warring states. Over time it became a symbol of China's desire to keep the world at a distance. In fact, Chinese leaders had such pride that they named their country the Middle Kingdom. To them, it was the center of the universe.

The Chinese had reason to believe that their civilization was the greatest in the world. They invented paper, gunpowder, silk weaving, the magnetic compass, the printing press, clockwork, the spinning wheel, and the water wheel. Chinese engineers were experts at digging canals, building dams and bridges, and setting up irrigation systems. To **irrigate** means to supply dry land with water by using ditches or canals. Chinese scientists made major discoveries in mathematics and medicine.

Starting in ancient times, China was governed by an **emperor**—a ruler of widespread lands and groups of people. A series of rulers from the same family was a **dynasty.** Chinese history is described by dynasties. The time line below highlights some important events and cultural contributions of several dynasties.

Ask Questions Think of three questions you might ask about the achievements of China.

▼ The Chinese made many important achievements during the Han dynasty. When did the Han rule China?

Major Dynasties of China

| 1500 B.C. | 1000 B.C. | 500 B.C. | A.D. 1 | A.D. 500 | A.D. 1000 | A.D. 1500 |

Shang
1700 B.C.–1100 B.C.
• Writing
• Wheeled chariots

Zhou
1100 B.C.–256 B.C.
• Confucius lived.
• First canals built

Qin
221 B.C.–206 B.C.
• China took its name from this dynasty.
• Great Wall built
• Standard weights and measures

Han
206 B.C.–A.D. 220
• Chinese trace their ancestry to this dynasty.
• Paper, compass, seismograph invented
• Buddhism comes to China from India.

Tang
A.D. 618–A.D. 907
• Art and poetry flourish.
• Chinese goods flow to Southwest Asia and Europe.
• First book printed

Song
A.D. 960–A.D. 1279
• Block printing
• Paper money

Ming
A.D. 1368–A.D. 1644
• Artists and philosophers make China the most civilized country in the world.

Qing
A.D. 1644–A.D. 1911
• Last dynasty ends with Emperor Pu Yi.

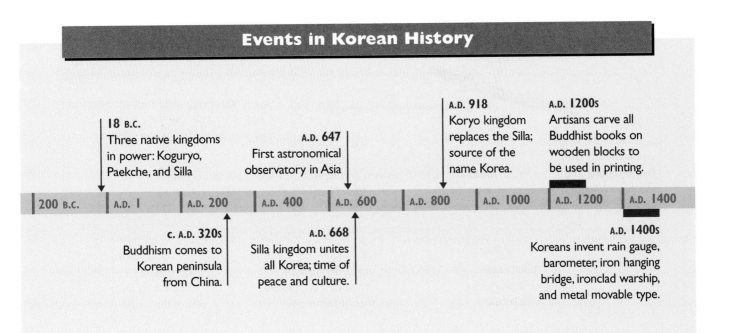

Events in Korean History

18 B.C.
Three native kingdoms in power: Koguryo, Paekche, and Silla

A.D. 647
First astronomical observatory in Asia

A.D. 918
Koryo kingdom replaces the Silla; source of the name Korea.

A.D. 1200s
Artisans carve all Buddhist books on wooden blocks to be used in printing.

200 B.C. | A.D. 1 | A.D. 200 | A.D. 400 | A.D. 600 | A.D. 800 | A.D. 1000 | A.D. 1200 | A.D. 1400

c. A.D. 320s
Buddhism comes to Korean peninsula from China.

A.D. 668
Silla kingdom unites all Korea; time of peace and culture.

A.D. 1400s
Koreans invent rain gauge, barometer, iron hanging bridge, ironclad warship, and metal movable type.

▲ Although Chinese culture influenced that of Korea, the Koreans made contributions of their own. What were some of them?

Korea and China Although Korea's original settlers came from north-central Asia, the country's history is closely tied to China. Around 1200 B.C., during a time of troubles in China, some Chinese moved to the Korean Peninsula. Later, other Chinese settled in the southern part of the peninsula. These migrations led to a transfer of Chinese knowledge and customs to the Koreans. A **migration** is a movement of people from one country or region to another to make a new home.

People have lived on the Korean Peninsula for thousands of years. But not until the Silla people gained control was the peninsula unified. The time line above highlights some of the major events and contributions during the country's early history.

Years of Japanese Isolation For much of Japan's history, **clans,** or groups of families who claimed a common ancestor, fought each other for land and power. Around A.D. 500, one clan, the Yamato (yah mah toh), became powerful. Claiming descent from the sun goddess, Yamato leaders took the title of emperor. Many emperors sat on Japan's throne. For a long time they had little power. Instead, shoguns (shoh gunz), or "emperor's generals," made the laws. Warrior nobles, the samurai (sam uh ry), enforced these laws. Together, the shoguns and samurai ruled Japan for more than 700 years.

At first, the Japanese favored trade with their East Asian neighbors. This did not last long, however. Japanese leaders came to believe that isolation, or separation, was the best way to keep the country united. Thus, Japan was isolated from the outside world for many hundreds of years. Although Japanese culture grew, the rest of the world knew little about it until Japan became interested in Western inventions. Japan finally was forced to trade with the West in the 1800s. The time line on the next page shows some key events in Japanese history.

▲ This comic mask is worn in *no* plays, a traditional form of Japanese drama.

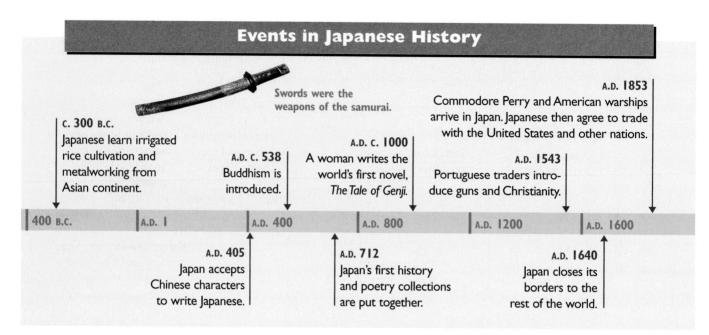

Events in Japanese History

Swords were the weapons of the samurai.

c. 300 B.C.
Japanese learn irrigated rice cultivation and metalworking from Asian continent.

A.D. c. 538
Buddhism is introduced.

A.D. c. 1000
A woman writes the world's first novel, *The Tale of Genji*.

A.D. 1543
Portuguese traders introduce guns and Christianity.

A.D. 1853
Commodore Perry and American warships arrive in Japan. Japanese then agree to trade with the United States and other nations.

| 400 B.C. | A.D. 1 | A.D. 400 | A.D. 800 | A.D. 1200 | A.D. 1600 |

A.D. 405
Japan accepts Chinese characters to write Japanese.

A.D. 712
Japan's first history and poetry collections are put together.

A.D. 1640
Japan closes its borders to the rest of the world.

▲ Japan has interacted with outside nations except for one period in its history. When was this? How long did it last?

West Meets East The West has been greatly influenced by the cultures of East Asia. Noodles and other Chinese food long ago became part of Western cooking. Eastern art influenced the design of Western architecture, gardens, furniture, and fabrics. Traders imported porcelain, pottery made from a fine white clay, from China, Japan, and Korea. Europeans and Americans called it "china" and tried to copy it.

The Spread of Culture

In ancient times, China was far ahead of the rest of the world in inventions and discoveries. Thus, it is not surprising that many Chinese discoveries spread to Korea and Japan. This **cultural diffusion,** or spreading of ideas, happened early. The teachings of Confucius were among the first ideas to be passed along. The religion of Buddhism (BOOD izm), which China had adopted from India, later spread to Korea and Japan.

Cultural diffusion also occurred between other lands. It was not always friendly. For example, Korean pottery so impressed the Japanese that they captured villages of potters and took them to Japan after an invasion in 1598. East Asian culture, as a whole, owes much to the early exchanges among China, Japan, and Korea. In each case, however, the countries changed what they borrowed until the tradition became their own.

Westerners in East Asia

Although East Asia was not interested in the rest of the world, the world was interested in East Asia. Marco Polo, an Italian merchant, is believed to have visited China in the 1200s. When he returned to Italy, he told people about China. He described a royal palace with walls covered in gold and silver. He told tales about people burning black rocks (coal) to heat their homes. His stories excited the imaginations and the greed of European monarchs and merchants.

The Opening of East Asia In spite of the efforts of China and Japan to remain isolated, Western nations could not be kept away. In the 1800s, Europeans and Americans began to produce great amounts of manufactured goods. East Asia seemed to be a good place to sell these products. Western trading ships began to sail to Asian ports.

Paper as We Know It

Cai Lun, an official of the Han dynasty, is said to have invented paper as we know it about 2,000 years ago. He made it from the bark of the mulberry tree or silk rags. In 1957, scientists discovered a small piece of paper in a Chinese tomb. It might have been made as early as 140 B.C.

Chinese papermakers first chopped up plants or other materials such as hemp rope or old fishing nets. They soaked these materials in water.

Workers pounded the mixture of water-soaked materials until it turned into a watery mush called pulp.

Workers dipped a mesh screen into the pulp. Water drained from the screen, leaving a layer of damp pulp on top. When the pulp dried, it was peeled off the screen to make a sheet of paper. Papermakers used starch or gelatin to strengthen the paper.

In 1853, U.S. Commodore Matthew Perry sailed with four warships to Japan to force it to grant trading rights to the United States. In a few years, the Japanese learned more about Western ways and inventions. They adapted what was useful to them, while preserving their own culture. Japan soon became the strongest nation in Asia.

The opening up of China to Europe was different. Foreign countries wanted to control parts of China and its wealth. As foreign powers entered China, it became clear that the country was not strong enough

Connect What do you think it would be like to live in a country isolated from others?

to protect itself. The British, French, Dutch, Russians, and Japanese gained control over parts of China. Other countries then feared losing the opportunity to share in China's riches. In 1899, the United States announced the policy that China should be open for trade with all nations equally. For a while, nations halted their efforts to divide up China.

New Forces in the Twentieth Century   Many Chinese blamed the emperor for the growing foreign influence. In 1911, revolution broke out in China. The rule of emperors ended, and a republic was set up.

Meanwhile, Japan was becoming more powerful. As Japan's industry grew, its leaders sought to control other Asian countries. They wanted to make sure that Japan would have resources to fuel its industries. Japanese attacks on other Asian and Pacific lands led to World War II in East Asia. After years of fighting, the United States and its allies defeated Japan. The United States then helped Japan recover and create an elected government.

After World War II, civil war broke out in China between two groups. The Nationalists wanted to strengthen China so it could manage its own affairs without other nations. The Communists wanted to break the power of the landlords and other wealthy people and drive out all foreign influences. The Communists won the civil war in 1949 and made China a **communist** nation. This means that the government owns large industries, businesses, and most of the country's land.

After World War II, Korea found itself divided into two parts. Communists ruled North Korea. South Korea turned to Western nations for support. In 1950, the two Koreas exploded into a bloody civil war. North Korea invaded South Korea. The United States sent 480,000 troops to help South Korea. The war dragged on for three years, killing about 37,000 U.S. soldiers. More than 2 million Korean soldiers and civilians lost their lives. Neither side won. The battle line at the end of the war, in 1953, remains the border between the two Koreas today.

SECTION 1 REVIEW

1. **Define** (a) civilization, (b) irrigate, (c) emperor, (d) dynasty, (e) migration, (f) clan, (g) cultural diffusion, (h) communist.

2. **Identify** (a) Confucius, (b) Commodore Matthew Perry, (c) Great Wall of China, (d) Middle Kingdom.

3. In what ways was ancient China an advanced civilization?

4. Explain how East Asian countries interacted with the West.

Critical Thinking

5. **Expressing Problems Clearly** Why would isolating a country from its neighbors help keep it united?

Activity

6. **Writing to Learn** Research an invention or a discovery of either the Chinese or the Koreans. Write and illustrate an advertisement for it that tells what it is and how it works. Explain the difference it might make in people's lives or why it is important.

People and Cultures

BEFORE YOU READ

Reach Into Your Background

Do you or a friend own something that has been handed down for generations? Perhaps it is something that was owned by a grandparent or great-grandparent. Perhaps someone bought it on a long-ago trip. List some of the ways in which people keep connections with earlier times.

Questions to Explore

1. How does East Asia's past affect modern-day culture?

2. Who are East Asia's many peoples?

Key Terms

commune   homogeneous
dialect   ethnic group
nomad

The Chinese game *weiqi* (wy chee) has ancient cultural roots. One player has 181 black stones standing for night. The other has 180 white stones standing for day. The goal is to surround and capture the opponent's stones. But to the Chinese, weiqi is more than a game. For centuries, Buddhists have used it to discipline the mind and show behavior. Masters can look at a game record to see exactly when players became too greedy and doomed themselves to defeat. Today, you can see people playing this ancient game in any park in China.

Tradition and Change

In East Asia, tradition mixes with change in a thousand ways. Businesspeople in Western suits greet each other in the traditional way—with a bow. Ancient palaces stand among skyscrapers. Everywhere in Japan, China, and the Koreas, reminders of the past mingle with activities of the present.

Communism and Change in China

When the Communists came into power in 1949, they began to make major changes in the Chinese way of life. To begin with, the government ended the old system of land ownership. It created **communes**, communities in which land is held in common and where members live and work together.

▼ This woman from Tibet, in the western part of China, reflects the traditions of her ethnic group in her headdress, jewelry, and the way she carries her baby.

The Ideal Family

YOU SHENG YOU YU ZHEN XING ZHONG HUA

The Chinese government uses billboard advertising to encourage people to limit the size of their families. **Critical Thinking** Why does the Chinese government want people to have small families?

Many Chinese farmers were bitter at losing their land. They were accustomed to living in family groups that worked together in small fields. The farmers resisted the communes. Food production fell, and China suffered terrible food shortages. Only when the government allowed some private ownership did food production grow.

The Communists also tried to slow China's population growth by attacking the idea of large families. Here, they had more success. Chinese couples are supposed to wait until their late twenties to marry. They are not supposed to have more than one child per family. Chinese families with only one child receive special privileges.

Under communism, the position of women has improved. Traditionally, Chinese women worked at home. Now most work in full-time jobs outside the home. One of the first laws the Communists passed allowed a woman to own property, choose her husband, and get a divorce. However, men still hold most of the power, and many marriages are still arranged.

The mixture of old and new affects the lives of all Chinese. The old traditions are strongest in rural areas. Yet even in the cities, a visitor sees examples of the old China. The streets are filled with three-wheeled cabs pedaled like tricycles. Tiny shops sell traditional cures made from herbs. These shops exist side by side with modern hospitals. Even as they are modernizing, the Chinese continue to respect their past.

Changing Korea   In Korea, daily life is still affected by long-standing traditions. The family is still important, though the average family is smaller today. A family still looks after the welfare of all its members. In rural areas, grandparents, parents, aunts, and uncles may live in one household. In the cities, a family is usually just parents and children.

As in China, modern ways are much more visible in urban areas. Most Koreans wear modern clothes. They save their traditional dress of trousers or a long skirt with a long jacket for holidays. Also, as is true all over the world, the role of women has changed. Earlier, women had few opportunities. Today, women can work and vote.

Japan's Blend of Old and New   Japan is the most up-to-date of the East Asian countries. Japanese work at computers in skyscrapers and ride home on speedy trains. Once they reach home, however, they may follow traditional customs. For example, they may change into kimonos, or robes. They may sit on mats at a low table to have dinner. Japanese students dress like students in the United States, though some wear the headbands of samurai warriors to show that they are getting ready for a challenge.

The Japanese use more modern technology than the rest of East Asia. Still, they try hard to preserve the past. The help given to Japanese artists is a good example. Some years ago, the Japanese saw that traditional arts and crafts were dying out. The government began offering lifetime salaries to some artists. The main task of these artists is to teach young people who will keep the ancient arts alive. Respected by all, these artists are referred to as National Living Treasures.

▼ In Beijing opera, an old form of Chinese drama, actors in rich costumes stage traditional myths and legends.

East Asia's People

East Asian cultures embrace both the old and the new. Within each of the area's countries, however, the people tend to share a single culture.

Connect What do you think it would be like to live in a country with a homogeneous population?

China: The Han and Others About 19 of every 20 Chinese people trace their ancestry to the Han, the people of China's second dynasty. As you can see on the map below, the Han live mostly in eastern and central China. Although they have a common language, they speak different **dialects,** or forms of a single language, from region to region. The other Chinese come from 55 different minority groups. These groups live mainly in the western parts of China.

Korea and Japan: Few Minorities Historians believe that the ancient Koreans were descended from many different groups of nomads from Mongolia. **Nomads** are people who have no settled home.

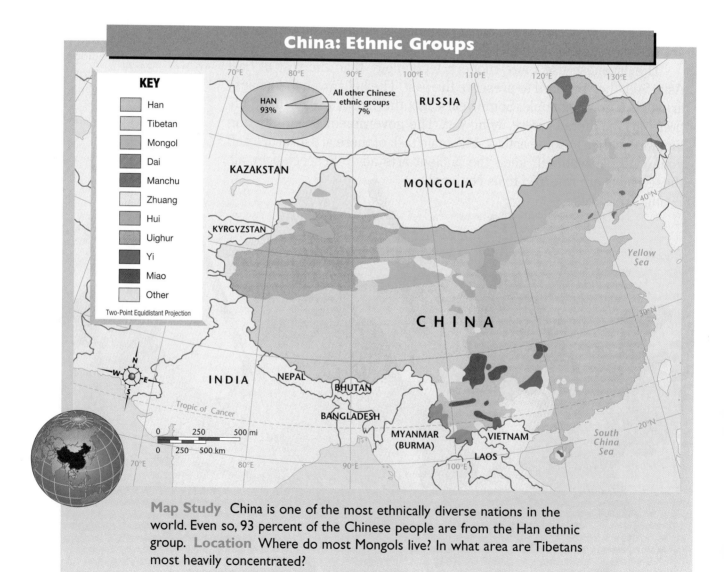

China: Ethnic Groups

KEY
- Han
- Tibetan
- Mongol
- Dai
- Manchu
- Zhuang
- Hui
- Uighur
- Yi
- Miao
- Other

Two-Point Equidistant Projection

HAN 93%

All other Chinese ethnic groups 7%

RUSSIA

KAZAKSTAN

MONGOLIA

KYRGYZSTAN

Yellow Sea

CHINA

INDIA NEPAL

BHUTAN

BANGLADESH

MYANMAR (BURMA)

VIETNAM

LAOS

South China Sea

Tropic of Cancer

0   250   500 mi
0   250   500 km

Map Study China is one of the most ethnically diverse nations in the world. Even so, 93 percent of the Chinese people are from the Han ethnic group. **Location** Where do most Mongols live? In what area are Tibetans most heavily concentrated?

The Country in the City

Chen Di
age 12
China

This painting shows a country scene in the city.
Critical Thinking How do you think the student artist feels about the countryside? Why?

They move from place to place in search of water and grazing for their herds. Over centuries, these groups lost their separate traditions. They formed one **homogeneous** (hoh muh JEE nee us) group. That is, the group's members were very similar. Today, even with the division of Korea into two countries, the population is quite homogeneous. There are few minority groups.

Because it cut itself off from the world for a long time, Japan has one of the most homogeneous populations on the Earth. Nearly all of the people belong to the same **ethnic group,** a group that shares language, religion, and cultural traditions. Minority groups are few. One notable minority group is the Ainu (EYE noo), who may have been Japan's first inhabitants. Small numbers of Koreans and Chinese also live in Japan. However, Japan has strict rules on immigration. It is hard for anyone who is not Japanese by birth to become a citizen.

SECTION 2 REVIEW

1. **Define** (a) commune, (b) dialect, (c) nomad, (d) homogeneous, (e) ethnic group.

2. How does East Asia reflect past and present traditions?

3. Why are the populations of Korea and Japan homogeneous?

Critical Thinking

4. **Recognizing Cause and Effect** Why do you think the Communists wanted to slow China's population growth?

Activity

5. **Writing to Learn** You want to make your permanent home in Japan. Write a letter to the Japanese government, asking officials to allow you to do so. Make your letter persuasive by pointing out all of the ways in which the country interests you.

China

TRANSFORMING ITSELF

BEFORE YOU READ

Reach Into Your Background
Think about the ways in which your community has changed during your lifetime. What new highways and buildings have been built? Are there new places for entertainment? Is there more traffic today? List all of the changes you know about in your community.

Questions to Explore
1. How has communism changed the lives of many Chinese?

2. What steps has China recently taken to improve its economy?

Key Terms
radical
free enterprise

Key People and Places
Mao Zedong
Red Guard
Taiwan

▼ China's streets are no longer packed with bicycles. In modern Shanghai, throngs of walkers share the streets with buses and other motor vehicles.

isiting China in the early 1980s, an American doctor named Jay Arena made the following comments:

> "Bicycles . . . bicycles . . . bicycles . . . 200 million of them (one out of every five Chinese owns one). Plain clothes . . . no jewelry . . . only stainless steel wristwatches. Courtesy . . . reasonable happiness . . . discipline; a relaxed people. Cities without pet cats, dogs, birds (keeping them is against the law). . . . Respect and affection for old people. . . ."

If you visited China today, you might share some of Dr. Arena's experiences. But you would also notice some changes.

During the early 1980s, for example, the streets of large cities were fairly quiet. Most people traveled by bicycle or bus. At this time, the total number of vehicles in all of China was 100,000. In 2000, over 11 million cars, buses, and trucks crowded the streets of major cities. When Dr. Arena visited China, few houses had running water or flush toilets. Today, China's major cities have high-rise apartment and office buildings. New roads connect rural areas to the cities. Change is speeding up as China works to become an industrial nation.

Tradition and Change

When the Communists took power in 1949 and formed the People's Republic of China, they had few friends among the major nations of the world. The United States had backed the Nationalists. The Soviet Union had been on the Communists' side, but later withdrew its support. The two nations disagreed about how a communist society should be run.

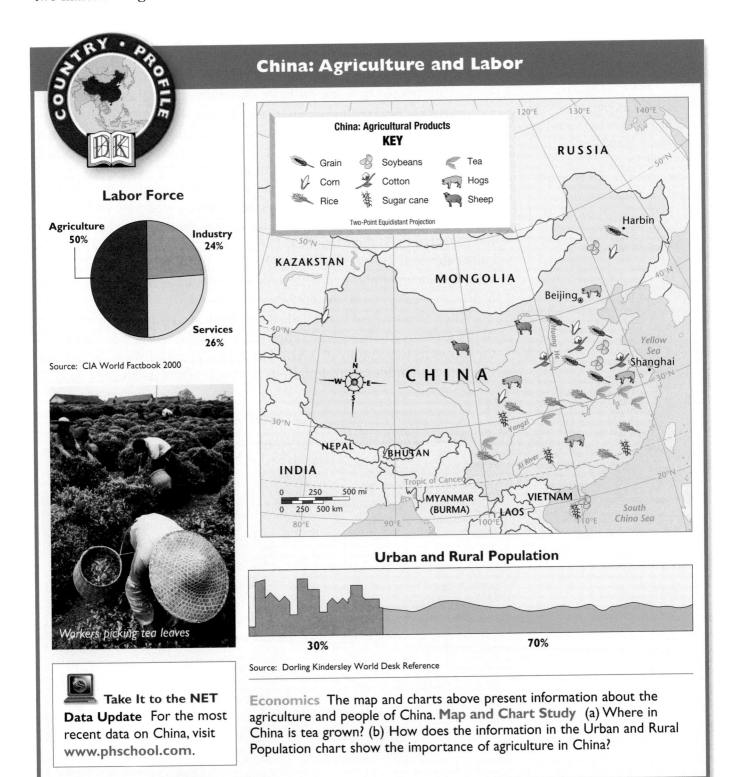

COUNTRY · PROFILE

China: Agriculture and Labor

China: Agricultural Products
KEY

Grain	Soybeans	Tea
Corn	Cotton	Hogs
Rice	Sugar cane	Sheep

Two-Point Equidistant Projection

Labor Force

Agriculture 50%
Industry 24%
Services 26%

Source: CIA World Factbook 2000

Workers picking tea leaves

Urban and Rural Population

30%   70%

Source: Dorling Kindersley World Desk Reference

Take It to the NET
Data Update For the most recent data on China, visit **www.phschool.com**.

Economics The map and charts above present information about the agriculture and people of China. **Map and Chart Study** (a) Where in China is tea grown? (b) How does the information in the Urban and Rural Population chart show the importance of agriculture in China?

Writing Chinese To write their language, the Chinese use characters, or symbols. Each one is a word or part of a word. To read and write, people must learn thousands of characters. Since 1949, the government has tried to make it easier to read and write Chinese. It adopted simpler forms of some characters. It also promoted the use of *pinyin*, a system of spelling the sounds represented by Chinese characters.

Huge problems faced the Communists when they took control. China had not had peace for almost a century. Most Chinese were extremely poor. Their methods of farming and manufacturing used few machines.

Under the leadership of Mao Zedong (mow zuh dung), China made huge changes. The government seized land from large landowners. In the cities, the government seized all factories and businesses. But Mao was not satisfied. Economic growth was too slow.

In the 1950s, Mao began a policy of **radical,** or extreme, change. This policy, called the "Great Leap Forward," turned out to be a giant step backward. The Communists rushed to increase production by forcing people to work on large communes. But they ignored the need for experience and planning. For example, they ordered a huge increase in steel production. Thousands of untrained workers built backyard furnaces for steel-making that never worked. Mao's policies, and natural disasters, resulted in a huge death toll.

In 1966, Mao introduced another radical policy called the Cultural Revolution. His aim was to create a completely new society with no ties to the past. He began the process by urging students to rebel against their teachers and their families. The students formed bands of radicals called the Red Guard. These bands destroyed some of China's most beautiful ancient buildings. They beat up and imprisoned many Chinese artists, professors, and doctors.

When the Red Guard raged out of control and began to threaten Mao's government, they were imprisoned, too. Mao called for an end to the Cultural Revolution in 1969. The three years of turmoil had left China in a shambles, with hundreds of thousands of its citizens dead.

China's Communist Takeover

"Under Mao's leadership, the people of the valleys and mountains." These words top a poster showing an image of Mao Zedong that celebrates the communist takeover of China in 1949. The purpose of posters like this was to make people feel a part of the revolution. **Critical Thinking** How are the people shown in the poster different from one another? Why do you think the artist made them different?

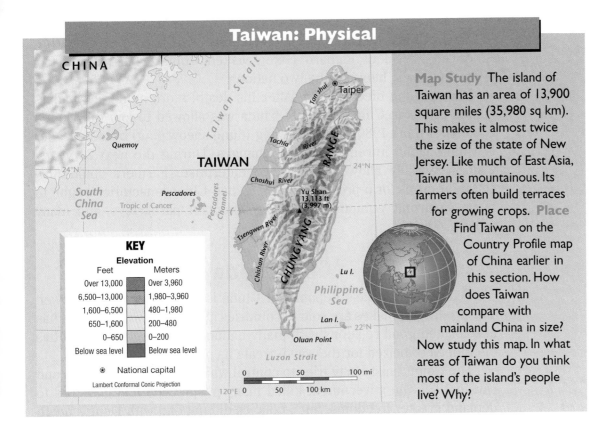

Taiwan: Physical

CHINA

Tan shui · Taipei

Taiwan Strait

Quemoy

TAIWAN

Tachia River

24°N · · 24°N

Choshui River

South China Sea

Pescadores

Tropic of Cancer

Pescadores Channel

Yu Shan 13,113 ft (3,997 m) ▲

Tsengwen River

Chishan River

CHUNG YANG

RANGE

Lu I.

Philippine Sea

Lan I.

22°N

Oluan Point

Luzon Strait

KEY
Elevation

Feet	Meters
Over 13,000	Over 3,960
6,500–13,000	1,980–3,960
1,600–6,500	480–1,980
650–1,600	200–480
0–650	0–200
Below sea level	Below sea level

⊛ National capital

Lambert Conformal Conic Projection

0   50   100 mi

120°E 0   50   100 km

Map Study The island of Taiwan has an area of 13,900 square miles (35,980 sq km). This makes it almost twice the size of the state of New Jersey. Like much of East Asia, Taiwan is mountainous. Its farmers often build terraces for growing crops. **Place** Find Taiwan on the Country Profile map of China earlier in this section. How does Taiwan compare with mainland China in size? Now study this map. In what areas of Taiwan do you think most of the island's people live? Why?

The Growth of Taiwan

After their defeat by the Communists in 1949, the Nationalists fled to Taiwan, an island 100 miles (161 km) off mainland China's southeast coast. They formed a new government called the Republic of China.

The Nationalists followed **free enterprise.** Under this economic system, people choose their own jobs, start private businesses, and can make a profit. Even in the 1950s, Taiwan's free enterprise economy was one of Asia's strongest. The Chinese on Taiwan started programs that increased farm output and brought in more money. This money helped Taiwan build new ports and railroads.

Taiwan also had the support of foreign countries. Both Taiwan and China claimed to be the "real" China. China said that Taiwan was its province. Taiwan said China was its province. At first, the United States and other western countries supported Taiwan. Taiwan sold computers and other electronic products to the rest of the world. Taiwan's economy grew dramatically. The quality of life greatly improved for its people.

China Faces Its Challenges

Meanwhile, many western countries refused to trade with China. At the same time some of Mao's policies, as you read, hurt the country. During the late 1970s, the Communists realized that they needed new policies in order to secure China's place in the world.

READ ACTIVELY

Ask Questions Think of questions you might like to ask about Taiwan.

First, China began repairing relations with the West. In 1972, American President Richard Nixon visited China. This historic trip opened up trade between the two nations.

Mao Zedong died in 1976. After his death, more moderate leaders gained power in China. In 1978, China was allowed to join the United Nations. Around 1980, Deng Xiaoping (dung sheow ping) became leader of China. Deng introduced many changes. During the next 20 years, China gradually allowed some free enterprise. Farmers could now sell their crops for a profit. Privately owned Chinese factories began to make electronic equipment, clothes, computer parts, toys, and many other products.

China Today

Today, the People's Republic of China is a major economic power. The products it makes are sold to countries all over the world. China has also formed good relations with many nations. Yet the government has often been criticized for the way it treats its people.

The Communist Party tries to control what Chinese people read and say. In 1989, the government killed many people who had gathered to demand greater freedoms. Such policies did not end with Deng's death in 1997. China's new leader, Jiang Zemin (zhang zuh min), followed Deng's lead in maintaining strict control over the Chinese people. However, the Internet and media make it hard to keep information from the Chinese people.

Many nations question how they should treat a country with such a poor human rights record. Still, most of them continue to remain trade partners with China. China's population makes it a huge market for goods, and China manufactures many items for other countries. In 2001, Beijing was chosen as the site of the 2008 Summer Olympics. People from all over the world will be there to see how China is facing its recent challenges.

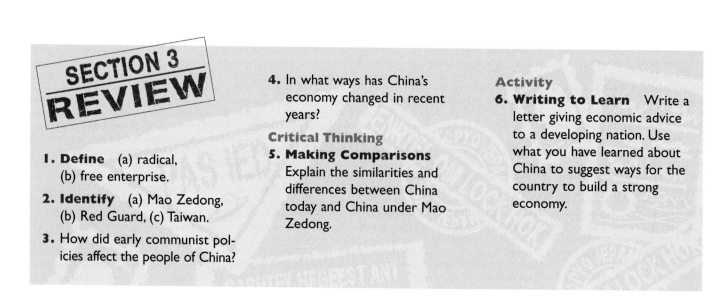

SECTION 3 REVIEW

1. **Define** (a) radical, (b) free enterprise.

2. **Identify** (a) Mao Zedong, (b) Red Guard, (c) Taiwan.

3. How did early communist policies affect the people of China?

4. In what ways has China's economy changed in recent years?

Critical Thinking

5. **Making Comparisons** Explain the similarities and differences between China today and China under Mao Zedong.

Activity

6. **Writing to Learn** Write a letter giving economic advice to a developing nation. Use what you have learned about China to suggest ways for the country to build a strong economy.

Japan

TRADITION AND CHANGE

Reach Into Your Background

What should a person think about when looking for a job? What makes a good job? Jot down some answers to these questions. Then compare your ideas with what you learn about working in Japan.

Questions to Explore

1. How did Japan become one of the most successful developed nations in the world?
2. How does modern culture exist side by side with traditional culture in Japan?

Key Terms

robot
subsidize
recession
discrimination

Employees of one Japanese electronics company gather each morning to sing the company song:

> "Sending our goods to the people of the world
> Endlessly and continuously,
> Like water gushing from a fountain.
> Grow, industry, grow, grow, grow!"

A Japanese car company hands out a weekly newsletter that includes pep talks to help its employees work more efficiently. In one year, workers cut the time it took to put together some car parts from 90 seconds to 45. At first, a packing task took workers an hour. Three years later, it took only 12 minutes.

A company that makes **robots,** computer-driven machines that do tasks once done by humans, holds an Idea Olympics each year. Employees compete in thinking up ideas to improve the company. Nearly half of the employees work on these ideas on their own time.

▼ Workers in neat uniforms exercise in unison at a seafood plant. The Japanese believe that such group activities make workers more productive.

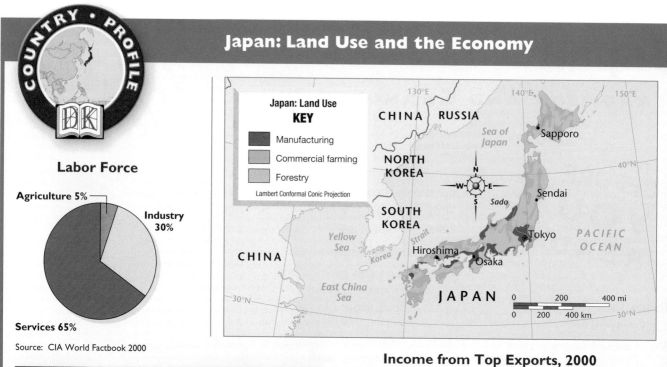

COUNTRY · PROFILE

DK

Labor Force

Agriculture 5%

Industry 30%

Services 65%

Source: CIA World Factbook 2000

Automobile factory in Japan

Income from Top Exports, 2000

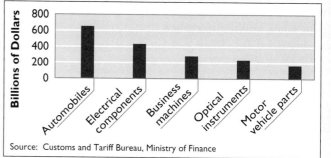

Billions of Dollars

800, 600, 400, 200, 0

Automobiles | Electrical components | Business machines | Optical instruments | Motor vehicle parts

Source: Customs and Tariff Bureau, Ministry of Finance

Economics The map and charts above present information about the land use and economy of Japan. **Map and Chart Study** (a) How is the land used on Japan's coast? How is the land used in Japan's interior? (b) What is Japan's top export?

Economic Ups and Downs

Take It to the NET
Data Update For the most recent data on Japan, visit **www.phschool.com**.

Some of Japan's ideas have come from outside the nation. Japan has long been known for adopting ideas from other nations and improving them. Once Japan finally opened its ports to other countries in the 1800s, it welcomed new ideas and inventions from the West. For years, the Japanese worked to build major industries. By the 1920s, Japan had become an important manufacturing country. Its economy depended on importing natural resources and exporting manufactured goods.

World War II and Beyond After World War II, Japan was in ruins. Only a few factories were still running. They made shoes from scraps of wood, and kitchen pots and pans from soldiers' steel helmets. The idea that the Japanese might soon be able to compete with the industrial giants of the West seemed impossible.

Tiny Computer Chips

In recent years, Japan has become a leader in computer technology. Here, a manager of a Japanese computer company displays dynamic random access memory, or DRAM, chips. These tiny chips, which measure about 0.5 inches (1 cm) by 0.75 inches (2 cm), are the "brains" of a computer. **Critical Thinking** How did the Japanese government help computer technology and other industries to grow?

Financial aid from the United States helped to rebuild industry. But the main reason Japan became a prosperous industrial nation was its ability to change and grow. The Japanese government helped industries by **subsidizing,** or economically supporting, them. This allowed companies to build large factories and buy modern machines. With more goods to sell, manufacturers could earn more money. Workers also earned more money, so they were able to spend more. This raised the demand for Japanese goods within Japan itself.

Since the 1960s, Japan has produced some of the world's most modern industrial robots. By the 1970s, the Japanese were making more watches and cameras than the Swiss and the Germans. By the 1980s, Japan made and sold a large share of the world's cars, electronic goods, skiing gear, and bicycles. Japan also produced huge amounts of steel, ships, televisions, and CDs.

Japan continued to improve on existing products. For example, the pocket calculator was invented in Britain. But the Japanese created better models. In addition, they had some new ideas of their own. You are probably familiar with personal stereos and small, hand-held electronic games. These were invented by the Japanese.

Success Brings Challenges By the 1980s, Japan had one of the world's largest and strongest economies. Japan was so wealthy that it loaned huge amounts of money to other countries. It also led the world in giving aid to developing nations.

Japan's economy depended on exports of its products to the rest of the world. Americans and Europeans eagerly bought Japanese products—particularly cars, television sets, and electronics. Yet Japanese people themselves did not buy many imported goods. Many of

Visualize Picture what an industrial robot might be like. What are some tasks it could do?

them worked too hard to want to spend money in their free time. Also, they preferred to save as much money as they could, which the government had encouraged in the past.

Other countries grew angry because though they bought many Japanese products, the Japanese did not buy theirs. This led to poor trade relations between Japan and other countries. On top of that, in the early 1990s the Japanese economy suffered a severe **recession.** A recession is when an economy and the businesses that support it slow down.

To overcome the recession, companies began laying off their employees. Unemployment in Japan rose. This had some long-term effects on workers. While companies used to hire workers for life, now they hired them only on a temporary basis. In the past, people were given special benefits just for being with a company for a long time. After the recession, many companies only gave benefits to those who they felt performed their jobs the best.

Japan still has one of the strongest economies in the world. As it has done in the past, it is likely to develop new ideas about how to stay strong in the face of its challenges.

The Modern and the Traditional

As elsewhere in East Asia, traditions are important in Japan. Times are changing, but change comes slowly. The role of women is one example. As in the past, being married is the most acceptable position for a Japanese woman. Large companies often have marriage bureaus to introduce their single employees.

School Outing

Like American schoolchildren, these Japanese students enjoy clowning for the camera. Unlike most U.S. students, though, they are dressed in school uniforms.
Critical Thinking What purpose do you think school uniforms serve?

Japan's hard-working wives and mothers support the economy. Japanese women are in charge of their households. They make housing and schooling decisions, handle the family finances, and take care of major purchases.

Japanese women often work before marriage. In the past, many worked in rice fields, fisheries, and factories, or as nurses or teachers. Today, though, some married women are venturing outside the home in a new direction—as part-time workers.

In the 1980s, the largest group of working women in Japan was the army of "office ladies." They served tea, did light cleaning, held doors, and answered the phone. Today, office ladies are rare. Instead, young graduates who want to work for a few years until they marry and middle-aged women with grown children are crowding the workplace. Often, these women work long hours beside male workers—who get higher salaries and good benefits.

At present, few women become managers in Japanese businesses. Even when they do, they may meet with job **discrimination**, or unequal treatment. For this reason, many young women are not willing to join Japanese firms. Instead, they look for jobs with foreign businesses in Japan. They are also finding jobs in newer fields where there is less discrimination.

Predict How do Japanese women balance the demands of work and family?

▼ Employees of an American computer firm discuss a technical problem at the company's Japan headquarters.

SECTION 4 REVIEW

1. **Define** (a) robot, (b) subsidize, (c) recession, (d) discrimination.

2. What are some reasons for Japan's economic success and for its recent economic downturn?

3. How do the roles played by women illustrate how tradition and change affect Japan today?

Critical Thinking

4. **Drawing Conclusions** How do you think the post-recession changes to hiring practices and benefits affected Japanese workers?

Activity

5. **Writing to Learn** Question several friends or family members about their attitudes toward their jobs. Are they loyal to their employers? Do they feel part of a team? Do they take pride in their work? What incentives do their employers offer? Write a short essay comparing American views with Japanese views.

The Koreas

A DIVIDED LAND

BEFORE YOU READ

Reach Into Your Background

What do you think it would be like to live in a country divided into two parts?

Suppose that part of your family lived in the other half and you could not visit or communicate with them. How would you feel?

Questions to Explore

1. How has South Korea become an economic success?
2. Why has North Korea been slower to develop?

Key Terms
diversify
famine

Key Places
Seoul
demilitarized zone

The Korean Peninsula is a tense and divided region. A visitor to South Korea's capital, Seoul (sohl), described that nation's defenses against its northern neighbor this way:

▼ South Korean troops patrol a section of the barbed-wire-topped fence that extends along the demilitarized zone. North and South Korea each fear they will be attacked by the other.

“If you head south from Seoul in a car, the . . . divider in the highway disappears soon after you leave the city, and for a long stretch, the road is broad and very flat. It becomes, in fact, an emergency airfield by which Seoul could be supplied—or evacuated [emptied]—in the event of war. North of the capital, the highway is marked every few miles by what appear to be overpasses for other highways that were never built. In fact, these massive concrete “bridges” are . . . designed to impede [block] assaulting tanks. In the DMZ, the 155-mile-long buffer zone between North and South Korea, the South Korean Army some time ago discovered three underground tunnels that were built during the past decade by the North Koreans.”

DMZ stands for “demilitarized zone.” It is a border area between North and South Korea in which no weapons are allowed. The DMZ holds back more than weapons and

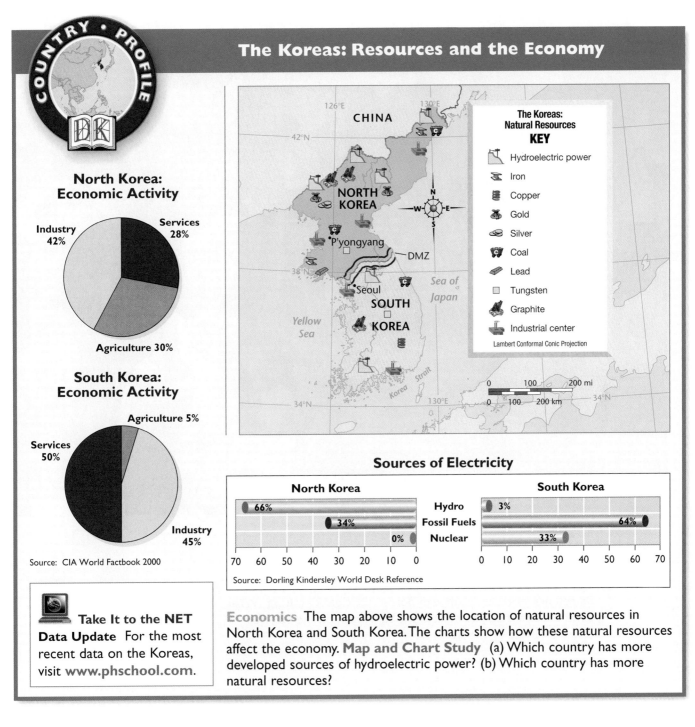

North Korea: Economic Activity

Industry 42%

Services 28%

Agriculture 30%

South Korea: Economic Activity

Agriculture 5%

Services 50%

Industry 45%

Source: CIA World Factbook 2000

The Koreas: Natural Resources
KEY

Hydroelectric power
Iron
Copper
Gold
Silver
Coal
Lead
Tungsten
Graphite
Industrial center

Lambert Conformal Conic Projection

CHINA

NORTH KOREA

P'yongyang

DMZ

Seoul

SOUTH KOREA

Sea of Japan

Yellow Sea

Korea Strait

0   100   200 mi
0   100   200 km

Sources of Electricity

	North Korea		South Korea
Hydro	66%		3%
Fossil Fuels	34%		64%
Nuclear	0%		33%

70 60 50 40 30 20 10 0   0 10 20 30 40 50 60 70

Source: Dorling Kindersley World Desk Reference

Take It to the NET
Data Update For the most recent data on the Koreas, visit **www.phschool.com**.

Economics The map above shows the location of natural resources in North Korea and South Korea. The charts show how these natural resources affect the economy. **Map and Chart Study** (a) Which country has more developed sources of hydroelectric power? (b) Which country has more natural resources?

troops, however. It keeps all people, supplies, and communication from passing between the countries. It also divides two countries that are on very different economic paths.

Economic Growth in South Korea

In the mid-1900s, South Korea had agricultural resources but few industries. A half-century later, South Korea has become a leading economic power. It is one of the world's fastest growing industrial centers.

South Korea is a democracy with an economy based on free enterprise. After World War II, South Korea's factories focused on making

READ ACTIVELY

Predict How does South Korea's economy differ from North Korea's economy?

In South Korea, groups often take to the streets to demand higher wages, better working conditions, new government programs, or friendlier relations with North Korea. Here, a group of college students march in such a parade, or demonstration, in Seoul. Sometimes, marchers clash with police. **Critical Thinking** What kinds of slogans do you think might be written on the colorful banners carried by the students?

cloth and processed foods. Later, it developed heavy industry. Today, South Korea is among the world's top shipbuilders. It has a growing electronics industry that exports radios, televisions, and computers. It has large refineries, or factories that process oil. This oil is then used to make plastics, rubber, and other products.

South Korea's change from a farming to an industrial economy has created a building boom. Factories, office and apartment buildings, and roads have sprung up to meet the needs of modern society.

The government of South Korea has focused on industry. But it has also helped farmers. Programs help farmers increase crop production. Other programs improve housing, roads, and water supplies and bring electricity to rural areas.

Despite its successes, South Korea faces a number of challenges. Like Japan, it lacks many natural resources. It must import large amounts of raw materials to keep industry running. Major imports are oil, iron, steel, and chemicals. The cost of living has grown, and wages often cannot keep up.

North Korea: Rich in Resources

North Korea is a communist country that has kept itself closed to much of the rest of the world. This has kept out new technology and fresh ideas. Yet North Korea is rich in mineral resources. Until the end of World War II, it was the industrial center of the Korean Peninsula.

Today, however, North Korea cannot compete with South Korea. It still manufactures goods in government-owned factories. These factories produce poor-quality goods. Little has been done to **diversify,** or add variety to, the economy.

Farming methods, too, are outdated in the north. Many farmers burn hillsides to prepare for planting crops. After a few years of this, the good soil can be washed away by rain. Then, the fields can no longer be farmed. In 1995, North Koreans faced **famine,** or a huge food shortage, and starvation. North Korean officials estimated about 220,000 people died from famine between 1995 and 1998. For the first time, North Korea asked noncommunist countries for aid.

In recent years, North Korea and South Korea have taken steps toward improving relations. South Korea provided North Korea with aid to help its northern neighbor overcome its food shortages and economic problems. In June 2000, the leaders of the two countries met in P'yongyang, the capital of North Korea, and agreed to strive for peace and cooperation among the nations. It was the first time leaders of the two nations had met since 1945. Communication between North and South Korea slowed in 2001, but both sides say they will continue peace-making efforts.

Peace for the Birds
Korea's DMZ is 2 1/2 miles (4 km) wide. Its north and south edges bristle with barbed wire and explosives. A million soldiers guard it. Yet this hostile area is a peaceful sanctuary for wildlife. The troops on both sides have an unspoken agreement not to disturb the creatures that live or migrate here.

SECTION 5 REVIEW

1. **Define** (a) diversify, (b) famine.
2. **Identify** (a) Seoul, (b) demilitarized zone.

3. Discuss the reasons for South Korea's economic success and recent downturn.
4. Why has North Korea's economy lagged behind South Korea's?

Critical Thinking
5. **Making Comparisons** How do the governments of North and South Korea affect their economies?

Activity Journal
6. **Writing to Learn** The division between North and South Korea has cut you off from family members. It has also influenced the way you live. Write a journal entry describing what it is like to live in either North or South Korea.

Reading Route Maps

Tony looked at the clock eagerly. In the last ten minutes of class, Mr. Nelson always held a discussion time, Tony's favorite part of the day.

Mr. Nelson spoke. "Ladies and gentlemen, today we're going to talk about something that has played a great role in the development of civilization. What do you think it is?"

There was silence for a moment as the students thought. "War," said one boy. "Computers," said another. "Books," said the girl behind Tony. After a few minutes, they ran out of ideas.

But then Mr. Nelson said, "What do you think about this one?" He picked up the chalk and wrote one word on the board: *Roads.*

Get Ready

Roads link people together as nothing else does. Roads let people travel to different lands. Roads are the lifeline of trade and the economy. Also, the people who travel on roads carry their ideas and customs with them. How would your life be different in a world without roads?

Roads are shown on route maps. A route is any way that people travel. There are sea routes and air routes. Most routes, however, are roads. To understand history, it helps to understand routes. To understand routes, you need to be able to read a route map.

Try It Out

Reading a route map is simply a matter of reading a map and the routes that are marked on it. Reading a map means reading the title, the key, the scale, the compass rose, and the labels on the map. This helps you understand what the map shows. You then find the routes on the map by following the lines that show them.

Try it out by reading a road map of your own community. Working with a small group, answer these questions:

A. What does the map key show?

B. How are types or sizes of roads shown?

C. What are the main roads that run north and south? East and west?

D. About how long is the longest road in town?

E. Locate your school on the map. What is the most direct route from your school to a major intersection in your community?

Apply the Skill

Now you have practiced with a modern route map of an area close to home. You have all the skills you need to read an ancient route map of an area far away.

The map below shows the Silk Road, which was a collection of trade routes dating from about 300 B.C. This road linked China to the West. Along it, traders carried not only many goods but also many ideas. The road, pictured in the Chinese painting on the opposite page,

had a very important effect on the development of cultures and the exchange of ideas. Use the route map of the Silk Road to complete the steps that follow.

1 Familiarize yourself with the map. The first step in reading any map is to figure out what it is about. What is the title of the map? In what region of the world was the Silk Road?

2 Understand what routes are shown. How is the Silk Road indicated? What was its western end point? What was its eastern end point? Through what major landforms did it pass?

3 Look at the physical features along the routes. Along the way, the Silk Road divides and then meets again. What physical feature lies between the divided sections of the road? Why do you think the road divides the way it does? What physical obstacles might have faced the travelers on the Silk Road?

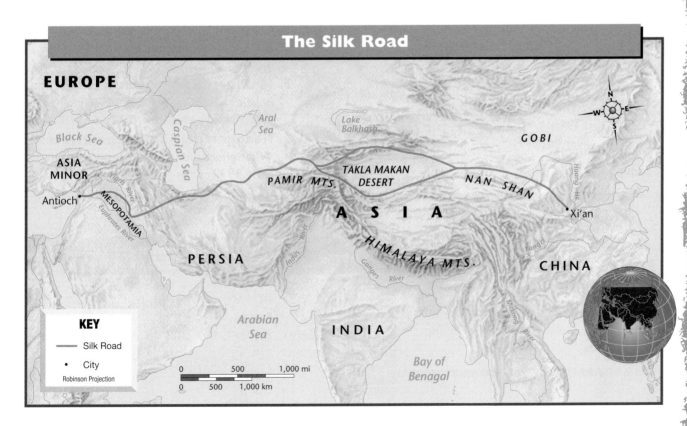

The Silk Road

KEY
—— Silk Road
•   City
Robinson Projection

0   500   1,000 mi
0   500   1,000 km

Review and Activities

Reviewing Main Ideas

1. Describe three major achievements of ancient East Asia.
2. In what ways did the West influence East Asia?
3. In what ways do tradition and change exist together in East Asian society?
4. How does China's population differ from the populations of Japan and Korea in terms of ethnic diversity?
5. What economic policies did the Chinese Communists introduce in the 1950s?
6. How did Mao Zedong's policies cause problems for China?
7. What abilities allowed the Japanese to build one of the world's most successful economies?
8. How do modern and traditional cultures exist together in Japan?
9. What economic problems has Japan faced in recent years?
10. Why is North Korea taking much longer than South Korea to improve and modernize its economy?

Reviewing Key Terms

Use each key term below in a sentence that shows the meaning of the term.

1. civilization
2. emperor
3. dynasty
4. migration
5. clan
6. cultural diffusion
7. commune
8. ethnic group
9. dialect
10. radical
11. subsidize
12. recession
13. discrimination
14. diversify

Critical Thinking

1. **Drawing Conclusions** Both ancient China and Japan attempted to isolate themselves from foreign influences. How did this affect both countries?
2. **Making Comparisons** Compare the policies of the communist government of China before and after the late 1970s.
3. **Recognizing Cause and Effect** What effect did Japan's recession of the early 1990s have on the country?

Graphic Organizer

Copy the chart onto a separate sheet of paper. Complete the chart by filling in the blanks.

	People	Type of Government	Type of Economy	Values and Traditions
China				
Japan				
North Korea				
South Korea				

Map Activity

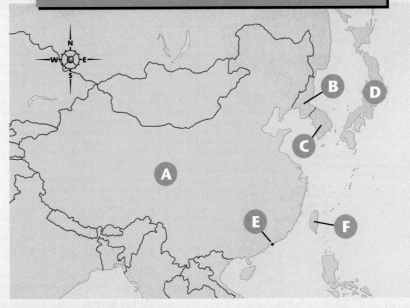

East Asia

For each place listed below, write the letter from the map that shows its location. Use the Atlas in the back of your book to help you.

1. Japan

2. China

3. Taiwan

4. South Korea

5. Hong Kong

6. North Korea

Writing Activity

Writing Sentences

Based on what you have read in this chapter, write five sentences describing how tradition and change exist together in East Asia. Then write five sentences describing how tradition and change exist together in the United States.

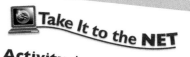

Take It to the NET

Activity Learn about the history, culture, and geography of the Korean Peninsula. What is the most interesting fact you learned about Korea? For help in completing this activity, visit www.phschool.com.

Chapter 2 Self-Test To review what you have learned, take the Chapter 2 Self-Test and get instant feedback on your answers. Go to www.phschool.com to take the test.

Skills Review

Turn to the Skills Activity. Review the steps for reading route maps. What is the purpose of a route map? Describe the different ways routes or roads can be shown on a route map.

How Am I Doing?

Answer these questions to check your progress.

1. Can I list some of the major cultural developments in East Asia?

2. Can I identify East Asia's many peoples?

3. Do I understand the impact that East Asia's various economies have had on its people?

4. Do I understand how tradition and change exist together in East Asia?

5. What information from this chapter can I include in my journal?

Poems

FROM SOUTH KOREA AND JAPAN

Reach Into Your Background

Think about looking up at the sky when no one else is around. You might see only a tiny cloud in the sunlight. You might hear only a bumblebee buzzing. If you were all alone, you might notice things that are normally very still and quiet.

Nature does not always shout to get your attention. Some poets look and listen in nature for small, still things. When you read these poems, you might think twice about a very simple thing. You might see something lovely or something new that once seemed very ordinary.

Look for still, silent images when you read the following poems by Kwang-kyu Kim from South Korea and by the Japanese poets Hashin and Jōsō.

Questions to Explore

1. What parts of nature are most important in these poems?
2. How do the poems change when you read them aloud?

Loneliness

No sky at all;
  no earth at all—and still
    the snow flakes fall. . . .

> *Hashin*
> Translated by
> Harold G. Henderson

Winter

Mountains and plains,
  all are captured by snow—
    nothing remains.

> *Jōsō*
> Translated by
> Harold G. Henderson

▲ "View of Mount Haruna Under the Snow," Japanese print, early 1800s.

◀ Mount Fuji,
Japanese print,
early 1800s.

The Birth of a Stone

In those deep mountain ravines
I wonder if there are stones
that no one has ever visited?
I went up the mountain
in quest of a stone no one had
    ever seen
from the remotest of times

Under ancient pines
on steep pathless slopes
there was a stone
I wonder
how long
this stone all thick with moss
has been
here?

Two thousand years? Two
    million? Two billion?

No
Not at all
If really till now no one
has ever seen this stone
it is only
here
from now on

This stone
was only born
the moment I first saw it

Kwang-kyu Kim
Translated by
Harold G. Henderson

Ask Questions Where
might this poem take
place?

Look Back

1. What do the three poems have in common?
2. What questions does the narrator of "The Birth of a Stone" ask about the stone?

Think It Over

3. Explain what the poet of "Winter" means by writing that the mountains and plains are captured by snow.

4. Why do you think the narrator in "Birth of a Stone" wanted to find a stone no one had ever seen?

Go Beyond

5. Think of a place where very few people have ever been. How would you feel if you saw something no one had ever seen?

6. Describe what you think it feels like to be alone in nature.

Ideas for Writing: Poem

7. Spend some time alone outside. You could be in a park, a forest, or any space under the sky. Try to find a place that is quiet, or visit it during a quiet part of the day. Look and listen for things you normally do not notice. Write a poem about what you find.

SOUTH AND SOUTHEAST ASIA

Physical Geography

This village is built on the Ganges (GAN jeez) River in the country of Bangladesh (bahn gluh DESH). The Ganges River begins in the mountains of India, runs through Bangladesh, and finally empties into the Bay of Bengal. To help you get to know this part of South Asia, do the following.

Write a letter
What would it be like to live in this village? Write a letter to a friend describing your life in this village.

Picture the seasons
Draw pictures of what you think the village would look like during the different seasons of the year. What do you suppose the climate is like in this village? Do you think it snows here? Why or why not?

Land and Water

BEFORE YOU READ

Reach Into Your Background

Mountains are the most important landform in South Asia. They affect where rain falls—rain that is needed for crops. Think about landforms in your state. Which do you think have the greatest effect on people's lives?

Questions to Explore

1. What are the major landforms of South and Southeast Asia?

2. How do the landforms affect the way people of South and Southeast Asia live?

Key Terms
subcontinent

Key Places
Himalaya Mountains
Ganges River
Indus River
Ring of Fire

Two hundred million years ago, the land now called the Indian **subcontinent** was attached to the east coast of Africa. A subcontinent is a large landmass that is a major part of a continent. Scientists believe that in those times, all of the Earth's continents were joined.

About 200 million years ago, the land shifted and cracked and the continents began to break apart. The Indian subcontinent split off from Africa and crept slowly toward Asia. The landmass moved so slowly that it took about four years to travel the length of an average pencil.

About 40 million years ago, the Indian subcontinent collided with Asia. Just as the front ends of cars crumple in a traffic accident, northern India and southern Asia crumpled where they met. This area is the huge Himalayan Mountain range. The Himalaya Mountains contain the tallest peaks in the world.

The Indian Subcontinent

The largest nation in South Asia is India. It extends from the Himalaya Mountains down to the narrow tip of the peninsula in the south. Pakistan and Afghanistan (af GAN uh stan) lie to

▼ A stream fed by melting snow zigzags down through the rugged Himalaya Mountains and across a field of wildflowers in the Lahaul Valley of northern India.

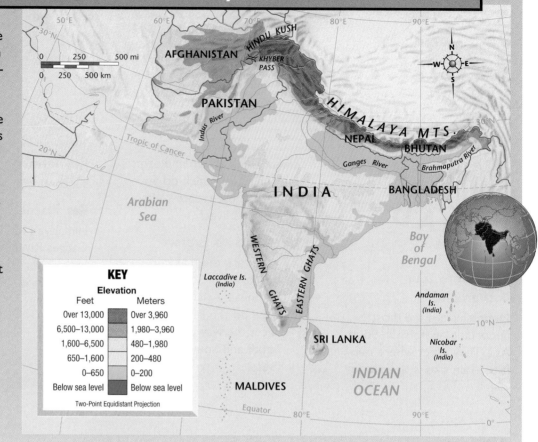

Huge, fertile plains cover the northern part of the Indian subcontinent. They stretch from the mouth of the Indus River to the mouth of the Ganges River. These plains are alluvial, which means they are made of soil deposited by rivers.

Movement What physical barriers do you think might have discouraged people who lived to the north of the subcontinent from moving onto its fertile plains?

KEY

Elevation

Feet		Meters
Over 13,000		Over 3,960
6,500–13,000		1,980–3,960
1,600–6,500		480–1,980
650–1,600		200–480
0–650		0–200
Below sea level		Below sea level

Two-Point Equidistant Projection

Predict What effects have the Himalaya Mountains had on the Indian subcontinent?

the west of India. Along India's northern border, the kingdoms of Nepal and Bhutan lie along the slopes of the Himalaya Mountains. To the east sits Bangladesh. The island nations of Sri Lanka (sree LAHN kuh) and the Maldives (MAL dyvz) lie off the southern tip of India.

A Natural Wall   The Indian subcontinent has many different landforms and contrasting regions. Perhaps the most dramatic is the Himalayan Mountain range. Find the Himalaya Mountains on the map above. Notice how they form a barrier between South Asia and the rest of the continent.

This huge mountain range stretches some 1,550 miles (2,500 km) from east to west. Mount Everest, the world's tallest mountain, is located in the Himalayas. Everest rises to 29,035 feet (8,850 m). That's about five and a half miles high! Another 30 mountains in the Himalayas soar above 24,000 feet (7,300 m).

As you know, the Himalaya Mountains were formed when two sections of the Earth's crust collided. This collision formed great folds in the Earth's surface. Over time, the movement of these sections has pushed the folds higher and higher. This mountain-building process is still going on today. Scientists estimate that Mount Everest is "growing" about 2 inches (5 cm) each year!

Rivers of Life The mighty Himalaya Mountains provide the subcontinent with one of its most valuable features: life-giving rivers. The two most important rivers in South Asia—the Ganges and the Indus—begin high in the mountains.

The Ganges River flows in a wide sweeping arc across northern India. After turning southward toward the sea, the Ganges is joined by the Brahmaputra (brah muh POO truh) River. They continue their journey through Bangladesh and empty into the Bay of Bengal.

The Indus River gives India its name. It flows westward from the Himalaya Mountains into the country of Pakistan. The lower part of the Indus flows through the hottest and driest part of the Indian subcontinent.

Rivers carry from the mountains the water and minerals necessary for good farming. The plains around the rivers, therefore, are quite fertile. As a result, the plains are heavily populated.

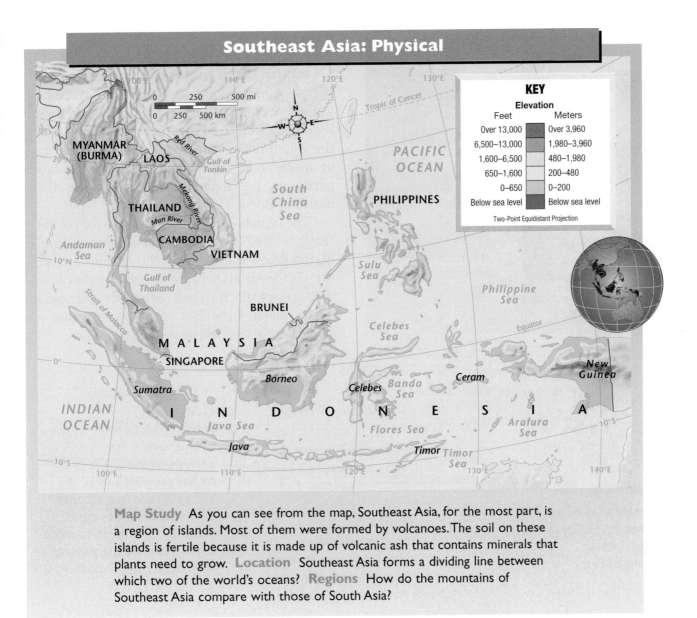

Southeast Asia: Physical

KEY

Elevation

Feet	Meters
Over 13,000	Over 3,960
6,500–13,000	1,980–3,960
1,600–6,500	480–1,980
650–1,600	200–480
0–650	0–200
Below sea level	Below sea level

Two-Point Equidistant Projection

Map Study As you can see from the map, Southeast Asia, for the most part, is a region of islands. Most of them were formed by volcanoes. The soil on these islands is fertile because it is made up of volcanic ash that contains minerals that plants need to grow. **Location** Southeast Asia forms a dividing line between which two of the world's oceans? **Regions** How do the mountains of Southeast Asia compare with those of South Asia?

Predict What do you think the Ring of Fire is?

▼ The yellow mineral called sulfur fills the baskets of this Indonesian miner. Sulfur is often produced by volcanic eruptions. It is used in making chemicals.

Southeast Asia

East of the Indian subcontinent and south of China lies the region called Southeast Asia. It is divided into mainland and island areas. The mainland is a giant peninsula that juts south from the main area of Asia. The islands extend east and west between the Indian and the Pacific oceans. Locate the mainland and the islands on the map on the previous page.

Mainland Southeast Asia The nations of mainland Southeast Asia are Vietnam, Cambodia, Laos (LAH ohs), Myanmar (MY ahn mar), Singapore, and Thailand (TY land). Singapore is the smallest of the mainland nations, located at the tip of the Malay Peninsula. The region is about one fifth the size of the United States. Much of this area is covered by forested mountains. The mountains run north and south. Most people live in the narrow river valleys between mountain ranges. Just as on the Indian subcontinent, rivers flow from the north and provide river valleys with the water and minerals necessary to grow crops.

Island Southeast Asia Four major nations make up island Southeast Asia: Malaysia (muh LAY zhuh), Brunei (broo NY), Indonesia, and the Philippines. The largest of the island nations is Indonesia. It is made up of more than 13,500 islands. Malaysia lies partly on the mainland and partly on the island of Borneo.

The islands of Southeast Asia are part of the "Ring of Fire." This is a region of volcanoes and earthquakes surrounding the Pacific Ocean. Most of the islands here are mountainous because they are actually the peaks of underwater volcanoes. People here live with the fear that a volcanic eruption will destroy their homes.

SECTION 1 REVIEW

1. **Define** subcontinent.

2. **Identify** (a) Himalaya Mountains, (b) Ganges River, (c) Indus River, (d) Ring of Fire.

3. What are the main rivers of South Asia?

4. Why are the river valleys of South and Southeast Asia more heavily populated than the mountainous regions?

Critical Thinking

5. **Making Comparisons** List and describe one similarity and one difference between South Asia and Southeast Asia.

Activity

6. **Writing to Learn** Write a two-paragraph description of a television show that focuses on the geography of South and Southeast Asia. Choose one feature, such as rivers, mountains, or islands to write about. Describe the pictures your show might include.

Climate and Vegetation

Reach Into Your Background

How do you feel after it rains for several days in a row? How about after several days of intense heat? South and Southeast Asia have climates that include both of these extremes. Read on to find out how people in the region feel about rain and heat.

Questions to Explore

1. What factors affect climate in South and Southeast Asia?

2. How is vegetation linked to climate in the region?

Key Terms

rain forest

Key Places

Ghat Mountains
Bangladesh
Vietnam

It is a scorching June day in Mumbai (Bombay), India. A hot breeze moves through the city streets like wind blowing from a huge oven. A water vendor pulls a water barrel on a wooden cart. "Water, only one rupee!" he shouts. Selling water, he makes about 40 rupees a day. That is less than $1 in the United States. An average field-worker in India makes only 15 rupees a day—about 30 cents.

Throughout India, schools remain closed. The grass on golf courses outside expensive hotels burns up. Movie theaters have only one show a day to save electricity. Much of India's electricity is produced by the force of fast-moving rivers. When water levels in the rivers fall, there is not enough force to generate power.

The rains brought by the summer monsoons are late again. The monsoons are seasonal winds. They are crucial to the lives of the people of South and Southeast Asia. All of India worries and waits for the first sign of the summer monsoons. If the rains are too late, crops will die and people will go hungry.

▼ Rain and mud are a source of fun for these Indian children. Each summer, they celebrate the return of the life-giving rains.

Predict How do you think monsoons affect the climate of South Asia?

Finally, after several more days, rain starts to fall. Some parts of India receive only a few drops. Other areas are blasted with strong storms and winds. The streets of Mumbai flood during the onslaught. Old buildings collapse.

But in rural parts of India, it is a time of joy and relief. The people here need the summer rains to grow crops. Once the rivers are flowing and the water tanks are full, the constant rain will lose its charm. But for now, people run into the streets and hold out their arms in joy.

The Climates of South Asia

The monsoons are the single most important factor in the climate of South Asia. There are two monsoon seasons. The summer monsoons blow across South Asia from the southwest. During the winter, the winds change direction and blow down from the northeast. Look at the land use and monsoons map in the Activity Atlas and note the directions of the monsoon winds.

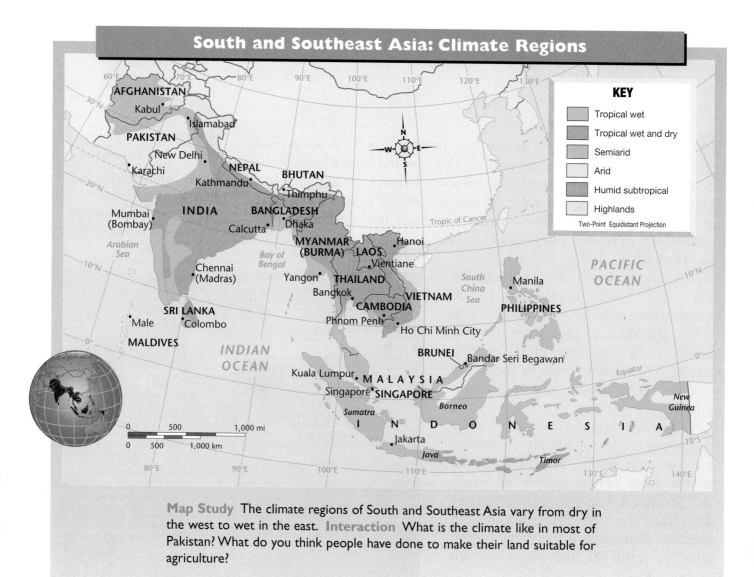

South and Southeast Asia: Climate Regions

KEY
- Tropical wet
- Tropical wet and dry
- Semiarid
- Arid
- Humid subtropical
- Highlands

Two-Point Equidistant Projection

Map Study The climate regions of South and Southeast Asia vary from dry in the west to wet in the east. **Interaction** What is the climate like in most of Pakistan? What do you think people have done to make their land suitable for agriculture?

The Summer Monsoons

From June to early October, steady winds blow air over the surface of the Arabian Sea and the Indian Ocean. This air picks up a great deal of moisture. Then, it passes over the hot land along the western tip of India and Sri Lanka. The change in temperature makes the air lose its moisture in the form of rain. As the air climbs up over the Ghat (gaht) Mountains, it loses even more moisture. By the time the air gets to the other side of the mountains, it has lost most of its moisture.

As the first heavy rains start falling near the coastline, the coastal lands cool down somewhat. So when the next moisture-filled air mass is blown in from the sea, it travels a little further inland before losing its supply of moisture as rain. In this way, the monsoon rains work their way inland until they finally reach the Himalaya Mountains. Just as the air traveling over southern India loses its moisture as it goes over the mountains, so, too, does the air that reaches the Himalaya Mountains. In fact, the southern mountain slopes of the country of Bhutan are drenched. They get as much as 300 inches (762 cm) of rain every summer.

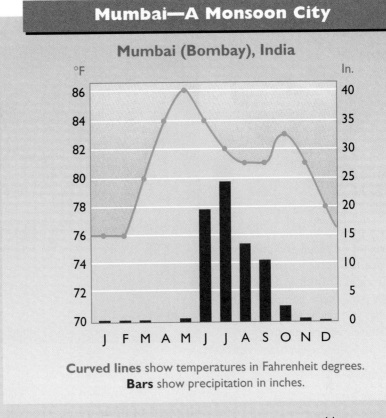

Mumbai—A Monsoon City

Mumbai (Bombay), India

Curved lines show temperatures in Fahrenheit degrees.
Bars show precipitation in inches.

Chart Study This climate graph shows the average monthly temperature and precipitation for Mumbai (Bombay), a city on India's west coast. As you can see on the graph, heavy rainfall occurs in June. This marks the beginning of the summer monsoons. **Critical Thinking** What effect do the summer monsoon winds have on the temperature in Mumbai?

The Winter Monsoons During the winter months in Asia, the monsoons change direction, and winds blow down from the frigid northeast. These winds move dry, cold air toward South Asia. But most of the bitter cold never gets there. The mighty Himalaya Mountains block the cold air. The nations of South Asia are spared. They enjoy dry weather, with temperatures averaging 70°F (21°C).

People and Monsoons The monsoon rains in Asia provide water for half the world's population. But the monsoons affect life in South Asia in other ways as well. In India, students start school in June, after the first rains have fallen. Their long vacation comes during the spring, when hot, stifling temperatures make it hard to concentrate on schoolwork.

In the country of Nepal, fierce monsoon rains can bring mudslides that destroy entire villages. The mud comes from hills that have been

India's Salt Lake During the hot months, the 90-square-mile (230-sq-km) Sambhar Lake in northwestern India is dry. Oddly, during this time the lake bed looks as though it is covered in snow. The white blanket is not snow but a sheet of salt. This salt supply was harvested as far back as the 1500s. It is an important resource for the region even today.

Amita
age 11
India

This park in an Indian city provides a green and pleasant place for many activities.
Critical Thinking How does this park scene compare with what you might see in a park in the area where you live?

Visualize Visualize rain pouring onto a bare dirt hillside. What do you think happens to such a hill if it rains a long time?

stripped of their trees. Trees keep soil from washing away during heavy rains. Many were cut down to create land for a growing population. Whole hillsides may wash away during rainstorms. In Bangladesh, swollen rivers overflow and flood two thirds of the land. In some years, crops and homes are destroyed and many people lose their lives. To protect against the floods, whole villages in Bangladesh are built on stilts.

The Climates and Vegetation of Southeast Asia

Look at the climate map of South and Southeast Asia at the beginning of this section. Notice that the climate regions in mainland Southeast Asia between Myanmar and Vietnam are similar to those in South Asia. On the west coast of Myanmar, there is a tropical wet climate, just as on the west coast of India. As you move east, the climate changes to tropical wet and dry, and then becomes humid subtropical.

However, when you get to the east coast of Vietnam, the pattern changes. The climate becomes tropical wet. It supports tropical **rain forests**—thick forests that receive at least 60 inches (152 cm) of rain a year. How is this possible? Don't the rains of the summer monsoons come from the southwest? Doesn't most of the summer rain fall on Myanmar?

Vietnam owes its lush coastal rain forest to the winter monsoons. As you already know, winds blow from the northeast during the winter in Asia. As the winter winds blow south from China toward Vietnam, they cross the South China Sea. The air picks up moisture, which it dumps as rain when it hits the coast of Vietnam. The Philippines and much of Indonesia also experience rainy seasons during the winter.

Rain forests like this one in Indonesia (left) may have more than 200 kinds of trees in a 2.5-acre (l-hectare) area. Around half of all the world's animal species live in rain forests. This Indonesian chameleon (below) changes color with changes in temperature and light. **Critical Thinking** What geographic factors make rain-forest growth possible in Southeast Asia?

As you can see on the climate map, much of Southeast Asia has a tropical wet climate. It is covered with rain forests. Southeast Asia contains the second-largest rain forest region in the world. The largest is in South America.

The rain forests of Southeast Asia are lush and thick. However, there are disadvantages to living in the tropical climate of Southeast Asia—typhoons. When typhoons hit land, the high winds and heavy rain often lead to widespread property damage and loss of life.

READ ACTIVELY

Connect What parts of the United States are subject to storms like typhoons?

SECTION 2 REVIEW

1. **Define** rain forest.

2. **Identify** (a) Ghat Mountains, (b) Bangladesh, (c) Vietnam.

3. Identify the climate zones you would pass through if you traveled eastward across mainland Southeast Asia.

4. Why does the rainy season occur during the summer in India and during the winter in Vietnam?

Critical Thinking

5. **Recognizing Cause and Effect** How might the climate of South Asia be different if the Himalaya Mountains were not there?

Activity

6. **Writing to Learn** Write three weather reports—one for the west coast of India in July, one for central India in December, and a third for the southeast coast of Vietnam in December.

Natural Resources

BEFORE YOU READ

Reach Into Your Background

Look around you. Can you identify the natural resources that were used to create any of the things you see? For example, what is your pencil made of? How many natural resources can you identify?

Questions to Explore

1. What natural resources do South and Southeast Asia have?

2. How are the resources located throughout the region?

Key Terms
surplus
cash crop

Key Places
Thailand
Java

▼ A sturdy scaffold made of bamboo easily supports the construction of this temple tower in Indonesia. The bamboo poles that run diagonally give added strength to the scaffold.

What grows up to 4 feet (1.2 m) a day, is stronger (for its weight) than both concrete and steel, and has flowers that bloom only once every 20 years? Hints: half of the world's people depend on this material for shelter and food. It is a natural material that can be used to make irrigation pipes, ropes, and bridges. A platform made from this material can support the weight of an elephant.

The answer is bamboo, a type of grass. Some kinds of bamboo look like regular grass. They grow only waist high in small bushes. Other kinds are much bigger. The giant bamboo, which grows deep in the forests of Asia, is about 25 inches (63 cm) around. It towers 120 feet (37 m) into the sky—as high as a 13-story building.

Asians have long recognized the value of this natural resource. "Bamboo is my brother," goes an old Vietnamese saying. And a Chinese poet who lived nearly a thousand years ago wrote, "It is quite possible not to eat meat, but not to be without bamboo."

Land and Water: Precious Resources

Most of the people of South and Southeast Asia make their living from the land. They live in small villages, where they build their own homes, often from bamboo, and grow their own food. Some use the same building and farming methods that their ancestors relied upon thousands of years ago.

Fertile River Valleys in South Asia Three out of four South Asians still live in the countryside. Most of these people are crowded into fertile river valleys. Here they grow whatever crops the soil and climate of their particular region will allow.

The Life of a Himalayan Farmer Far up in the Himalaya Mountains, near the sources of the mighty rivers of South Asia, live the people of Nepal and Bhutan. The resources they need come from the beautiful land around them.

If you had been born in a small village in Nepal or Bhutan, you would look up at the high mountain peaks with respect. You might spend your day helping your parents tend to the crops of rice, corn, wheat, or barley growing on the terraced slopes. You might pass each day tending a herd of yaks. These are shaggy, oxlike animals that graze on the grassy slopes of the Himalaya Mountains. Your clothing would be made from yak hide and hair. Your diet would include yak milk and meat.

READ ACTIVELY

Ask Questions Think of three questions to ask about how people live in South and Southeast Asia.

Herding in the Himalayas

A herder drives his yaks across a high meadow in the Himalaya Mountains (left). Yaks provide the people of the Himalayas with milk and meat. The yaks' shaggy coats (below) can be used to make cloth, mats, or tent coverings.

Visualize Visualize a house on stilts during a summer downpour. Can you see a reason for putting a house on stilts?

Fertile River Valleys in Southeast Asia The river valleys between the mountain ranges of mainland Southeast Asia are home to millions of people. Like the people of South Asia, they live in small villages and usually grow their own food. In fact, rural Southeast Asia produces enough rice to feed people in the countryside and in the cities. Thailand produces so much extra rice that it has become a world leader in rice export. In the past, Cambodia, Myanmar, and Vietnam have also produced a rice **surplus,** or more than is needed.

The Life of a Thai Farmer Life in small farming villages in Southeast Asia differs greatly from the life of a farmer in Nepal or Bhutan. If you had been born in a small village in Thailand, you would probably live in a bamboo house built on stilts near a river. During the monsoon rains, the river might flood, and you would paddle home after school in a small boat. During the dry season, your family's prized possession, a water buffalo, would live between the stilts under your house. There it would be safe from wild animals.

Most of your time would be taken up with growing rice. Soon after planting seeds in boxes, you would transplant the sprouts to the fields just before the rains. Throughout the growing season, you would keep the fields flooded. You would carefully weed between the rice plants. And, at harvest time, you would cut down the rice plants, using a knife or a sickle. All this is hard but needed work. In Thailand, as in many Southeast Asian countries, rice is the most important part of all meals.

▼ Tea is an important cash crop in Sri Lanka. These workers can pick about 40 pounds (18 kg) of tea a day. Harvesting tea is a job traditionally done by women.

Cash Crops Some countries of South and Southeast Asia produce cash crops such as tea, cotton, and rubber. A **cash crop** is one that is raised to be sold for money on the world market.

Cash crops often bring in a great deal of money, but they may also cause problems. They can make the economies of a region dependent on world prices for the crops. When prices are high, the people who produce the crops are able to buy food. But when world prices fall, the cash crops do not bring in enough money. Because you cannot eat tea or rubber, the people who produce these crops sometimes go hungry.

▲ The mineral wealth of South and Southeast Asia includes valuable gems. Myanmar, Thailand, Sri Lanka, and India are the source of fine rubies and sapphires.

Other Resources of South and Southeast Asia

South and Southeast Asia are rich in mineral and rain forest resources. Tapping these resources, however, has led to serious problems for the countries of this region.

Mineral Resources of South and Southeast Asia The earth beneath India holds a vast supply of mineral wealth. Iron ore and coal are plentiful. Other important minerals include copper, limestone, and bauxite—an ore used to make aluminum. India has only a small amount of oil. Because of this, India relies heavily on hydroelectric and nuclear power for energy.

The nations of Southeast Asia are also rich in minerals. Indonesia, Myanmar, and the small kingdom of Brunei contain large deposits of oil. Malaysia is the world's leading exporter of tin. And iron can be found in the Philippines, Vietnam, and Malaysia.

Simply having mineral resources does not mean that a country is rich and its people live well. It is risky to depend heavily on money from the export of minerals, just as it is risky to rely on cash crops. When world prices for these minerals fall, so do the profits.

It is better for nations to use their resources to help create their own industries. In recent years, the nations of Southeast Asia have begun to build up their industries. However, they continue to export large amounts of raw materials. The challenge for South and Southeast Asia in the future will be to use their mineral resources to modernize their own nations.

LINKS TO SCIENCE

Brunei's Big House Brunei, on the northwestern coast of the island of Borneo, is only about the size of the state of Delaware. Yet this tiny nation boasts the world's biggest palace, the home of the Sultan of Brunei. This building covers 50 acres (20 hectares)—about the area of 36 football fields—and has 1,788 rooms. The Sultan and the people of Brunei have grown rich from the oil and natural gas resources of the area.

Rain Forests: A Fragile Resource Large areas of South and Southeast Asia have a tropical climate that supports rain forests. These forests contain a great variety of plant and animal life. They are a valuable source of bamboo and timber; dyes, oils, and chemicals used in industry; and medicines to treat diseases. They also produce food products—coffee, bananas, nuts, and spices.

However, the rain forests are in danger. Huge sections of them have been cut down to make more farmland and living space for a growing population. On the island of Java in Indonesia, more than 90 percent of the rain forest has been cleared for farms and tree plantations. Similar destruction is found in every nation of this region with rain forests.

The Asian rain forests contain valuable trees. Teakwood was once used to build ships and is now in demand for furniture. Teak trees take hundreds of years to mature. When the rain forest is thinned by logging, the trees are gone forever. The forest may not have a chance to grow

Rain Forest Destruction in Southeast Asia

KEY
Extent of rain forest, 1996
Extent of rain forest, 1966
Two-Point Equidistant Projection

Map Study Rain forests have only a thin layer of topsoil. When people clear rain forests for farms, the topsoil often is washed away by heavy rains. Or it wears out after just a few years. Then people must clear more land for crops. **Place** Where is the 1996 extent of rain forest the same as it was in 1966?

The orangutan makes its home in the rain forests of Indonesia. Orangutans like this mother and baby spend most of their lives high in the trees. This quiet, shy animal is an endangered species. **Critical Thinking** What do you think will happen to orangutans if Indonesian rain forests are cut down? Why?

back. The logging of rain forest trees was once carried out slowly. Workers used handsaws to cut the trees and elephants to drag the timber from the forest. But recently, logging has become faster. Chain saws, bulldozers, and trucks now cut and clear the trees.

A Step Toward Conservation   Another challenge for the nations of South and Southeast Asia is to balance the need for economic growth with the need for rain forests. Thailand has made some progress toward conserving its remaining rain forests. In 1988, hundreds of people were killed by huge mudslides. The mudslides occurred because trees that had held the soil on the hillsides had been cut down. In 1989, logging in Thailand was banned.

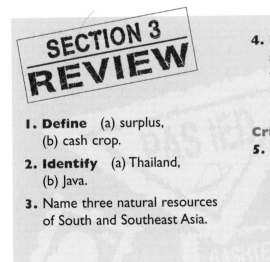

SECTION 3 REVIEW

1. **Define**   (a) surplus, (b) cash crop.

2. **Identify**   (a) Thailand, (b) Java.

3. Name three natural resources of South and Southeast Asia.

4. How do natural resources affect how people live? Give two examples of natural resources and describe their effects on people.

Critical Thinking

5. **Expressing Problems Clearly**   The island nation of Sri Lanka is one of the world's leading producers of tea. What might happen to the people of Sri Lanka if tea prices fell very low?

Activity

6. **Writing to Learn**   Write a diary entry from the point of view of a farmer living in South or Southeast Asia. What daily tasks might you describe? What would you notice about the weather? Use information from this chapter, conclusions you drew from this information, and your imagination.

Using Isolines to Show Precipitation

If you ever visit Mawsynram, remember to take an umbrella.

Mawsynram, a city in India, is the rainiest place on the Earth. On average, Mawsynram receives about 463 inches (11,873 mm) of rain per year. That is more than ten times as much rain as most cities in the United States receive! It rains an average of $1\frac{1}{4}$ inches in Mawsynram every day.

Mawsynram is in Asia. You will also find the world's largest dry region in the world in Asia—the Arabian Peninsula. While Mawsynram is getting drenched, parts of the Arabian Peninsula do not see rain for years at a time.

It is hard to imagine how the wettest and the driest places in the world can be on the same continent. Asia is the world's largest continent. Rainfall varies greatly all the way across it.

Get Ready

On maps, the amount of precipitation is often shown by isolines. The word *isoline* comes from the Greek word *isos,* which means "equal," and the Latin word *linea.* Isolines are lines on a map that connect parts of an area that are equal in some way. On a map that shows precipitation, they outline areas that have about the same amount of precipitation.

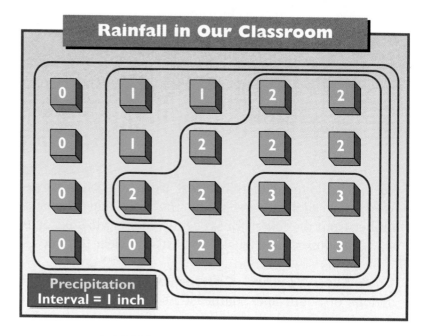

Rainfall in Our Classroom

Precipitation Interval = 1 inch

Try It Out

To see how isolines are used to show precipitation, make a simple isoline map of "rainfall" in your own classroom.

A. **Make it rain.** Take plastic or paper cups of the same size and place one on each desk in your classroom. Fill four cups in one corner of the classroom with three inches of water each. Surrounding those four cups, fill eight cups of water with two inches of water each. Next to these cups, fill three cups each with one inch of water. Leave the remaining cups empty. The arrangement of your cups will vary slightly, depending on your classroom.

B. **Draw a map.** On the board, draw a rough map of your classroom. Draw a box to show each desk.

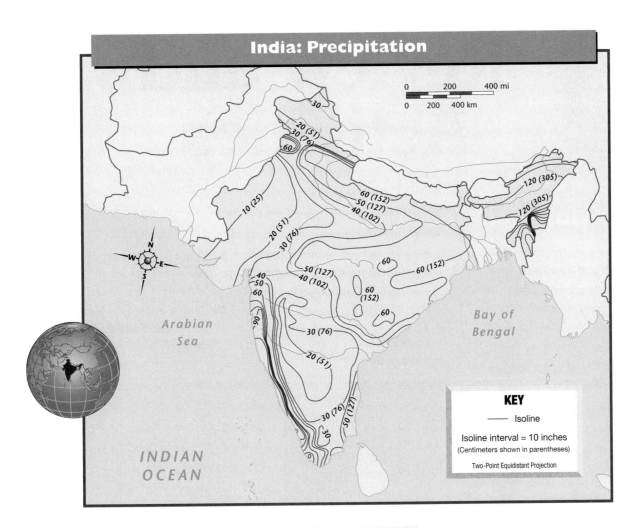

India: Precipitation

0   200   400 mi
0   200   400 km

30

20 (51)
30 (76)
60

60 (152)
50 (127)
40 (102)

120 (305)
120 (305)

10 (25)

20 (51)
30 (76)

50 (127)
40 (102)

60

60 (152)

60
(152)

60

*Arabian
Sea*

40
50
60

90

30 (76)

20 (51)

*Bay of
Bengal*

KEY

—— Isoline

Isoline interval = 10 inches
(Centimeters shown in parentheses)

Two-Point Equidistant Projection

30 (76)
50 (127)

30

0

**INDIAN
OCEAN**

C. Record the precipitation on the map. Count the inches of "rainfall" in each cup. Write each measurement in the box that shows that desk on the map.

D. Draw isolines. Draw one isoline around the entire area of all desks. This line shows the base level of no rainfall. Then draw a single line around the entire area that has *at least* one inch of rainfall. This will also enclose areas with two and three inches of rainfall.

Just inside the one-inch isoline, draw an isoline that surrounds the desks with at least two inches of rainfall. Be sure not to include the desks with only one inch of rainfall. Inside the two-inch isoline, draw an isoline that surrounds only the desks with three inches of rainfall.

E. Read your map. Look at the isolines on your map and think about how they help you to visualize the differences in precipitation throughout your classroom.

Apply the Skill

The same process is used on a larger scale to draw precipitation maps of large regions, countries, or whole continents. The map above is a precipitation map that uses isolines to show average amounts of rainfall in India. Use it to complete the following steps.

1 Study the isolines. What is the interval, or difference in amount of precipitation, between isolines? How much rain does the rainiest part of India receive each year? How much rain does the driest part receive?

2 Use the isolines to find useful information. Where is the rainiest part of India? Where is the driest part?

Review and Activities

Reviewing Main Ideas

1. Describe two major landforms in South and Southeast Asia.
2. How do landforms affect the people living in South and Southeast Asia?
3. How does climate affect the vegetation growing throughout South and Southeast Asia? Give two examples.
4. What are monsoons, and how do they affect rainfall in South and Southeast Asia?
5. What mineral and agricultural resources do South and Southeast Asia have?
6. Why are the rain forests of South and Southeast Asia in danger?

Reviewing Key Terms

Use each key term below in a sentence that shows the meaning of the term.

1. subcontinent
2. rain forest
3. surplus
4. cash crop

Critical Thinking

1. **Recognizing Cause and Effect** Why would cash crops affect rain forests?
2. **Making Comparisons** What are two similarities between South and Southeast Asia? What are two differences?

Graphic Organizer

Copy the chart onto a sheet of paper. Then fill in the empty boxes to complete the chart.

	Major Landforms	Climate and Vegetation Regions	Natural Resources
South Asia			
Southeast Asia			

Map Activity

South and Southeast Asia

For each place listed below, write the letter from the map that shows its location.

1. Vietnam

2. Nepal

3. India

4. Bangladesh

5. Borneo

6. Thailand

7. Himalaya Mountains

Writing Activity

Writing a Plan

Suppose you were planning a trip to South and Southeast Asia. Write a day-by-day plan for your trip. Explain what places you would visit and when you would go. Include information about the climate, landforms, and natural resources of the regions in your plan. Begin with this entry: "July 1: Fly from New York to Mumbai (Bombay), India. Arrive in Mumbai at 3:00 P.M."

Take It to the NET

Activity Read an article about the impact of a proposed dam in Thailand. What are the advantages and disadvantages of building the dam? For help in completing this activity, visit www.phschool.com.

Chapter 3 Self-Test To review what you have learned, take the Chapter 3 Self-Test and get instant feedback on your answers. Go to www.phschool.com to take the test.

Skills Review

Turn to the Skills Activity.

Review the use of isolines to show precipitation. Then answer the following questions: (a) What is an isoline? (b) Could isolines connect areas of equal snowfall? Why or why not?

How Am I Doing?

Answer these questions to help you check your progress.

1. Can I describe the major landforms of South and Southeast Asia?

2. Do I know how the monsoons affect the climate and vegetation of South and Southeast Asia?

3. Do I know the natural resources that can be found in the nations of South and Southeast Asia?

4. What information from this chapter can I include in my journal?

SOUTH AND SOUTHEAST ASIA

Cultures and History

PICTURE ACTIVITIES

The picture above shows a religious festival in India. Begin your study of India and other countries in South and Southeast Asia by completing the following activities.

Study the picture
What does the picture tell you about the role of religion in every-day life in South and Southeast Asia?

Choose a person
Pick one of the people in the picture. Write a short description of the person. What is the person wearing? What do you think he or she is doing?

The Cultures of South Asia

BEFORE YOU READ

Reach Into Your Background

Holidays and celebrations are one part of culture. What holidays or celebrations do you or people you know take part in? Think about the things you do to celebrate. Do you eat turkey on Thanksgiving? Do you belong to a group that marches in a parade on the Fourth of July? What else do you do?

Questions to Explore

1. How did invasions affect the cultures of South Asia?
2. What ancient traditions influence the cultures of South Asia today?

Key Terms

caste
colony
boycott
partition

Key People

Siddhartha Gautama
Asoka
Mohandas K. Gandhi

In 1922, scientists digging near the Indus River came upon the ruins of an ancient city they called Mohenjo-Daro (moh HEN joh DAH roh). The city was amazingly well planned, with wide, straight streets and large buildings. It had a sewer system and a large walled fortress. Mohenjo-Daro was part of a civilization that developed about 4,500 years ago.

The people who lived there were part of one of the world's oldest civilizations. Over the centuries, many other people moved into the region. Some came peacefully. Others marched in with swords in their hands. All of these invaders contributed to South Asian culture.

South Asian culture, in turn, influenced cultures of other regions. Hinduism (HIN doo izm) and Buddhism, two religions that developed in South Asia, are practiced by hundreds of millions of people.

New Religions

Between 2000 B.C. and 1500 B.C., invaders known as Aryans (AIR ee unz) swept down on the people of the Indus Valley. Look at the map on the next page and note the route the Aryans took. The Indus Valley farmers were no match for the Aryan soldiers in horse-drawn chariots. The Aryans took control of

▼ The people of Mohenjo-Daro built their city on mounds of earth to protect it from the floods of the Indus River.

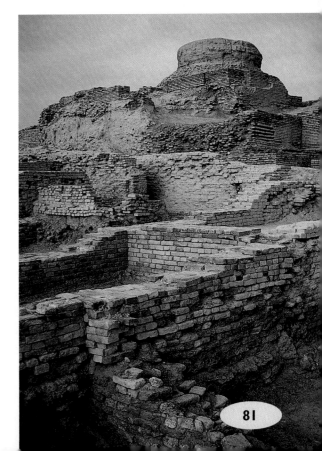

Map Study The Aryan people came from Central Asia. Over time, they used iron tools to clear areas of thick rain forests along the Ganges River. **Place** Why do you think the people of the Indus Valley and the Aryans settled where they did?

KEY

Indus Valley Civilization, c. 2400–1550 B.C.

Chandragupta Maurya's Empire, 330–298 B.C.

Aryan invasion, c. 1500 B.C.

Asoka's Empire, c. 273–232 B.C.

Two-Point Equidistant Projection

CHINA

• Harappa

Mohenjo-Daro •

Indus River

Ganges River

Arabian Sea

INDIA

Bay of Bengal

INDIAN OCEAN

0   300   600 mi
0   300   600 km

READ ACTIVELY

Predict What do you think are the main religions of South Asia?

the area. In time, the Aryans moved eastward to the Ganges River, laying claim to much of northern India.

The Aryans ruled northern India for more than 1,000 years. They introduced new ways of living. For instance, they divided people into three classes—priests, warriors, and ordinary working people. This division grew out of Aryan religious writings called the Vedas (VAY duz). In time, the Aryans drew the conquered people into their class system. By 500 B.C., there was a strict division of classes. Europeans later called it the caste system. Each **caste,** or class, had special duties and work.

The caste system became a central part of a new system of belief that also emerged from Aryan religious ideas and practices. This system of beliefs, Hinduism, is one of the world's oldest living religions.

Hinduism Hinduism is unlike other major world religions. It has no one single founder. However, it has many great religious thinkers. Also, Hindus worship many gods and goddesses, but they believe in a single spirit. To Hindus, the various gods and goddesses represent different parts of this spirit. As an old Hindu saying states: "God is one, but wise people know it by many names." Today, Hinduism is the national religion of India and has 700 million followers here.

Buddhism   Buddhism, like Hinduism, developed in India. According to Buddhist tradition, its founder was a prince named Siddhartha Gautama (sihd DAHR tuh goh TUH muh). He was born in about 560 B.C., in present-day Nepal. Gautama was a Hindu of high caste. He lived a privileged life, safe from hunger and disease.

When he was 29 years old, Gautama left home to learn about his kingdom. For the first time, he saw people who were hungry, sick, and poor. He became so unhappy that he gave up his wealth. He pledged his life to finding the causes of people's suffering.

Eventually, Gautama found what he believed was the solution. He taught that people can be free of suffering if they give up selfish desires for power, wealth, and pleasure. He then became known as the Buddha, or "Enlightened One." People of all backgrounds, princes and ordinary people alike, flocked to hear his sermons.

For some time after the Buddha's death, Buddhism had a huge following in India. Over time, however, it almost completely died out there.

Great Empires

Buddhism had its greatest following in India in the 200s B.C., during the time of a great empire. For hundreds of years, India was divided into many small kingdoms. No one ruler emerged to unite them.

Ask Questions Think of three questions you might ask about the teachings of the Buddha.

Languages of South Asia

Country	Major Languages	Major Religions
Afghanistan	Pashtu, Dari	Islam
Bangladesh	Bengali (official), English	Islam, Hinduism
Bhutan	Dzongkha (official), Gurung, Assamese	Buddhism, Hinduism
India	Hindi (official), English (official), and 14 other languages	Hinduism, Islam, Christianity, Sikhism
Nepal	Nepali (official) and many others	Hinduism, Buddhism, Islam
Pakistan	Urdu (official), English, Punjabi, Sindhi	Islam
Sri Lanka	Sinhala (official), Tamil (official), and English (official)	Buddhism, Hinduism, Christianity, Islam

Chart Study The chart shows the major religions and languages of South Asia. In India, for example, the people speak over 1,000 different languages and dialects. Note that an official language is one chosen by a nation and used for government business. **Critical Thinking** Why do you think English is a major language in several South Asian countries?

The Maurya Empire   Around 330 B.C., however, a fierce leader named Chandragupta Maurya (CHUN druh gup tuh MAH ur yuh) conquered many kingdoms. By the time of his death in 298 B.C., he ruled an empire that covered much of the subcontinent.

Chandragupta's grandson, Asoka (uh SOH kuh), continued the conquests. This soon changed, however. After one bloody battle, Asoka gave up war and violence and freed his prisoners. Later he changed his beliefs to Buddhism and vowed to rule peacefully.

Asoka kept his word. He showed concern for his people's welfare. He made laws requiring people to treat each other with respect. He spread the peaceful message of Buddhism throughout his empire.

The Maurya empire collapsed not long after Asoka's death. More than 1,500 years would pass before another empire as great ruled India.

The Mughal Empire   In the A.D. 700s, people from the north began moving into northern India. They introduced Islam to the area. Islam is the set of beliefs revealed to the prophet Muhammad. He began teaching these beliefs around A.D. 610 in Southwest Asia. Islam spread westward into North Africa and eastward into Central and South Asia.

Among these Muslims, or followers of Islam, who settled in India were the Mughals (MOO gulz). They arrived in the 1500s and established an empire. Akbar (AK bar), who ruled the Mughal empire from 1556 to 1605, allowed all people to worship freely, regardless of their religion. He also supported the arts and literature.

Akbar's grandson, Shah Jahan (shah juh HAHN), built many grand buildings. Perhaps the greatest is the Taj Mahal (tahzh muh HAHL). He had it built as a magnificent tomb for Mumtaz (mum TAHZ) Mahal, his

Buddhism in India

The religion founded by the Buddha (right) had its greatest following during the rule of Asoka. The stone lions (left) topped one of the pillars that Asoka set up all over India. Asoka had Buddhist writings carved on these pillars. After Asoka's death, Buddhism nearly died out in India, but missionaries carried the religion to Japan, Korea, China, and Vietnam.

It took 20,000 workers 22 years to finish the Taj Mahal, the stunning monument Shah Jahan built to his wife.

wife. The cost of this and other of Jahan's building projects was enormous. It drained the empire of money and, eventually, helped to cause the empire's collapse in the 1700s.

The Jewel in the Crown During the 1700s, 1800s, and 1900s, European nations established many colonies in Asia, Africa, and the Americas. A **colony** is a territory ruled by another nation, usually one very far away. Through trade and war, the nations of Europe made colonies of most of South Asia. Britain took over most of the region, including India. Because of the riches it produced, the British called India the "jewel in the crown" of their empire.

While Britain treasured its empire, many Indians treasured their freedom. A strong independence movement grew up. Its greatest leader was Mohandas K. Gandhi (GAHN dee). He called for people to resist British rule. However, Gandhi stressed that they should do this through nonviolent means. For example, he urged a boycott of British goods. A **boycott** means a refusal to buy or use goods and services. Gandhi was jailed many times for opposing British rule. This only made him a greater hero to his people. Gandhi's efforts played a major part in forcing Britain to grant India its freedom in 1947.

READ ACTIVELY

Ask Questions What questions do you have about how India won its freedom from Britain?

Mohandas K. Gandhi urged Indians to resist the British by following Hindu traditions. He preached the Hindu idea of *ahimsa*, or nonviolence and respect for all life. Because of his nonviolent approach, Indians called him *Mahatma*, or "Great Soul." **Critical Thinking** Why do you think that Gandhi's nonviolent methods proved so successful?

Independence was soon followed by the horror of religious warfare. During the struggle for freedom, Hindus and Muslims had worked together. However, Muslims were a minority. Many feared that their rights would not be protected in a land with a Hindu majority. In 1947, Hindus and Muslims agreed on the **partition,** or division, of the subcontinent into two nations. India would be mainly Hindu. Muslims would be the majority in Pakistan.

This did not stop the fighting. About 1 million people were killed. Gandhi himself was murdered. Conflict between the two nations continued. In 1971, for example, Indian troops helped East Pakistan break away from Pakistan to form the nation of Bangladesh (bahn gluh DESH). Even today, India and Pakistan continue to view each other with distrust.

SECTION 1 REVIEW

1. **Define** (a) caste, (b) colony, (c) boycott, (d) partition.

2. **Identify** (a) Siddhartha Gautama, (b) Asoka, (c) Mohandas K. Gandhi.

3. How did the Aryan invasion shape South Asian culture?

4. What religions have influenced the cultures of South Asia?

Critical Thinking

5. **Drawing Conclusions** Why do you think jailing Gandhi made him more of a hero to the people of India?

Activity

6. **Writing to Learn** Write a letter in which the Buddha explains to his family why he gave up his wealth.

The Cultures of Southeast Asia

Reach Into Your Background

Southeast Asia has a great deal of cultural diversity, or variety.

Think about the idea of diversity. The United States is culturally diverse, too. Why do you think this is so?

Questions to Explore

1. Why is Southeast Asia a culturally diverse region?

2. What effects did colonial powers have on Southeast Asia?

Key Terms

nationalist
dictator

Key Places

Angkor Wat
Philippines

D eep in the rain forests of Cambodia lies Angkor Wat—the largest temple in the world. Angkor Wat is a Hindu temple. It was built in the A.D. 1100s by the Khmer (kuh MEHR). The Khmer empire included Cambodia and much of Laos, Thailand, and Vietnam. In the 1100s, the empire enjoyed great wealth. Wearing gold and pearls, the king rode on an elephant whose tusks were wrapped in gold. The ruins of Angkor Wat stand as proof of a great civilization.

A Region of Diversity

The Khmer empire was one of many kingdoms in Southeast Asia. Unlike the Khmer empire, however, the other kingdoms were small. Geography had much to do with this. Southeast Asia's mountains kept people protected and apart. People had little contact with those who lived outside their own valley. Each group developed its own special way of life. These factors created a region with a variety of cultures.

Through the centuries, traders, explorers, and travelers passed through Southeast Asia. They brought new ideas and new religions to the region. The people of Southeast Asia blended these new ideas with their own traditions to create unique ways of life.

▼ Angkor Wat is almost one square mile (2.6 sq km) in area. Its inner walls are covered with carvings of figures from Hindu myths.

These Cambodian girls are learning traditional dances of Southeast Asia. The dances of this region are based on dances of India. They often retell ancient Hindu legends. Each hand gesture has a special meaning. **Critical Thinking** Why do you think the dances of Southeast Asia are based on those of India?

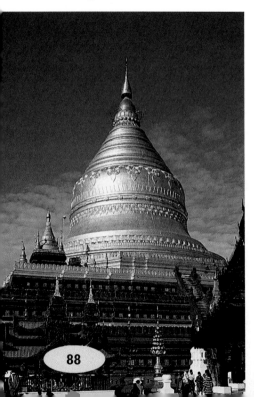

▼ The Shwe Dagon Pagoda crowns Yangôn, Myanmar's capital city. This famous Buddhist temple is covered with gold.

The Influence of China   In spite of the mountains, the kingdoms of Southeast Asia always worried about invasion from their powerful neighbor to the north—China. From time to time, Chinese armies swept into Southeast Asia. In 111 B.C., the Chinese took over Vietnam. They ruled the country for more than 1,000 years. During that time, the Vietnamese began using Chinese ways of farming. They also began using the ideas of Confucius to run their government.

The Religions of Southeast Asia   The Indians were another influence on Southeast Asia. Nearly 2,000 years ago, Indian traders sailed across the Indian Ocean to the lands of Southeast Asia. Indians introduced the religion of Hinduism to the region. Today, there are Hindus in Bali, in Indonesia, and in parts of Malaysia. Around A.D. 100, Indians brought Buddhism to Southeast Asia. Buddhists eventually outnumbered Hindus in the region. There are many Buddhists in Myanmar, Thailand, Laos, Vietnam, and Cambodia today.

During the 800s and 900s, Arab traders introduced Islam to Southeast Asia. Today, Islam is the religion of millions in Malaysia, Indonesia, the southern Philippines, and other countries. In fact, Indonesia has the largest Muslim population in the world.

European missionaries brought Christianity to the area in the 1500s. Today, most Filipinos are Christian. There are small groups of Christians in other Southeast Asian countries, too.

Colonial Rule in Southeast Asia

Europeans brought more than Christianity to Southeast Asia. Traders from Europe arrived in the region in the 1500s. They hoped to gain control of the rich trade in silks, iron, silver, pearls, and spices. At first, Portugal, the Netherlands, and other European nations built trading posts here. From these small posts, Europeans expanded their power. By the 1800s, European nations had gained control of most of Southeast Asia.

Effects of Colonial Rule Outside nations took over Southeast Asian land in order to gain control of the economy. The ruling powers forced their colonies to grow cash crops. On the island of Java, the Dutch forced farmers to grow and sell coffee. This caused rice production to fall. There was not enough food for people to eat.

Colonial rulers built a network of roads, bridges, ports, and railroads in Southeast Asia. Good transportation was essential for the economic

Visualize Visualize a road, bridge, canal, or railroad in your community. How does it make moving people and goods across your region easier?

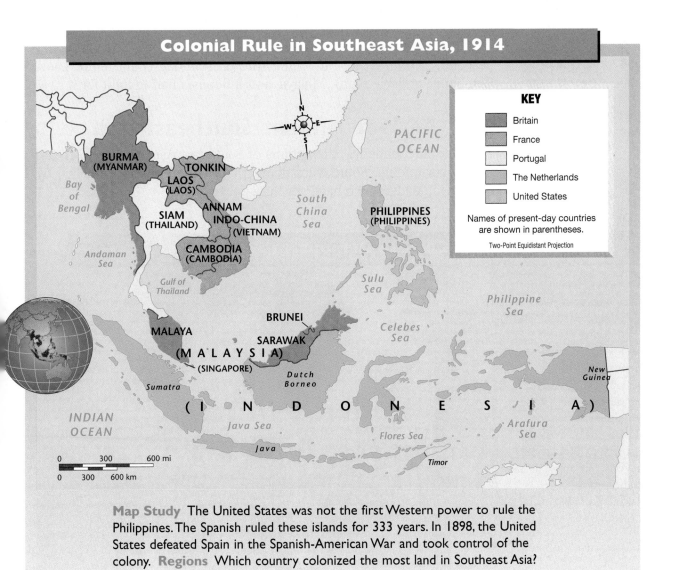

Colonial Rule in Southeast Asia, 1914

KEY

- Britain
- France
- Portugal
- The Netherlands
- United States

Names of present-day countries are shown in parentheses.

Two-Point Equidistant Projection

Map Study The United States was not the first Western power to rule the Philippines. The Spanish ruled these islands for 333 years. In 1898, the United States defeated Spain in the Spanish-American War and took control of the colony. **Regions** Which country colonized the most land in Southeast Asia?

CITIZEN HEROES

Working Together East Timor takes up half of a small island several hundred miles from the capital of Indonesia, Jakarta. A former Portuguese colony, East Timor was invaded by Indonesia in 1975 and ruled harshly. Some people, however, fought back. Carlos Filipe Ximenes Belo, a Roman Catholic bishop, and José Ramos-Horta, a politician, worked peacefully on behalf of the Timorese people. They were awarded the 1996 Nobel Peace Prize for their efforts. In 1999, East Timor voted to become an independent nation.

success of the colonies. It made it easier to move people and goods across the region. The colonial powers also built schools and universities, which helped to produce skilled workers for colonial industries. In addition, education gave some Southeast Asians the skills to become teachers, doctors, government workers, and more. These educated Southeast Asians would eventually lead the struggle for freedom.

Fighting for Freedom   By the early 1900s, nationalists were organizing independence movements throughout Southeast Asia. A **nationalist** is someone who is devoted to the interests of his or her country. By the time World War II broke out in 1939, the Japanese had begun to move into Southeast Asia. During the war, the Japanese drove out the colonial powers. Many Southeast Asians hoped that a Japanese victory would end colonialism in the region. However, Japanese rule proved to be as harsh as that of the former colonial powers.

After the Japanese were defeated in World War II, Western nations hoped to regain power in Southeast Asia. But Southeast Asians had other hopes. They wanted independence.

Most Southeast Asian countries did gain independence. Some, like the Philippines and Burma (now called Myanmar), won their freedom peacefully. Others, like Indochina (the present-day countries of Laos, Cambodia, and Vietnam), Malaya, and Indonesia had to fight for it.

An Independent Southeast Asia

After independence, the nations of Southeast Asia worked to create new governments. Some were democratic. Others were controlled by **dictators,** leaders who have absolute power.

Anti-Chinese Demonstrations

During the 1990s, many Indonesians came to resent people of Chinese descent. The Chinese in Indonesia tended to do very well in their businesses. Though a small part of Indonesia's population, they were an important part of the economy. Indonesians also feared China's power in aiding communist groups throughout Southeast Asia. This anti-Chinese demonstration took place in Jakarta in 1996.

Corazon Aquino (KOR uh zahn uh KEE noh) is shown here campaigning during the 1986 elections in the Philippines. She had restored democracy to the nation after dictator Ferdinand Marcos (MAHR kohs) had been forced to flee. Aquino served as president of the Philippines for six years.

Indonesia won its independence in 1945. In 1965, the army took control of the country. Two years later, General Suharto (soo HAR toe) became president. Suharto used violence to stay in power. During his rule, Indonesia's economy grew rapidly. In 1998, however, an economic collapse brought inflation and food shortages. Indonesians blamed Suharto, and forced him to resign. The next year, Indonesia held its first free elections. Having taken this step toward democracy, Indonesians could concentrate on fixing the economy.

Problems still remained for some people in Indonesia. The East Timorese had lived on the island of Timor for hundreds of years. In the 1600s Portugal took control of the island. In 1975, Indonesia invaded and later annexed East Timor. The Indonesian government ruled the territory harshly. Many people were killed as the Indonesian government tried to suppress a growing movement for independence. Finally, Indonesia's president allowed the East Timorese to choose between remaining part of Indonesia or forming their own independent nation. In September of 1999, the East Timorese voted overwhelmingly for independence.

Though the East Timorese finally had gained independence, their struggle was far from over. Right after the vote, pro-Indonesia militias in East Timor began to terrorize those who had voted for independence. In an attempt to stop the violence, the United Nations sent a peace-keeping force to the island. In addition, the president of Indonesia agreed to set up a commission to investigate human rights violations. Still, the future of East Timor remains uncertain, and the East Timorese have many obstacles to overcome before they can build a new nation.

READ ACTIVELY

Connect How did the United States gain its independence? What type of government was created in the United States when it became independent?

SECTION 2 REVIEW

1. **Define** (a) nationalist, (b) dictator.

2. **Identify** (a) Angkor Wat, (b) the Philippines.

3. How did China and India affect the cultures of Southeast Asia?

4. (a) Why were many Southeast Asians hopeful when the Japanese invaded the region during World War II? (b) Why were they disappointed?

Critical Thinking

5. **Expressing Problems Clearly** What challenges face the independent nations of Southeast Asia?

Activity

6. **Writing to Learn** Write a speech urging Southeast Asians to support independence from European rule.

India

IN THE MIDST OF CHANGE

Reach Into Your Background

What if you had little choice when it came to choosing a job? Suppose that you were expected to work in the same occupation as the rest of your family—an occupation that your family has worked at for hundreds of years. Write a few sentences telling how you would feel about this situation.

Questions to Explore

1. How has independence affected life in India?
2. How are the roles of men and women in India changing?

Key Terms
quota
purdah
parliament

Key People
Indira Gandhi

The whole village had turned up for the Hindu religious service—everyone from members of the highest caste to those of no caste, the Untouchables. After the service, the people sat down to a meal. No one seemed to mind who was sitting next to them. At the end of the meal, lower caste members and Untouchables began to clean up the dining room. Some higher caste members told them to stop, then did the work themselves. Stunned, an Untouchable said, "This is the first time in my life to see such a sight."

A Changing Society

Why did the Untouchable express surprise? Because of the ancient traditions, such as the caste system, in which Indian culture is rooted.

The Caste System Traditional Hindu society divides its followers into four castes. The castes put people in order from the bottom of society to the top. Below the lowest caste are the Untouchables. They are a "casteless" or outcast Hindu group.

Over thousands of years, the caste system grew complex. The main castes divided into hundreds of groups, or subcastes. The people in each subcaste had

▼ An Indian barber shaves a customer. Many barbers in India work in the open air.

COUNTRY · PROFILE

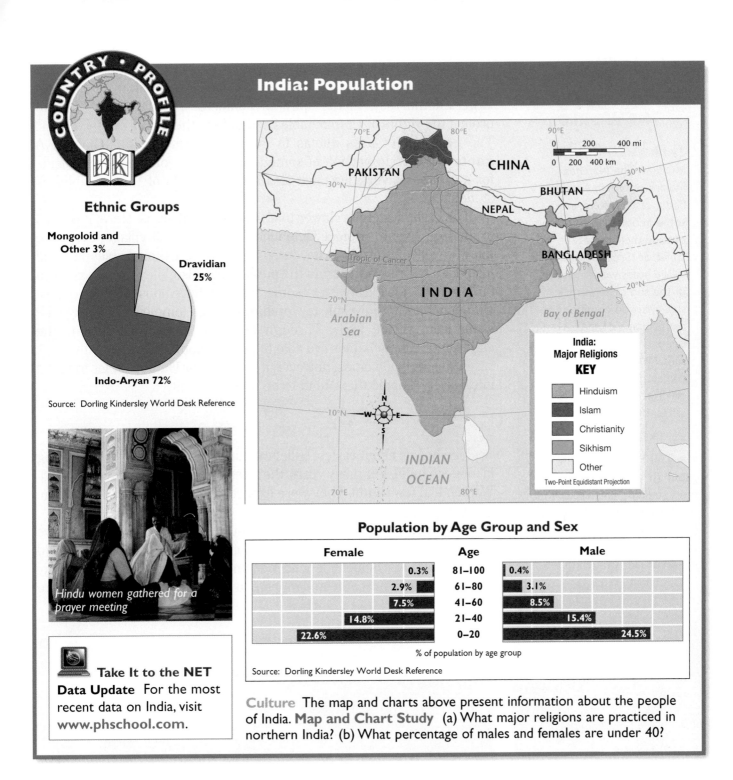

Ethnic Groups

Mongoloid and Other 3%

Dravidian 25%

Indo-Aryan 72%

Source: Dorling Kindersley World Desk Reference

Hindu women gathered for a prayer meeting

Take It to the NET
Data Update For the most recent data on India, visit **www.phschool.com.**

India: Major Religions
KEY
- Hinduism
- Islam
- Christianity
- Sikhism
- Other

Two-Point Equidistant Projection

Population by Age Group and Sex

Female	Age	Male
0.3%	81–100	0.4%
2.9%	61–80	3.1%
7.5%	41–60	8.5%
14.8%	21–40	15.4%
22.6%	0–20	24.5%

% of population by age group

Source: Dorling Kindersley World Desk Reference

Culture The map and charts above present information about the people of India. **Map and Chart Study** (a) What major religions are practiced in northern India? (b) What percentage of males and females are under 40?

---

the same job. Shopkeepers, barbers, and weavers, for example, each had their own subcaste. The caste system gave Hindus a sense of order. But for the Untouchables, life was hard. Untouchables could do only the dirtiest work. They were not allowed to mix with people of higher castes.

The System Weakens Today, however, the caste system is weakening. During India's struggle for independence, Mohandas Gandhi began to fight for the rights of Untouchables. He took Untouchables as his pupils. He called them *Harijans,* or children of God.

Castes Among the Natchez The Natchez Indians of North America had a caste system. In it, some people had to marry outside their caste. The Chief, or Great Sun, and village heads were members of the sun caste. Female suns married commoners, or members of the lowest caste. Their children were suns. Male suns also married commoners, but their children belonged to a caste called "honored people."

▼ ▶ This street scene in Jaipur (JY poor), northern India (below), illustrates well the hustle and bustle of Indian city life. In the country-side outside Jaipur (right), however, life is much quieter.

After independence, India became a democracy. With more than three times the population of the United States, India is the world's largest democracy. In the spirit of democracy, India passed laws to protect the rights of Untouchables and to help them improve their lives. The government uses quotas to guarantee jobs to Untouchables. A **quota** is a certain portion of something, such as jobs, that is set aside for a group. Universities must also accept a quota of Untouchables as students.

The caste system is slower to change in rural areas. Here, it is hard to enforce laws to protect Untouchables. In a small village, everyone knows everyone else's caste. In some villages, Untouchables are still forbidden to draw water from the public well. Also, they may be allowed only certain jobs. However, some villages have loosened the rules. Untouchables now are able to worship at village temples. They may take water from village wells. Through India's public school system, the children of Untouchables are able to go to school.

In the crowded cities, however, it is easier for Untouchables to blend into society. People there tend to be more tolerant.

Women in India

Like beliefs about castes, beliefs about men and women are changing in modern India. For many years, the roles of men and women were rigid. Women had few rights. They were expected to marry and have children.

Women Gain Rights Gandhi urged women to play an active part in India's fight against Britain. Women took part in boycotts and prepared leaflets. Since independence, Indian women have gained many rights. They can now vote and engage in business. They are now free to

take part in public life, as well. In 1966, a woman, Indira Gandhi, became prime minister. She was the daughter of Jawaharlal Nehru (juh WA hur lal NAY roo), India's first prime minister.

Changing Roles for Indian Women In addition to gaining legal rights, women have changed their roles in other ways. Many Muslim women no longer follow the custom of **purdah,** or covering their heads and faces with veils. Many Indian women today have careers and work outside the home. More and more women are entering the fields of science and health care. For example, India has a high percentage of women doctors.

Also, more Indian women than American women hold high government positions. For example, Roda Mistry, who lives in the city of Hyderabad, in central India, is president of the Indian Council on Social Welfare. Before reaching this position, Mistry was a member of the Indian **parliament,** or lawmaking body. She also served as Minister of Tourism and Minister of Women's and Children's Welfare in the Indian government. In her work for the Council on Social Welfare, Mistry has set up shelters for orphans. She also has started programs designed to help poor women find work. Mistry is a well-respected political leader. Her grandchildren call her *Mamaiji*, which means "Grandmother, Sir."

Indira Gandhi

Indira Gandhi served as prime minister of India for all but three years during the period from 1966 to 1980. Conflict between the Indian government and Sikhs, a religious minority, led to Gandhi's death in 1984. She was assassinated after she ordered an attack on a temple held by armed Sikhs.

READ ACTIVELY

Connect Think about the men and women in your family. How are their lives similar and different?

SECTION 3 REVIEW

1. **Define** (a) quota, (b) purdah, (c) parliament.

2. **Identify** Indira Gandhi.

3. How is the caste system different in cities and rural villages?

4. What rights have women gained since independence?

Critical Thinking

5. **Drawing Conclusions** Why do you think the Indian government has taken the lead in helping Untouchables?

Activity

6. **Writing to Learn** Write a letter to Roda Mistry. Include some questions you would like to ask her about the roles of women in India.

Pakistan

ECONOMIC PROGRESS

BEFORE YOU READ

Reach Into Your Background

Jot down several goals that you have achieved. Put a star beside those that required the help of other people. Who helped you achieve your goals? How did they help?

Questions to Explore

1. What has Pakistan done to help its farmers?
2. What industrial growth has taken place in Pakistan?

Key Terms
drought
textile
automotive industry

Key Place
Kashmir

▼ Only about 6 percent of Kashmir's land is good for growing crops. Here, farmers have built terraces so they can grow crops on sloping land.

Water. Everyone needs it to survive. Many of us take it for granted. We turn on the tap, and water pours out. But many countries in the world lack water resources. **Drought,** or a long period without rain, is a major problem in Pakistan. It is one cause of the conflict over the region of Kashmir (KAZH mihr).

Kashmir is a land of high mountains and beautiful lakes. The Indus River flows from the high mountains of Kashmir. Therefore, whoever controls Kashmir, controls the water flow of the Indus River. This water is necessary to farmers. They need it to irrigate their crops. Without the Indus River, Pakistan would be a dry, hot desert.

Kashmir is bordered by Pakistan, India, China, and Afghanistan. Both Pakistan and India claim Kashmir. Both wish to control the waters of the Indus. The conflict over Kashmir has led to battles between India and Pakistan. This is how important water is to the region.

An Agricultural Nation

Pakistan fears losing control of the waters of the Indus River. Most Pakistanis are farmers. They rely on the waters to irrigate their fields. Through hard work and clever farming methods, they grow large amounts of wheat, cotton, and sugar cane. Pakistani farmers grow so

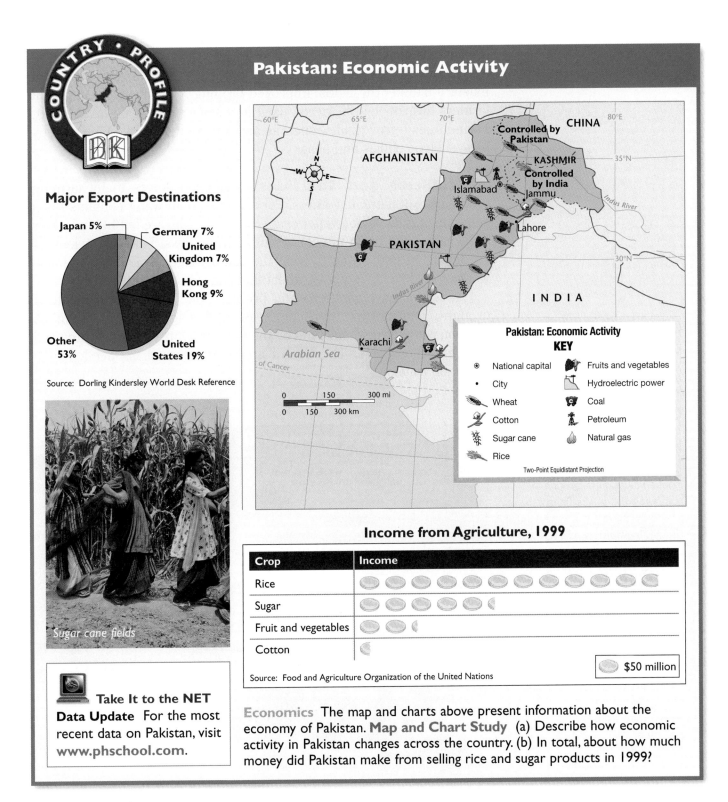

COUNTRY · PROFILE

Pakistan: Economic Activity

Major Export Destinations

Japan 5%
Germany 7%
United Kingdom 7%
Hong Kong 9%
United States 19%
Other 53%

Source: Dorling Kindersley World Desk Reference

Sugar cane fields

Pakistan: Economic Activity KEY

⊛ National capital	Fruits and vegetables
• City	Hydroelectric power
Wheat	Coal
Cotton	Petroleum
Sugar cane	Natural gas
Rice	

Two-Point Equidistant Projection

Income from Agriculture, 1999

Crop	Income
Rice	⬭⬭⬭⬭⬭⬭⬭⬭⬭⬭⬭⬭
Sugar	⬭⬭⬭⬭⬭◖
Fruit and vegetables	⬭⬭◖
Cotton	◖

⬭ = $50 million

Source: Food and Agriculture Organization of the United Nations

Take It to the NET
Data Update For the most recent data on Pakistan, visit **www.phschool.com.**

Economics The map and charts above present information about the economy of Pakistan. **Map and Chart Study** (a) Describe how economic activity in Pakistan changes across the country. (b) In total, about how much money did Pakistan make from selling rice and sugar products in 1999?

Predict What do you think farmers in Pakistan do to make sure that their crops get enough water?

much rice, they export it to other countries. The great advances the country has made in agriculture could easily be lost without the much-needed water.

Irrigation Produces Larger Crops   Pakistanis on the Indus Plain have built thousands of canals and ditches to move water to their fields. In this way, farmers maintain a steady flow of water, even during droughts. As more land is irrigated, more acres are farmed. This increases the amount of crops.

At harvest time, the bright yellow flowers of Pakistan's five kinds of mustard blanket the fields. Improved farming methods allow Pakistani farmers to grow lentils, beans used in a spicy dish called *dhal* (dahl). Farmers also grow fruits, such as apricots and mangoes, and vegetables, such as chilies and peas.

Problems and Solutions   Irrigation solves many farming problems. But it creates others. For example, river water contains small amounts of salts. When water evaporates, the salts are left behind. Over time, salts build up in the soil. Plant growth slows. Pakistani scientists are trying to find a way to treat the salt-damaged soil. They are also working to develop a type of wheat that can grow in salty soil.

Pakistanis have another water problem, one that is the opposite of drought. During the monsoon season, damaging floods occur. A solution is the large dams built by the government. The dams catch and hold monsoon rains. The waters are then released, as needed, into irrigation canals.

Wheat Harvest in Pakistan

These Pakistani farmers are removing the husks from wheat grains by tossing the wheat into the air. In addition to such age-old practices, they also use modern farming methods. For example, they plant seeds developed by scientists that produce bigger crops. Since farmers started doing this in the 1960s, wheat production has doubled. Pakistan now grows more wheat than Kansas and Nebraska combined.

A Pakistani worker checks a handful of pills to make sure they have the correct coating. The making of pharmaceuticals (fahr muh SOOT ih kulz), or medicines and pills, is an important new industry in Pakistan.

Industrial Growth

In addition to helping farmers, dams such as the Tarbela—on the Indus River in northern Pakistan—speed industrial growth. Dams can release rushing water to create hydroelectric energy. In Pakistan, hydroelectric power plants produce electricity to run **textile,** or cloth, mills and other factories. Most industry is located near the sources of hydroelectric power, on the Indus Plain.

Industries Based on Agriculture At independence, Pakistan had few factories. Pakistan has worked hard to build its economy through agriculture and industry. Today, Pakistan is one of the most prosperous countries in Asia. Even so, only a few Pakistanis can afford such things as refrigerators, telephones, and cars. The typical Pakistani family earns about 29,400 Pakistani rupees each year. That is equal to about $490.

Pakistan began its industrial growth by building on what its people knew best: farming. More than half of Pakistan's industrial output comes from turning crops such as cotton into manufactured goods such as socks.

Industries: From Steel to Crafts Although most industry in Pakistan relates to farming, the nation has other industries. The chemical industry produces paint, soap, dye, and insect-killing sprays. The **automotive industry** is one that puts together vehicles such as

A Geologist's Dream The mountains in Pakistan's Salt Range are of little interest to most people except geologists. These scientists learn about the Earth by studying its rocks. This area of Pakistan offers a detailed picture of the Earth's history. It has a series of rocks that range from 570 million years to less than a million years in age.

Traditional Crafts

Many people in Pakistan work in small workshops producing traditional crafts. This worker from Karachi makes wooden trays and boxes that are inlaid with metal designs. Other traditional craft items produced in Pakistan include lace, carpets, pottery, and leather goods. **Critical Thinking** How might the development of traditional crafts help Pakistan's economy?

Connect What products do you use that may have been made in Pakistan?

cars, vans, pickup trucks, tractors, and motorcycles. Several steel mills allow Pakistan to make almost all the steel it needs. This saves money. Producing steel is less costly than buying it from other countries.

Millions of Pakistanis work in small workshops, instead of in large factories. Workshops produce field hockey sticks, furniture, knives, saddles, and carpets. Pakistan is famous for its beautiful carpets. Some sell for as much as $25,000 in Pakistan—and $50,000 in New York or London.

Pakistanis are working hard to improve their future. By building industries and modernizing agriculture, they hope to raise their quality of life.

SECTION 4 REVIEW

1. **Define** (a) drought, (b) textile, (c) automotive industry.

2. **Identify** Kashmir.

3. Why is the Indus River crucial to Pakistani farmers?

4. What industries have emerged since Pakistan became a nation?

Critical Thinking

5. **Expressing Problems Clearly** Why is Kashmir important to both India and Pakistan?

Activity

6. **Writing to Learn** Write a dialogue between an Indian and a Pakistani in which each expresses his or her opinion about the fate of Kashmir.

Vietnam

A REUNITED NATION

Reach Into Your Background

Write down two or three things you know about the

Vietnam War. As you read this section, revise your list, adding new information.

Questions to Explore

1. What conflicts have divided Vietnam?
2. How are the Vietnamese rebuilding their economy?

Key Terms

refugee

Key People and Places

Ho Chi Minh
Ngo Dinh Diem
Ho Chi Minh City

It is summer in northern Vietnam. Villagers cut, harvest, and plow rice fields just as their parents and grandparents did. Unlike their parents and grandparents, however, these villagers are making money. Rice farmers in the village of Phu Do return from the fields to a second job: noodle-making. Farmers in Son Dong carve religious statues from wood in their free time. Potters in Bat Trang, goldsmiths in Dong Sam, embroiderers in Thuong Tin—all are earning money from age-old crafts. Their success helps to rebuild the economy of Vietnam.

▼ These Vietnamese women are making dishes and bowls in a traditional way. It takes great skill to form smooth, round pots from clay without using a potter's wheel.

Decades of Conflict and War

The people of Vietnam are ending a long period of struggle. The struggle began when they fought for independence from France after World War II. Then the country was divided, and civil war followed. North Vietnam fought South Vietnam and its ally, the United States.

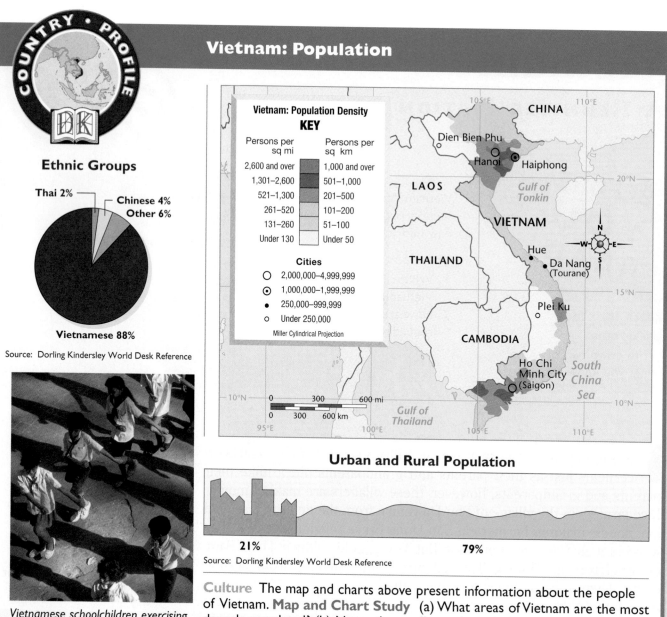

Ethnic Groups

Thai 2%

Chinese 4%
Other 6%

Vietnamese 88%

Source: Dorling Kindersley World Desk Reference

Vietnam: Population Density
KEY

Persons per sq mi | Persons per sq km
2,600 and over — 1,000 and over
1,301–2,600 — 501–1,000
521–1,300 — 201–500
261–520 — 101–200
131–260 — 51–100
Under 130 — Under 50

Cities
○ 2,000,000–4,999,999
◉ 1,000,000–1,999,999
• 250,000–999,999
○ Under 250,000

Miller Cylindrical Projection

CHINA

Dien Bien Phu
Hanoi   Haiphong
Gulf of Tonkin

LAOS

VIETNAM

THAILAND

Hue
Da Nang (Tourane)

Plei Ku

CAMBODIA

Ho Chi Minh City (Saigon)

South China Sea

Gulf of Thailand

Urban and Rural Population

21%   79%

Source: Dorling Kindersley World Desk Reference

Culture The map and charts above present information about the people of Vietnam. **Map and Chart Study** (a) What areas of Vietnam are the most densely populated? (b) Name the smaller major ethnic groups in Vietnam.

Vietnamese schoolchildren exercising

Take It to the NET
Data Update For the most recent data on Vietnam, visit **www.phschool.com**.

In the mid-1800s, France took over Vietnam as a colony. Vietnam resented French rule. They wanted to have their own government on their own soil. In 1946, they listened to the call to arms of independence leader Ho Chi Minh (hoh chee MIN):

> ❝ Let him who has a rifle use his rifle, let him who has a sword use his sword. And let those who have no sword take up pickaxes and sticks. ❞

Under Ho Chi Minh, the Vietnamese Communists defeated the French. The United States and other democracies did not want Vietnam to become a communist country. After the French defeat, a treaty divided

◄ The United States began sending troops to Vietnam in the mid-1960s. By 1968, more than 500,000 troops were there. About 58,000 Americans died in the Vietnam War.

Vietnam into northern and southern parts. The northern half was controlled by Communists. The treaty said that, eventually, an election would be held to reunite the country under one government.

These elections were never held. Ngo Dinh Diem (noh DIN deh EM), the leader of South Vietnam, refused to uphold his part of the treaty. Instead, he held a vote on whether he should keep ruling South Vietnam. Diem won the election. However, Diem made many enemies within South Vietnam. He ruled until 1963, when he was killed by political opponents.

During these years, Ho Chi Minh and the Communists were trying to take over the south by force. In 1959, they launched a war to achieve this goal. Ho Chi Minh's forces were called the Viet Cong. As they threatened South Vietnam, the United States took an active role in the war. At first, the United States sent thousands of military advisors to help the South Vietnamese. Later, hundreds of thousands of American troops arrived. Through the 1960s, the United States sent more and more troops to Vietnam. By 1968, there were more than 500,000 U.S. troops fighting in Vietnam.

By the 1970s, Vietnam had been at war for more than 30 years. The United States government realized it was fighting a war it would never win. In addition, thousands of people in the United States were calling for an end to the war. By 1973, the United States finally ended its part in the war.

After the War

After the United States pulled out, North Vietnam conquered the south. In 1976, the country was reunited under a communist government. Vietnam had been devastated by the war. Millions of Vietnamese had been killed or wounded. Homes, farms, factories, and forests had

Water Puppets In Vietnam, a type of puppet theater uses a pond for a stage. Water puppet shows started centuries ago. In them, a puppeteer guides wooden figures so that they appear to wade through the water. The puppets are attached to rods and strings hidden underwater. Audiences sit at the water's edge. Stage settings of trees and clouds are also placed on the pond.

been destroyed. Bombs had torn cities apart. Fields were covered with land mines, or hidden explosives. The Vietnamese people were worn out. Still ahead was the huge effort of rebuilding.

The Vietnamese Rebuild   In the years after the war, the communist government in Vietnam strictly controlled the lives of its citizens. As time passed, however, it was clear that the economy was not growing. Like the Chinese, the Vietnamese had to adapt their approach to economic growth. Although it is still a communist country, Vietnam now allows some free enterprise. This has helped many Vietnamese improve their lives.

Most Vietnamese live in rural areas. In spite of some progress, these areas remain poor. Whole families live on a few hundred dollars a year. Most houses have no indoor toilets or running water. Children suffer from a lack of healthy food. Vietnam is still among the poorest nations in Asia.

▼ Modern cranes and construction projects reflect the growing economy of Vietnam. Here, construction workers lay the foundations for a new office building in Ho Chi Minh City.

Rebirth in Ho Chi Minh City   Vietnam's greatest successes have been in rebuilding its cities. Hanoi in the north is the capital. The city of Saigon (sy GAHN) was renamed Ho Chi Minh City. It is the most prosperous city in Vietnam and is the center of trade. Americans who visit Ho Chi Minh City find some of the same things they would find at home. They eat American-style ice cream, drink soda, and watch cable news networks on television. Well-off Vietnamese also feel comfortable here. They buy designer clothing and watches, stereo systems, video recorders, and jewelry. Many of these people run restaurants or hotels, buy and sell land or buildings, or own factories.

Northern Vietnam has been much slower to modernize than the south. Still, the desire for economic success has taken hold in that part of the country. One elderly Vietnamese who fought in the war now says, "I'm astonished by what I see of America on television—automobiles, refrigerators, private homes. Such abundance! The United States ought to be our model."

◀ Like people in many parts of the world, these young Vietnamese women enjoy traveling by motorbike. These vehicles are cheaper than cars and speedier than bicycles.

Le Van Cam, an artisan in a village in the north, explained his economic success story in the new Vietnam:

"A few years ago, I managed a [factory] that produced rice bowls. My family lived in one room, and all I had was a bicycle. Since the reforms, I've been running my own company. Now I have a big house, a television set, a videocassette recorder, even a washing machine. If I had a garage, I'd buy a car."

Visualize Visualize a family living in one room. Then visualize the same family living in a big house. How is life in a big house different from life in one room?

Thousands of former **refugees,** people who flee their country because of war, have returned to Ho Chi Minh City. Many developed valuable skills in other lands. Some ex-refugees attended business and law schools in the United States. Today, they use their knowledge of Vietnam and the West to help wealthy foreigners do business in Vietnam.

SECTION 5 REVIEW

1. **Define**   refugee.
2. **Identify**   (a) Ho Chi Minh, (b) Ngo Dinh Diem, (c) Ho Chi Minh City.

3. What conflicts have divided Vietnam?
4. What successes has Vietnam had in rebuilding its economy?

Critical Thinking
5. **Understanding Points of View**   Why do you think Saigon was renamed Ho Chi Minh City after the war?

Activity
6. **Writing to Learn**   Imagine that you are a Vietnamese living in Saigon in 1954. Explain your attitude towards Ngo Dinh Diem and Ho Chi Minh.

Identifying the Central Issue

Have you ever said to someone, "That's not the point!" or "You just don't get it"?

You probably have. Suppose you want to talk to a friend about the big play in a football game. You say, "Wasn't that a great catch Jimmy Brown made?" Then your friend replies by saying, "The closest defender to him was 20 yards away."

You might say, "That's not the point!"

It is frustrating when someone you are talking to does not "get it," or understand your main point. It is just as difficult when you do not "get," or really understand, something you read, because you know that understanding what you read is necessary for you to do well in school and beyond.

Get Ready

Another way to say "getting the point" is "identifying central issues." All the many ideas that relate to a topic are its issues. For example,

the issues related to a trip to the zoo include the animals, the weather, the crowd, the snacks, and the parking lot. The list is almost endless. But the central issue of a trip to the zoo—the most important idea—is the animals. Can you see why this is so? The central issue is the single most important idea about a topic. All of the other issues are less important than the basic idea behind the zoo—people go to see animals.

Identifying central issues is the way you understand the most important ideas about any topic.

Try It Out

Any paragraph has a central issue, often expressed in the first sentence or two. This is usually followed by details that support the central issue by giving examples or further explanation. When you read a paragraph, be sure to make note of the details and see how they support the central issue.

Read the following paragraph. Then look at the four statements that follow the paragraph. Which statement best describes the central issue of the paragraph—statement A, B, C, or D?

Like the United States, India has a very diverse population. However, diversity in India has developed somewhat differently from here. For example, the majority of today's American ethnic and cultural groups have come to this country in the last 200 years. Many of India's cultures, on the other hand, have entered the country through many centuries of invasion and migration. Other cultural groups have evolved through many years of isolation from other groups.

A. Some Indian cultures have been isolated for many years.

B. Cultural diversity in India developed differently than it did in the United States.

C. American ethnic groups have immigrated recently.

D. Both the United States and India have many different ethnic groups.

Apply the Skill

In Section 1 of this chapter, read the paragraphs under the heading "New Religions." After you have read the paragraphs, read the statements listed below. Which statement identifies the central issue—statement A, B, C, or D?

A. Aryans invaded the Indus Valley in 1500 B.C.

B. In a caste system, each class has special duties and work.

C. One result of the Aryan invasion of northern India was the formation of Hinduism.

D. The Aryans introduced their class system to India.

Review and Activities

Reviewing Main Ideas

1. What lasting effect did the Aryan invasion have on South Asia?
2. Give proof of Siddhartha Gautama's continuing influence in South and Southeast Asia.
3. What effect did colonial rule have on the development of Southeast Asian economies?
4. How has the caste system weakened since India's independence?
5. Why is helping farmers a major concern of the Pakistani government?
6. Why did the Vietnam War break out?
7. How is Vietnam building its economy today?

Reviewing Key Terms

Use each key term below in a sentence that shows the meaning of the term.

1. caste
2. colony
3. boycott
4. partition
5. nationalist
6. dictator
7. quota
8. parliament
9. purdah
10. drought
11. textile
12. automotive industry
13. refugee

Critical Thinking

1. **Recognizing Bias** Ho Chi Minh spoke of "liberating" South Vietnam when he tried to reunite it with North Vietnam. Why do you think he used the word *liberate*?
2. **Making Comparisons** Compare recent changes in the roles of women in India and the United States.

Graphic Organizer

Copy the web onto a sheet of paper. Then fill in the empty ovals to complete it.

Cultures of South and Southeast Asia

big differences between cities and farms

Map Activity

South and Southeast Asia
For each place listed below, write the letter from the map that shows its location.

1. India

2. Pakistan

3. Vietnam

4. Bangladesh

5. Pacific Ocean

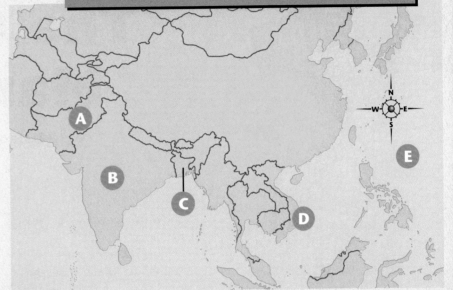

Writing Activity

Write a Newspaper Editorial
Choose one conflict that you read about in this chapter. Write a newspaper editorial that gives your point of view on the conflict.

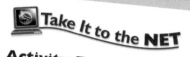 **Take It to the NET**

Activity Take a photographic tour of India and see how the people who live there interact with the environment. For help in completing this activity, visit **www.phschool.com**.

Chapter 4 Self-Test To review what you have learned, take the Chapter 4 Self-Test and get instant feedback on your answers. Go to **www.phschool.com** to take the test.

Skills Review

Turn to the Skills Activity.
Review the steps for identifying central issues. Then look back at Section 1 and answer the following questions: (a) What is the central issue? (b) How did you identify the central issue?

How Am I Doing?

Answer these questions to help you check your progress.

1. Do I understand how geography helped shape the cultures of South and Southeast Asia?

2. Can I explain the cultural diversity of these two regions?

3. Can I identify some historic events that shaped the cultures and beliefs of South and Southeast Asians?

4. What information from this chapter can I include in my journal?

LITERATURE

FROM

The Clay Marble

BY MINFONG HO

BEFORE YOU READ

Reach Into Your Background

Think of someone you admire. What special gift or quality does that person have? Some people have the ability to show us a new way of looking at things.

In 1980, civil war in Cambodia forced thousands of Cambodians to leave their homes and move to refugee camps near the border of Thailand and Cambodia. Among these refugees lived many children. There was very little food, and living conditions were poor. *The Clay Marble* tells the story of twelve-year-old Dara, who lives in one such camp. Dara's friend Jantu, another girl in the camp, makes toys out of little scraps and trinkets she finds at the camp.

Questions to Explore

1. What is Jantu's special gift?
2. What does Dara learn from Jantu?

It amazed me, the way she shaped things out of nothing. A knobby branch, in her deft hands, would be whittled into a whirling top. She would weave strips of a banana leaf into plump goldfish or angular frogs. A torn plastic bag and a scrap from some newspaper would be cut and fashioned into a graceful kite with a long tail. A couple of old tin cans and a stick would be transformed into a toy truck.

Whenever Jantu started making something, she would withdraw into her own private world and ignore everything around her. Leaving me to mind her baby brother, she would hunch over her project, her fierce scowl keeping at bay anybody who might come too close or become too noisy. But if I was quiet and kept my distance, she didn't seem to mind my watching her.

And so I would stand a little to one side, holding the baby on my hip, as Jantu's quick fingers shaped, twisted, smoothed, rolled whatever material she happened to be working with into new toys.

"How do you do it?" I asked her one day, after she had casually woven me a delicate bracelet of wild vines.

"Well, you take five vines of about the same length—elephant creeper vines like this work

well—and you start braiding them, see. Like this . . . "

"No, I don't mean just this bracelet," I said. "I mean the goldfish, too, and the kites and toy trucks and . . ."

"But they're all different," Jantu said. "You make them different ways."

"But how do you know what to make? Is there some . . . some kind of magic in your hands, maybe?"

Jantu looked puzzled. "I don't know," she said, turning her hands over and examining them with vague interest. They looked like ordinary hands, the finger-nails grimy, the palms slightly callused. "I don't see anything there," she said. "Nothing that looks like magic." She shrugged and dismissed the subject.

Yet the more I watched her, the more convinced I became that Jantu's hands were gifted with some special powers, some magic. How else could anyone explain how she made that wonderful mobile, of two delicate dolls husking rice?

Even from the start, I knew it was going to be something special. For three days Jantu had kept me busy scrounging up a collection of old cloth and string. Then, as I sat cross-legged watching her, she fashioned two straw dolls in sarongs and straw hats and, with dabs of sticky rice, glued their feet onto a smooth branch. Carefully she tied strings connecting the dolls' wrists and waists, so that when one doll bent down, the other one straightened up. Each doll held a long thin club, with which, in turn, one would pound at a tiny mortar as the other doll lifted up its club in readiness. Jantu held up the mobile and showed me how a mere breath of wind would set the two dolls in motion.

Pound and lift, up and down, the two dolls took turns crushing the rice with exactly the same jerky rhythm that real village women pounded it to get the brown husks off. There were even some real grains in the miniature mortar set between the two dolls. It was the cleverest thing I had ever seen.

sarong *n.* (suh RAWNG) a loose garment made of a long strip of cloth wrapped around the body

mortar *n.* a dish in which seed or grain is pounded or ground

READ ACTIVELY

Visualize Picture the two dolls in motion. What does the toy look like?

▶ These Cambodian children are in a refugee camp in Thailand.

recruit *v.* to persuade someone to join
resistance army *n.* an army of people resisting, or opposing, the group holding political power in a country
saunter *v.* to walk in an idle or casual manner
retrieve *v.* to get something back again

Children crowded around Jantu, pressing in from all sides to watch her work it. "Let me hold it," I begged, standing next to Jantu. "I helped you find the stuff for the dolls."

Jantu nodded. Breathlessly I held it carefully and blew on it. It worked! One of the dolls bent down and pounded the mortar with its club. The other doll straightened up and waited its turn. I was still engrossed with it when someone shouted a warning: "Watch out, Chnay's coming!"

Even in my short stay at the camp, I'd heard of Chnay. He liked to break things, and he was a bully. An orphan, Chnay made his way to the Border alone. Too young to be recruited into the resistance army, Chnay roamed the fields by himself, scrounging for food and sleeping wherever he liked.

Chnay sauntered up and shoved his way through to us.

"What've you got there?" he demanded.

"Nothing," I said, trying to hide the toy behind me.

Laughing, Chnay snatched it away from me. One of the dolls was ripped loose and dropped to the ground.

As I bent over to retrieve it, Chnay pushed me aside. "Leave it," he said. "That's for kids. Look what I have." He thrust his arm out. It was crawling with big red ants, the fierce kind that really sting when they bite. "I'm letting them bite me. See?" he bragged. Already small fierce welts were swelling up on his arm, as some ants kept biting him.

"That's dumb!" I exclaimed. Dodging behind him, I tried to snatch the mobile back from him.

Chnay flung the toy to the ground, scattering straw and red ants into the air.

I grabbed on to his hand, but he was taller than I, and much stronger. He shoved me aside and stomped on the dolls until they were nothing but a pile of crushed sticks and rags. Then, kicking aside a boy who stood in his way, Chnay strode off, angrily brushing red ants off his arm.

I squatted down beside the bits of dolls and tried to fit them together, but it was no use. The delicate mobile was beyond repair. I could feel my eyes smarting with angry tears. "I should've held on to it more tightly," I said bitterly. "I shouldn't have let him grab it away from me."

Jantu knelt next to me and took the fragments of the dolls out of my hands. "Never mind," she said quietly, putting them aside. "We can always start something new."

"But it took you so long to make it," I said.

Idly Jantu scooped up a lump of mud from a puddle by her feet and began to knead it in her hands. "Sure, but the fun is in the making," she said.

She looked down at the lump of mud in her hands with sudden interest. "Have you ever noticed how nice the soil around here is?" she asked. "Almost like clay." She smoothed the ball with quick fingers, then rolled it between her palms.

When she opened her palm and held it out to me, there was a small brown ball of mud cupped in it. "For you," she announced.

I looked at it. Compared to the delicate rice-pounding mobile, this was not very interesting at all. "I don't want it," I said. "It's just a mud ball."

"No, it's not. It's a marble," Jantu said. Her eyes sparkling, she blew on it. "There! Now it's a magic marble."

I took it and held it. Round and cool, it had a nice solid feel to it. I glanced at Jantu. She was smiling. Slowly I smiled back at her.

Maybe, I thought, maybe she did put some magic in the marble. After all, why else would I feel better, just holding it?

READ ACTIVELY

Connect When have you changed the way you feel about something? What made you change?

EXPLORING YOUR READING

Look Back

1. What does Dara think about Jantu's ability to make toys?

2. What did Chnay do to Jantu's dolls?

Think It Over

3. How does Jantu feel about her own abilities?

4. Why do you think Chnay behaves the way he does?

5. What does Dara learn from Jantu?

Go Beyond

6. How might you learn from Jantu to see something differently in your own life?

7. Describe a person you know and admire. What can you learn from that person?

Ideas for Writing: Short Story

8. Write a story about a person who learns something from the example of another person. Write about at least two characters, and be sure that your story has a beginning, a middle, and an end. In your story, show the moment when the person first understands what there is to learn.

SOUTHWEST AND CENTRAL ASIA

Physical Geography

PICTURE ACTIVITIES

The photo above shows natural sandstone arches in Israel, a country in Southwest Asia. Study the picture. Then start your study of this region by doing the following activities.

Write a caption
Write a short caption for the photo that describes the arches.

Decide what to wear
Think about what the weather would be like in the place shown above. Would it be hot or cold? Would it be wet or dry? Would the temperature vary or stay the same? Make a list of the clothing you would pack for a week-long visit to the location.

Land and Water

BEFORE YOU READ

Reach Into Your Background

Every place in the world has physical features that are unique. What physical features stand out in the area in which you live? Is there a lake, a stream, a hill, or a plateau that everyone in your community knows about? Write down a phrase or two that would help describe this feature to a stranger.

Questions to Explore

1. What are the major landforms of Southwest and Central Asia?
2. Why are Southwest and Central Asia considered a crossroads?

Key Term
oasis

Key Places
Rub al-Khali
Tigris River
Euphrates River
Hindu Kush
Pamirs
Mediterranean Sea

The Rub al-Khali (roob ahl KHAH lee), or "Empty Quarter," of the Arabian peninsula is the largest all-sand desert in the world. Almost nothing lives in this flat, hot territory. Ten years may pass between rainfalls. One sand dune may weigh millions of tons. And the sand dunes do not stay in one place—they gradually move because they are blown by the wind.

The Dry World

A visitor to the nations of Southwest and Central Asia will see more than just sand, however. The region also includes snowcapped mountains, green valleys, and seacoasts. Look at the physical map of Southwest and Central Asia on the next page. What nations contain mountains? What nations have seacoasts?

Vast Expanses of Desert Despite the region's diversity, its nickname, "the Dry World," is accurate. Southwest and Central Asia contain some of the Earth's largest deserts. The Rub al-Khali is almost as big as the state of

▼ The sands of the Rub al-Khali seem to go on forever. Its shifting dunes make it almost impossible to explore or map.

Pavlodar

Akmola ⊛   Semey
Karaganda   •Lake
             Zaysan

K A Z A K S T A N   Lake
                     Balkhash

Ural River

Istanbul   Black Sea

Izmir   Ankara ⊛   Aral
                     Sea   Syr Darya   •Almaty

GEORGIA   Tbilisi   UZBEKISTAN   ⊛Bishkek
                                    KYRGYZSTAN
ARMENIA   AZERBAIJAN   Tashkent ⊛
Yerevan   •Baku   KARA KUM   Dushanbe⊛ ⊛TAJIKISTAN
T U R K E Y   Amu Darya   PAMIR MTS.

CYPRUS   •Tabriz   Caspian Sea   TURKMENISTAN   HINDU KUSH
Nicosia ⊛   Ashkhabad ⊛
Mediterranean Sea
LEBANON   SYRIA   Meshed•
Beirut ⊛   Damascus   Tigris River
Jerusalem ⊛ ⊛Amman   Tehran ⊛
ISRAEL   IRAQ   Euphrates River   I R A N
JORDAN   Baghdad ⊛   ZAGROS MOUNTAINS   •Isfahan
          Shatt al-Arab
KUWAIT
⊛Kuwait

S A U D I   BAHRAIN   OMAN
A R A B I A   Manama⊛   Persian Gulf   Tropic of Cancer
          Doha⊛ QATAR   •Abu Dhabi   Strait of Hormuz
Riyadh ⊛   UNITED   ⊛Muscat
Jidda •Mecca   ARAB EMIRATES   Arabian
          OMAN   Sea

Red Sea   RUB AL-KHALI

Sanaa •   YEMEN
Aden •
Bab al-Mandab   Gulf of Aden   Socotra
                                 (Yemen)

KEY

Elevation

Feet	Meters
Over 13,000	Over 3,960
6,500–13,000	1,980–3,960
1,600–6,500	480–1,980
650–1,600	200–480
0–650	0–200
Below sea level	Below sea level

⊛ National capital

• Other city

Two-Point Equidistant Projection

0   250   500 mi
0   250   500 km

Map Study Southwest and Central Asia is an area of great geographic diversity. Few people live in the area's mountains and deserts. Its rivers and plains, however, have always attracted settlers. **Place** From looking at this map, where do you think would be a good place to settle?

Visualize Visualize the contrast between an oasis and a gravelly desert.

Texas. In Central Asia, the Kara Kum covers 70 percent of Turkmenistan (turk mun ih STAHN). Most parts of the Dry World get little rain. Water is very valuable in dry regions.

Some of the region's deserts are covered with sand. In others, the land is strewn with pebbles, gravel, and boulders. Travelers passing through any of these dry regions are relieved when they find an **oasis** (oh AY sis), a place where fresh water is available from an underground spring or well. Sometimes, the oasis has enough water to support a community of people. Palm trees provide shade from the sun. Farmers can grow fruits and vegetables. Shepherds can raise livestock such as camels, sheep, and goats.

The Importance of Rivers Few plants grow in most Southwest and Central Asian deserts. However, some of the most fertile soil in the world lies along the Tigris, Euphrates (yoo FRAYT eez), and Ural rivers. When these rivers flood, they deposit rich soil along their banks. More people live in river valleys than anywhere else in the region.

Rivers are not only important as sources of water. They also provide means of transportation. The Tigris and Euphrates rivers, for example, both begin in Turkey and make their way south. They combine to form the Shatt-al-Arab Channel, in Iraq. This channel empties into the Persian Gulf, and gives Iraq its only outlet to the sea.

Mountains as Borders Many rivers begin in Southwest and Central Asia's rugged mountains. These mountains serve as borders between countries and regions. To the east, mountains separate Central and East Asia. The Hindu Kush separate Tajikistan (tah jeek ih STAHN) from Afghanistan. The Pamirs (pah MIHRZ) divide Tajikistan and China.

Sea to Shining Sea Like the mountains of Central Asia, the seas of Southwest Asia separate regions and countries. The Red Sea separates Southwest Asia and Africa. The Mediterranean Sea forms Southwest Asia's western border. The Black Sea borders Turkey to the north. And the Caspian Sea forms part of the boundary between Southwest and Central Asia.

An African Desert Africa's Sahara is the world's largest desert. It is as big as the United States. The Grand Erg Occidental and the Grand Erg Chech are huge sand dunes in the Sahara. They can appear on maps because they stay in one place. Most sand dunes are moved by the wind. Some have been known to move as far as 60 feet (18 m) in a single day in violent winds.

◀▲ The Sea of Galilee (left) is the starting point of Israel's National Water Carrier. This system of pipelines and channels carries water west to the country's coastal cities and south to the Negev Desert. In dry Southwest Asia, plastic shelters are used to keep the moisture in, not to keep the rain out (above).

The Turkish city of Istanbul is located on two continents—Europe and Asia. This picture shows a view from the European part of the city looking out across the Sea of Marmara. The building in the center of the picture is the Blue Mosque. It is unusual because it has six minarets. Most mosques have only four of these tall towers. **Critical Thinking** What in the picture suggests that the Sea of Marmara is a busy trade route?

A Crossroads of Continents

Southwest Asia is often called the Middle East. But the Middle East is not in the middle or the east of any continent. Geographers prefer to call it Southwest Asia. The word *middle* is correct in one way, however. In Istanbul, Turkey, you can go from Asia to Europe and never leave the city. This is because the city is built on both sides of a narrow strip of water that forms part of the border between the two continents. To go from Asia to Africa, catch a bus in the Israeli city of Taba and ride to the African nation of Egypt. Southwest and Central Asia are at the crossroads where North Africa, Asia, and Europe meet.

SECTION 1 REVIEW

1. **Define** oasis.
2. **Identify** (a) Rub al-Khali, (b) Tigris River, (c) Euphrates River, (d) Hindu Kush, (e) Pamirs, (f) Mediterranean Sea.
3. What are some of the deserts, rivers, mountain ranges, and seas that can be found in Southwest and Central Asia?
4. What continents meet within Southwest and Central Asia?

Critical Thinking
5. **Recognizing Bias** Some of the people who live in Southwest and Central Asia object to the term *Middle East.* Why do you think they object to this term?

Activity
6. **Writing to Learn** Write a description of one of the landforms discussed in this section.

Climate and Vegetation

Reach Into Your Background

The climate that you live in affects the food crops that are grown in your area. Think of some foods that are grown where you live. What are some foods that must be brought in from places with different climates?

Questions to Explore

1. What are the main climates and types of vegetation in Southwest and Central Asia?

2. How do the climate and vegetation affect the people of Southwest and Central Asia?

Key Terms

wadi
arable land

In the winter, the citizens of eastern Kazakstan (kah zahk STAHN) wrap themselves in fur to brave the freezing temperatures. Snow covers the ground as far as the eye can see. Livestock must dig through the ice to feed on the tough grass that lies under it. But the straight, lonely roads of the countryside never need to be plowed. Engineers built the roads slightly higher than the surrounding flatland. The fierce winds keep the roads free of snow.

Nearly 2,000 miles (3,220 km) away, in Iraq, temperatures can climb above 100°F (38°C) in the summer. It is so hot that the air seems to shimmer. Windstorms kick up so much dust that people wrap themselves in robes for protection. And it is so dry that herders and their animals must travel long distances to find water.

Dry Regions

Southwest and Central Asia are regions of huge climate extremes. They have scorching summers followed by bitterly cold winters. In some places, temperatures change drastically every day. When the sun goes down, the temperature often falls 20°F (11°C). Winter or summer, however, one thing remains the same: Southwest and Central Asia are among the largest dry regions on the Earth. Droughts are common here.

▼ This young Bedouin boy may go months without seeing rain. Where he lives— Qatar in Southwest Asia— receives only about 4 inches (10 cm) of rain a year.

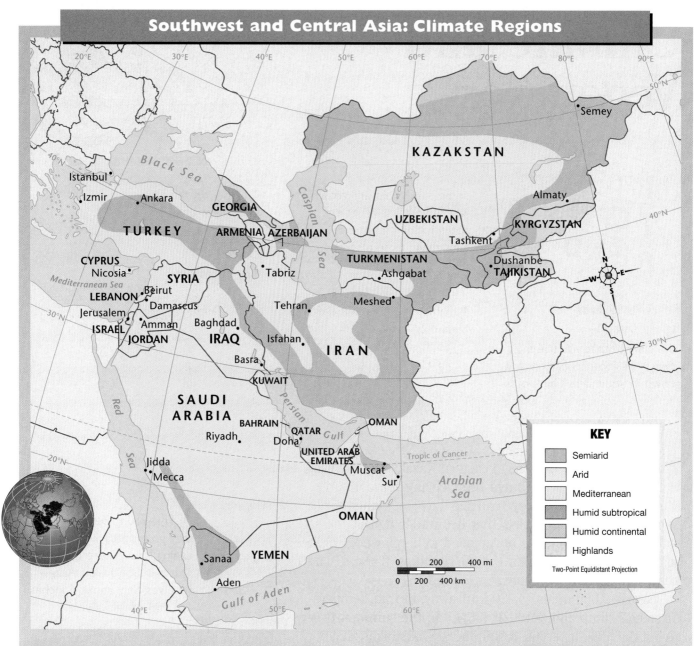

Southwest and Central Asia: Climate Regions

KEY

	Semiarid
	Arid
	Mediterranean
	Humid subtropical
	Humid continental
	Highlands

Two-Point Equidistant Projection

Map Study This map shows clearly why this area is called "the Dry World." Its most common climates are arid and semiarid. Next is the Mediterranean climate. Areas where humid subtropical and humid continental climates are found are small. **Place** The city of Ashgabat in Turkmenistan is over 1,000 miles (1,609 km) from the Mediterranean Sea, yet it has a Mediterranean climate. How can this be?

Predict How do you think people adapt to living in very dry areas?

Adapting to Harsh Conditions Even in dry conditions, some plants survive. Plants that grow well in Southwest and Central Asia have adapted to the harsh climate. Some plants survive by growing quickly. They are fully grown before the hottest and driest time of the year. Others have thick, oily skins to protect them from the heat.

Water Where There Was None To grow crops in these regions, however, people must often irrigate their land. Saudi Arabia, for example, has no permanent rivers. It has **wadis** (WAH deez), waterways

120 ASIA AND THE PACIFIC

▲ Muhammad bin Abdallah Al Shaykh inspects one of the date palms on his farm. These trees produce a sweet, nourishing fruit. In addition, the trunk provides timber, and leaves provide fuel and the makings of baskets and rope.

that fill up in the rainy season but are dry the rest of the year. Rainfall is scarce. People here irrigate their crops by pumping water from deep underground wells.

In other parts of Southwest and Central Asia, wells are not as necessary. People use water from rivers and streams to irrigate the dry areas of the country. Pipes and canals carrying water from rivers snake across the land. This way, the snows melting off the mountains in Tajikistan, for example, can water dry plains that have soil suitable for farming.

A Family Farm in Saudi Arabia   Muhammad bin Abdallah Al Shaykh (moo HAM ud bin ub DUL lah al SHAYK) and his family now raise crops on what was once a huge, sandy plain in Saudi Arabia. Only thornscrub, a kind of short, stubby shrub, grew here. Before Muhammad and his family could grow any crops on their land, they had to dig a well more than 600 feet (183 m) into the ground to find water.

Muhammad's family also dug irrigation canals throughout their 20 acres (8 hectares) of farmland. They planted trees to help protect the farm from the fierce desert winds. Then they planted date palms. Dates are an important crop in Southwest Asia. The palms survive well in desert conditions. The picture above shows Muhammad checking on his date palms.

Dates are not the only crop grown by Muhammad's family. They also grow cucumbers, tomatoes, corn, and large crops of alfalfa. The extremely long roots of alfalfa plants can find moisture deeper in the ground. Growing plants with long roots is one way that farmers adapt to a climate of hot summers and cold winters.

Water and Population

Although much of Southwest and Central Asia is extremely dry, some areas are more suitable for living. People tend to settle near coasts, oases, and rivers. The Mediterranean Coast and the river valleys of the Tigris and Euphrates are heavily populated.

Water and Farming

In the dry lands around the city of Avalos in central Turkey, water is scarce. Farmers have to work very hard to raise a few vegetables (right). In the Dalaman River valley in southwest Turkey, water is plentiful. Farmers can grow cash crops such as cotton (below).

READ ACTIVELY

Connect What parts of the United States have plenty of arable land?

Most workers in Southwest and Central Asia work on farms. In Turkey and Syria, agriculture is the most important economic activity. But the amount of **arable land,** or land that can produce crops, is limited. In some places, the soil is not fertile. Sometimes there is not enough water to go around. In other places, mountains make it hard to farm. Under such conditions, people have a hard time making a living.

People are using technology to solve some of these problems. In Turkey, people built the Ataturk Dam so they could increase the amount of arable land. A dam blocks the flow of a river so that its water forms a large lake. Water stored in such a lake can be released as it is needed to irrigate land. Scientists and farmers are also developing ways to grow more crops in less space. As industry develops, fewer people will have to make a living farming. But in the meantime, the people of Southwest and Central Asia will continue to grow crops in a dry world.

SECTION 2 REVIEW

1. **Define** (a) wadi, (b) arable land.
2. Describe the climate of Southwest and Central Asia.

3. How has the climate of Southwest and Central Asia affected where people live and what they grow?

Critical Thinking

4. **Expressing Problems Clearly** Few places in Southwest and Central Asia receive enough rainfall for growing crops. What challenges does this create for the people who live in the region?

Activity

5. **Writing to Learn** Write a paragraph describing how the climate that you live in affects you.

Natural Resources

BEFORE YOU READ

Reach Into Your Background

The lifestyle of Americans today depends on oil products, such as gasoline. For example, every item found in a grocery store was brought there by vehicles powered by gasoline. Think back on the last few days. How would your life have been affected if no gasoline had been available?

Questions to Explore

1. How has petroleum affected Southwest and Central Asia?

2. Why is water considered a most precious resource?

Key Terms

petroleum
nonrenewable resource
standard of living

Key Places

Kuwait
Almaty
Aral Sea

In February 1991, day seemed like night in the oil fields of Kuwait (koo WAYT). Smoke filled the air, and flames shot hundreds of feet into the sky. Iraq was at war with Kuwait near Southwest Asia's Persian Gulf. As Iraqi troops retreated from Kuwait, they set fire to more than 700 oil wells.

The world watched the war in the Persian Gulf with horror. People worried about how the raging oil fires might harm the environment. They also worried that Kuwait's oil reserves might be destroyed forever, or that the price of oil would rise sharply. People around the world relied on Persian Gulf oil. A rise in oil prices could mean hard times for people in most countries.

Petroleum: Black Gold

The oil mined in Kuwait is **petroleum** (puh TROH lee um), which formed from the remains of ancient plants and animals. It is found under the Earth's surface. Petroleum deposits take millions of years to form. Petroleum is a **nonrenewable resource**—one that cannot be replaced once it is used. Petroleum is the source of gasoline and other fuels. People all over the world depend on petroleum to fuel cars and trucks, provide energy for industry, and heat homes.

▲ At the time of the Persian Gulf War, burning oil wells in Kuwait spread air pollution to Iraq, Iran, and other areas of Southwest Asia.

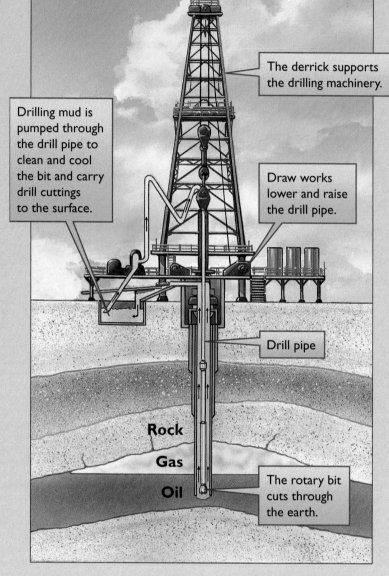

The derrick supports the drilling machinery.

Drilling mud is pumped through the drill pipe to clean and cool the bit and carry drill cuttings to the surface.

Draw works lower and raise the drill pipe.

Drill pipe

Rock

Gas

Oil

The rotary bit cuts through the earth.

To obtain petroleum, workers must drill through layers of rock to reach deposits of oil under the Earth's surface. They begin by building a tall framework called a derrick. The derrick is usually 80 to 200 feet (24 to 61 m) high. It has a system of pulleys and cables that raise and lower the drilling equipment. Some oil deposits are as much as 3.75 miles (6 km) under the Earth's surface. When oil is reached, the drilling equipment is removed. Then, special pipes that let the oil flow up to the surface are put in place.

Predict What effect do you think reserves of petroleum have on the countries of Southwest and Central Asia?

Petroleum can be found in only a few places around the globe. As a result, petroleum-rich countries play a key role in the world's economy. Southwest Asia is the largest oil-producing region in the world. Central Asia also has a large supply of it. Both regions are greatly affected by their oil wealth.

Southwest Asia: Resources Divided Unequally

Petroleum is Southwest Asia's number one export. Oil wealth allows many Southwest Asian countries to increase the standard of living, or quality of life, of their people. These countries have enough money to build excellent schools and hospitals and import goods from other countries. They can also import workers. Most of the people living in oil-rich Kuwait are citizens of other countries. Workers from Sudan, Jordan, and Lebanon poured into tiny Kuwait to work. This flow of people is common in the region.

Southwest Asia has more than half of the world's oil reserves. But some countries in the region have little or no oil. These countries tend to have a lower standard of living than their oil-rich neighbors. Why? They do not have the income that petroleum brings. However, these countries benefit from oil wealth in one way. When their citizens work in oil-rich nations, they bring money home.

Central Asia: Attracting Attention Central Asia, too, is rich in natural resources. Kazakstan's oil reserves have changed the face of Almaty (al MAH tee), its largest city. Almaty used to be a quiet city.

HEROES

Working Together After the Iraqi Army set fire to Kuwait's oil wells, a group of brave oil-firefighters from Texas, led by a man named Red Adair, saved the day. They smothered the fires with nitrogen. The work was dangerous; firefighters breathed smoke; the heat melted desert sands into glass. It took eight months to put out the fires.

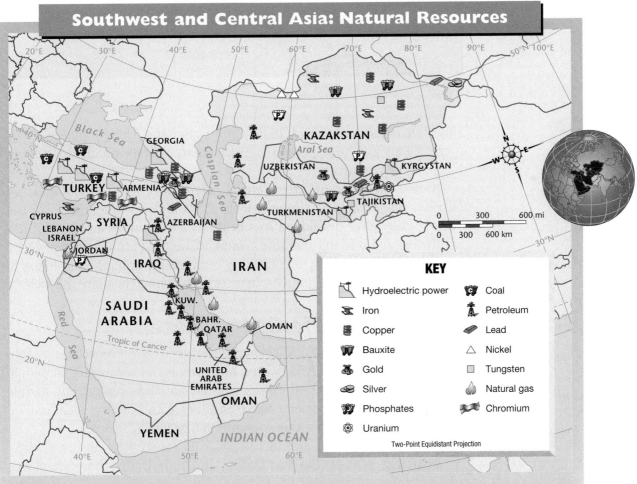

Southwest and Central Asia: Natural Resources

KEY

- Hydroelectric power
- Iron
- Copper
- Bauxite
- Gold
- Silver
- Phosphates
- Uranium
- Coal
- Petroleum
- Lead
- Nickel
- Tungsten
- Natural gas
- Chromium

Two-Point Equidistant Projection

Map Study Saudi Arabia has about one fourth of the world's oil reserves. Its oil fields are located in the eastern part of the country and under the Persian Gulf. **Movement** Why is the location of Saudi Arabia's oil fields an advantage? Look at the physical map at the beginning of Section 1. What would be the disadvantages of having oil fields in the Rub al-Khali?

► Today, Almaty is a bustling industrial city. However, it is easy to find peaceful scenes like this one. It shows a Russian Orthodox church at the end of a quiet lane.

Visualize Visualize water rushing through a creek. Then visualize the creek bed dry, with no water in it. How could a creek be full of water one week and dry the next?

Now businesspeople from Italy, China, and the United States travel there. Many of these people are in Almaty to talk about developing Kazakstan's resources.

Kazakstan is one of three Central Asian countries that contain large oil reserves. Uzbekistan (ooz bek ih STAN) and Turkmenistan are the others. They have developed less of their petroleum reserves than has Southwest Asia. Many countries want to help Central Asia develop a larger oil industry. They are offering equipment, training, and loans to Central Asia's oil-rich countries. In return, they hope to share the wealth.

Life-Giving Water

Petroleum is the natural resource that brings the most money into Southwest and Central Asia. Water, however, is the resource that people need most. In addition to the uses you have already read about, people use water to create electricity. Since Southwest and Central Asia have an arid climate, the water in this region must be used carefully.

Making Water Go Farther   In Saudi Arabia, there are places where a torrent of muddy water may cut through the dry earth. Along the banks of this rushing wadi, vegetation may sprout. It is a welcome bit of green in the brown landscape. Two weeks later, however, a visitor to the same place may find that the water has disappeared and the creek bed is dry. Throughout much of Southwest and Central Asia, rivers, lakes, and wadis are dry for part of the year. The water they sometimes hold must be used while it is there. Then other sources must be found. As the population in Southwest and Central Asia grows, the demand for water grows, too.

There are few permanent water sources in the region. Southwest and Central Asian countries must conserve the water that they have. In Saudi Arabia, people dig deep wells to tap into water below the surface. People in Kazakstan have built several dams along the Syr Darya (sihr DAR yah) River. They use the water supply created by the dams to irrigate crops.

Stretching Sources to Their Limits   The nations of this region have continued to build irrigation systems. But irrigation cannot solve the problem of water scarcity. Too much irrigation can use up the water that is available.

The Aral (A rul) Sea in Central Asia was once the world's fourth-largest lake. Now many boats here rest on dry earth. Two of the rivers that feed the sea were channeled to raise cotton crops in Uzbekistan and Kazakstan. With so much less water flowing into it, the Aral Sea is drying up.

In an area with little rainfall, water that is channeled from a river cannot be replaced. When a river runs through more than one nation, each nation is affected by the others' irrigation systems. For example, in 1989, Turkey built a giant dam on the Euphrates River. Turkey cut the flow of the Euphrates into Syria and Iraq while it filled the lake behind the dam. The dam created new farmland and a supply of electricity for Turkey. But the other countries through which the Euphrates flowed suffered.

The countries of Southwest and Central Asia are trying to work together to preserve their water. They are also trying to make the best use of their oil reserves. Managing these precious resources is important not only to these nations, but to the rest of the world.

LINKS TO SCIENCE

Dead Sea Alive With Minerals The Dead Sea, a lake between Israel and Jordan, is too salty to support fish or plant life. But it does help support Israel's economy. The sea is full of minerals. The Israelis take out potash—a mineral used for explosives and fertilizer—as well as table salt and other minerals for export.

SECTION 3 REVIEW

1. **Define**   (a) petroleum, (b) nonrenewable resource, (c) standard of living.

2. **Identify**   (a) Kuwait, (b) Almaty, (c) Aral Sea.

3. What benefits has oil brought to Southwest and Central Asia?

4. List three important uses of water.

Critical Thinking

5. **Making Comparisons** Do you think a person in Chicago looks at water in a different way than a person in Southwest and Central Asia does? What about someone living near the deserts of the southwestern United States?

Activity

6. **Writing to Learn**   The economy of Southwest and Central Asia depends on oil and water. Write a paragraph explaining ways in which water and oil can be conserved.

Interpreting Graphs

ook at the picture to the right. It is a standard-size oil barrel. The barrel is about the size of a large trash can. It holds 42 gallons.

Imagine ten of these barrels, filled with oil, standing together in a corner of your classroom. Now imagine 20. Is your classroom filled up yet? If you stacked them, how many could fit into the room? You could probably squeeze in a few hundred.

If just a few hundred barrels of oil would fill your classroom, imagine how much space 22 billion barrels would fill! You probably can't even picture so many barrels. Yet it is important for people to visualize huge numbers like these, because they often represent facts we need to understand.

What kind of visual tool might help you to think about and compare such large numbers? You might try using a graph.

Get Ready

Graphs are helpful because they show a large amount of information in a simple, easy-to-read way. A common type of graph is the bar graph. To help you understand bar graphs, try making a simple one yourself.

Try It Out

Which season is the busiest for birthdays in your class—spring, summer, fall, or winter? You can graph this simple data using the following steps.

A. Gather information. Write down the names of the four seasons: spring, summer, fall, and winter. Poll the class on their birth dates. Count the number of birthdays that occur in the spring and write that number down on your paper next to the word *spring*. Do the same for the other three seasons.

B. Draw the frame of your bar graph. Using the empty graph below as a model, draw and label the horizontal and vertical axes. The horizontal axis is called the *x*-axis. Along this axis you will show the categories of your data—spring, summer, fall, and winter. The vertical axis is called the *y*-axis. The *y*-axis shows value. In your graph, this means the number of birthdays. Make both your *x*-axis and *y*-axis 6 inches long. Space your categories evenly along the *x*-axis. Space your values evenly along the *y*-axis, beginning with zero.

C. Title your bar graph. Write a title above the graph. The title should tell what the graph is about.

D. Draw the bars. Now use the information you gathered in Step A to finish your graph. Begin at the category Spring. Draw a bar beginning from the *x*-axis. The bar should rise only as high as the number on the *y*-axis that matches the number of students having spring birthdays. Do the same for the other three seasons.

E. Study your bar graph. Just by glancing at the bar graph, you can tell when most of the students in your class have birthdays. During which season does your class have the fewest birthdays?

Apply the Skill

Now here's your chance to work with a bar graph that shows very large numbers. Follow these steps to read the bar graph.

① **Study the labels and the axes.** The title indicates the subject matter of the graph. The labels tell you what each axis represents. What is the subject matter of this bar graph? What information does the horizontal axis show? What information does the vertical axis show? In what order are the countries listed?

② **Analyze the data in the bar graph.** Which country produces the most oil? Which country produces the least? How much oil does Iraq produce in one year? What about the United Arab Emirates? Which country produces about half as much oil as Saudi Arabia?

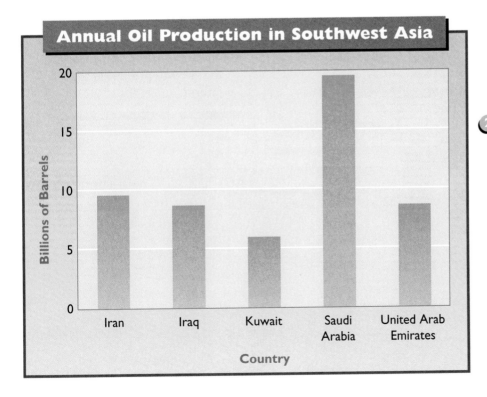

Review and Activities

Reviewing Main Ideas

1. (a) Name one major desert found in Southwest or Central Asia. (b) Name one sea. (c) Name one river. (d) Name one mountain range.
2. Describe why the region of Southwest and Central Asia is known as a crossroads.

3. How does climate affect what grows in Southwest and Central Asia?
4. How does the availability of water in Southwest and Central Asia affect where people settle in the region?

5. What benefits have Southwest and Central Asia gained from their oil reserves?
6. Why is it important for Southwest and Central Asia to conserve water?

Reviewing Key Terms

Match the definitions in Column I with the key terms in Column II.

Column I

1. land that produces crops
2. a measure of the quality of life
3. a type of oil formed from the remains of ancient plants and animals and found underneath the Earth's surface
4. a waterway that fills up in the rainy season but is otherwise dry
5. a natural resource that cannot be replaced once it is used
6. a place in a dry region where fresh water is available from an underground spring or well

Column II

a. nonrenewable resource

b. oasis

c. wadi

d. standard of living

e. arable land

f. petroleum

Critical Thinking

1. **Recognizing Cause and Effect** Most of Southwest and Central Asia has an arid or semi-arid climate. What are three effects of this lack of water?
2. **Expressing Problems Clearly** The populations of Southwest and Central Asian countries are growing very quickly. What challenges might this growth present in the future?

Graphic Organizer

Copy the chart onto a separate sheet of paper, then fill in the empty boxes to complete the chart.

Country	Natural Resources	Major Bodies of Water	Major Areas of Population
Iraq			
Kazakstan			
Saudi Arabia			
Turkey			
Uzbekistan			

Map Activity

Southwest and Central Asia

For each place listed below, write the letter from the map that shows its location.

1. Rub al-Khali

2. Euphrates River

3. Pamirs

4. Mediterranean Sea

5. Kuwait

6. Saudi Arabia

7. Turkey

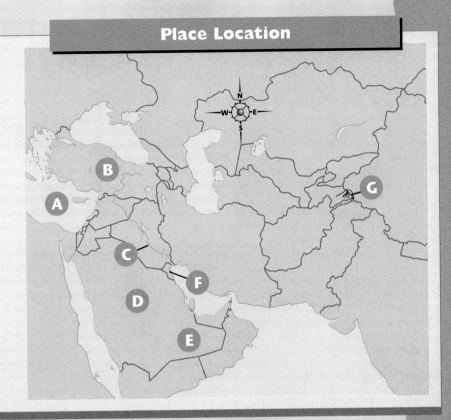

Writing Activity

Writing a Pamphlet

In order to have enough water to meet the needs of the population, irrigation systems must be used throughout Southwest and Central Asia. Sometimes these irrigation systems can cause environmental problems or deprive other countries of water. Select a country in Southwest Asia. Write a pamphlet that describes the advantages a dam might bring to this country. Also, mention possible problems the dam might bring and offer solutions to those problems.

Take It to the NET

Activity Learn more about the geography of Saudi Arabia. Use what you have learned to give a typical daily weather report on a region of your choice. For help in completing this activity, visit www.phschool.com.

Chapter 5 Self-Test To review what you have learned, take the Chapter 5 Self-Test and get instant feedback on your answers. Go to www.phschool.com to take the test.

Skills Review

Turn to the Skills Activity.

Review the six steps for making and interpreting a bar graph. Then complete the following: (a) What makes bar graphs an easy way to get information? (b) List the steps for reading a graph. Should you always do them in the order given? Why or why not?

How Am I Doing?

Answer these questions to help you check your progress.

1. Can I identify the main geographic features of Southwest and Central Asia?

2. Do I understand how climate has affected the vegetation and population in this region?

3. Can I identify two of the most important natural resources in Southwest and Central Asia?

4. What information from this chapter can I include in my journal?

SOUTHWEST AND CENTRAL ASIA

Cultures and History

PICTURE ACTIVITIES

This photo shows the ruins of a ziggurat, a pyramid-like structure in Southwest Asia. People living in what is now the country of Iraq built ziggurats between 2200 B.C. and 500 B.C. The ziggurats were different from the pyramids of ancient Egypt. First, the ziggurats did not have any rooms inside. They were made out of solid mud brick. Second, the sides of each ziggurat were terraced, or shaped like stairs. People planted trees and gardens on the terraces.

Study the picture
How do you think people climbed to the top of the ziggurat? Why do you think people built the ziggurat? How might they have used it?

Consider the architecture
Suppose that you were going to build a model of the ziggurat. How would you start? What materials would you use? What are some of the main steps that would be part of your building process?

The Cultures of Southwest Asia

Reach Into Your Background

Every society has rules. What are some of the rules that you must follow at school, at home, and in your community? What would happen if no one followed these rules?

Questions to Explore

1. What were some of the achievements of the ancient cultures of Southwest Asia?

2. Why has Southwest Asia had a long history of conflict?

Key Terms
deity
muezzin

Key Places
Mesopotamia
Iraq
Palestine

H ammurabi's Code was written about 3,800 years ago in Southwest Asia. People have described its laws as demanding "an eye for an eye." But there was more to the code than that:

> "If the robber is not caught, the man who has been robbed shall formally declare whatever he has lost . . . and the city and the mayor . . . shall replace whatever he has lost for him.
>
> . . .
>
> If a person is too lazy to make the dike of his field strong and there is a break in the dike and water destroys his own farmland, that person will make good the grain [tax] that is destroyed."

The law punished people harshly for wrongdoings. But it also offered justice to people who had been hurt through no fault of their own.

Mesopotamia

Hammurabi ruled the city of Babylon from about 1800 B.C. to 1750 B.C. He united the region along the Tigris and Euphrates rivers. This region is called Mesopotamia, which means "between the rivers."

Map Study Southwest Asia was the location of some of the world's earliest civilizations. Written language—an important feature of civilizations—was first developed in this area. The people of Mesopotamia used a writing system made up of wedge-shaped marks. This tablet (below) shows the calculations for the area of a piece of land. Southwest Asia also is the birthplace of Judaism, Christianity, and Islam. Jerusalem, Bethlehem, Mecca, and Medina all have religious connections. **Location** Between which two rivers is Mesopotamia located?

KEY

• City

Lambert Azimuthal Equal-Area Projection

The people of Mesopotamia developed a system of writing. They also produced ideas about law that still affect people today. For example, they believed that all citizens must obey the same set of laws.

People had lived in Mesopotamia for thousands of years, long before Hammurabi united it. By 3500 B.C., the people made the area a center of farming and trade. The Tigris and Euphrates rivers flooded every year, leaving fertile soil along their banks. People dug irrigation ditches to bring water to fields that lay far from the river. Irrigation helped them to produce a crop surplus, or more than they needed.

Many people settled in Mesopotamia. They invented the sailboat and used it to travel on the rivers, trading goods. They developed writing because they needed it to record business deals. People here also exchanged ideas with people from other regions—ideas about agriculture, law, and religion.

Birthplace of Three Religions

Three of the world's religions—Judaism, Christianity, and Islam—have their roots in Southwest Asia. Judaism began when Abraham began practicing it in Mesopotamia around 2000 B.C. Almost 2,000 years later, Jesus, the founder of Christianity, began preaching in what is now Israel. In about A.D. 600, Islam's prophet, Muhammad, began teaching in what is now Saudi Arabia.

People who practice Judaism, Christianity, and Islam all worship the same **deity,** or God. They all study the Bible as part of their heritage. Of the three religions, Islam has by far the most followers in the region today. They are called Muslims.

The sights and sounds of Islam are everywhere in Southwest Asia. One sound is the call of the **muezzin** (moo EZ in), a person whose job is to summon Muslims to pray. Five times a day, wherever they are, Muslims stop what they are doing and pray. In large cities, the call to prayer is broadcast over loudspeakers.

Arabic-speaking Arabs are the largest ethnic group in the region, and Islam is their main religion. But not all Southwest Asians are Arabs. Many Southwest Asians do not speak Arabic and many people, including Arabic-speaking Arabs, practice religions other than Islam.

Judaism is centered in Israel, although Jews live in every part of the world. At the heart of Judaism is the Torah, five books that make up the Jews' most sacred text. The Torah contains the Ten Commandments, laws that Jews believe God gave them through the prophet Moses. The laws established both religious duties toward God and rules for moral and ethical behavior.

Christianity is firmly rooted in Judaism. Jesus, the founder of the Christian religion, was a Jew. Christians adopted the Torah as the first five books of the Old Testament in the Bible. Like Islam and Judaism, Christianity began in Southwest Asia and spread throughout the world.

READ ACTIVELY

Visualize Visualize what it would be like to live where everything stopped for prayer five times a day. What might such a town look like? What would it sound like?

Jerusalem, Crossroads of Three Religions

Jerusalem, capital of the country of Israel, is an ancient city. People have been living there since 1800 B.C. Jerusalem is holy to Jews, Christians, and Muslims because events important to their religions took place there. To the left is the silver dome of a Christian church. The golden-domed building is called the Dome of the Rock. It stands over the rock from which Muslims believe the prophet Muhammad rose into heaven to speak with God.

Critical Thinking Do you think it is easy for three religions to share a holy city? Why or why not?

Conflicts and Challenges

Aswir Shawat is a Kurd from the town of Halabja, Iraq. Kurds are an ethnic group whose people live throughout Southwest Asia. Kurds practice Islam, but have their own language and culture. However, they do not have a country of their own. Their desire for a country has led to conflicts between Kurds and the governments of Iran, Iraq, and Turkey. Shawat describes what happened to him when the Iraqi army attacked his hometown in 1991:

READ ACTIVELY

Predict What do you think might happen if two groups of people claimed the same land?

> "Over 5,000 Kurdish people were killed at Halabja, and thousands were injured. My brother and I were saved from death because a few hours before the bombing, we had gone out of town to a village for some reason. . . . We had to go with thousands of people towards the border to Iran. I walked with my grandmother and brother. Nobody took anything with them. We left all our things in Halabja. When we got to Iran, they took us to a camp and gave us a tent. At the camp, we found our mother and grandfather."

Many people in Southwest Asia have had experiences like Shawat's. The region is a crossroads for Asia, Africa, and Europe. As a result, many groups live here. Religious and ethnic differences have led to disputes.

After World War I, a conflict broke out between Arabs and Jews in Southwest Asia. Judaism has its roots in Southwest Asia. Over the centuries, a few Jews continued to live in their homeland. But many had migrated to other parts of the world. In the late 1800s, Jews from around the world began to dream of returning to Palestine, an area along the eastern shore of the Mediterranean Sea. This alarmed the Arabs who lived there.

▼ This Kurdish settlement is located in eastern Turkey. Kurds also live in the neighboring countries of Armenia, Iran, Iraq, and Syria. However, they long for their own homeland. Notice the minaret—the tall tower to the right in the picture. Most Kurds, like the majority of Southwest Asians, are Muslims.

Palestine was their homeland, too. When some Jews began moving to Palestine at the end of World War I, tensions rose.

Jews continued to migrate to Palestine during the 1930s. During World War II, millions of Jews in Europe were killed solely because they were Jewish. After the war, many of those who had survived decided to go to Palestine. The United Nations voted to divide Palestine into separate Arab and Jewish states. But neither side was happy with the borders that were chosen. The result was war.

In 1948, Jews formed their own state, Israel. Their state was recognized by the United Nations. Since then, the Arabs of Palestine have lived as refugees in other Arab nations or in Israel, under Israeli rule. Israel has fought a number of bloody wars with the Arab nations that border it.

Arabs and Israelis have been working toward peace. Yasser Arafat is chairman of the Palestinian Liberation Organization (PLO), which seeks to create a Palestinian nation on Israeli land. Israel and the PLO agreed that Palestinians could govern themselves in some Israeli-occupied lands. Then in 1998, Arafat and Israeli Prime Minister Benjamin Netanyahu signed the Wye agreement. This agreement called for Israel to give Palestinians more land, and to release some Palestinian prisoners from Israeli jails.

Though the Wye agreement was easy to sign, carrying it out proved to be difficult. For years neither side could agree on the exact terms. Tensions between the two groups increased. In 2000, fighting broke out among Israelis and Palestinians once again. By early 2001, hundreds of people had been killed. Arafat and Israel's new prime minister, Ariel Sharon, had much work ahead of them to try to work out a peace agreement.

A Handshake for Peace

Former Israeli Prime Minister Yitzhak Rabin (left) shook hands with Yasser Arafat (right). In 1995 U.S. President Bill Clinton invited the two leaders to the White House, where they signed a peace agreement between Israel and the PLO. This event paved the way for the Wye agreement. Although the terms of the agreement could not be settled upon, it is hoped that Arafat and Israel's new prime minister can work them out. **Critical Thinking** Why do you think that many people considered the 1995 meeting a historic occasion?

SECTION 1 REVIEW

1. **Define** (a) deity, (b) muezzin.

2. **Identify** (a) Mesopotamia, (b) Iraq, (c) Palestine.

3. Describe three achievements of the civilizations of ancient Mesopotamia.

4. What three religions have their roots in Southwest Asia?

5. What caused tensions between Arabs and Israelis?

Critical Thinking

6. **Identifying Central Issues** What conflicts over land have existed in Southwest Asia?

Activity

7. **Writing to Learn** Write a paragraph explaining why writing helps people engaged in trading goods.

The Cultures of Central Asia

▼ Signs written in the Russian Cyrillic alphabet, like the one on the window below, still can be seen throughout Kazakstan.

Hard currency only
продажа товаров за скв

Have you ever wished you could change your name? In 1995, the people of Kazakstan did just that. Their republic used to be known as Kazakhstan. The "h" in Kazakhstan was added by Russians to make the name easier to pronounce in Russian.

Russians had a history of misnaming the Kazaks. When Russians first met the Kazaks, they wanted to avoid confusing them with the Cossacks, a southern Russian ethnic group. So Russians called the Kazaks the *Kyrgyz* (kihr GEEZ). Finally, they began calling the Kazaks *Kazakhs* and their country *Kazakhstan*. When the "h" was dropped in 1995, the Kazaks finally had a name for their country that reflected who they really were.

Meeting Place of Empires

Kazakstan is the largest country in Central Asia. But the Kazaks are not Central Asia's only ethnic group. Because of the region's central location, dozens of ethnic groups have settled here. Russians still live here, too. Each group that settled in Central Asia brought new ideas and ways of doing things.

The rugged Caucasus Mountains are located in western Central Asia (left). In the mountainous areas of Tajikistan, traveling can be difficult even in the mountain valleys (below).

Early History Central Asia is a rugged land. It contains broiling deserts and rocky mountains. Many of Central Asia's ethnic groups first made a living as nomadic herders. They herded livestock across the deserts and the **steppes,** or treeless plains. The nomads took their livestock to places where they knew they could find food and water. On the way, they met other groups and exchanged ideas and customs.

Over 2,000 years ago, a trade route called the Silk Road linked China and Europe. The Silk Road brought the people of Central Asia into contact with the people of East Asia, Southwest Asia, and Europe. For hundreds of years, caravans brought Chinese silk to the West. They carried items such as glass, wool, gold, and silver to the East. Along with goods, the traders exchanged ideas and inventions. Cities like Samarkand, in the country of Uzbekistan, sprang up along the route. These cities became wealthy centers of trade and learning.

The Silk Road generated wealth, but it also attracted invaders. Waves of foreign conquerors fought to control Central Asia. Sometimes the conquerors came from the West. Sometimes they came from the East. Although some ruled for hundreds of years, none lasted. Eventually, a new invader would conquer the area.

Each conqueror left a mark on the region. For example, an ancient Asian people called Persians left large buildings built from stone. In the 300s B.C., the Greeks, led by their warrior king, Alexander the Great, ruled for only a short while. But when they left, their ideas about military organization and strategy remained.

READ ACTIVELY

Predict Why do you think the trade route across Central Asia was called the "Silk Road"?

The people of Central Asia represent many different cultures. On the left, a girl takes a short break from picking cotton on a farm in Tajikistan. On the right, a young family waits for a bus on a city street corner in Kazakstan.

LINKS

ACROSS TIME

Lands for Empires In the 1200s, much of Central Asia was part of the largest land empire the world has ever known. Genghis Khan (GEN giz kahn), a leader of Mongolia, to the north of China, united his nomadic people into a strong fighting force. He conquered much of China and then swept west over Central Asia. At his death in 1227, his empire stretched from the Sea of Japan to the Caspian Sea.

About A.D. 700, the Muslim empire spread across large stretches of Central Asia. The Muslims had the greatest impact on the culture of the region. Many of the people of Central Asia adopted Islam. Today, most people in this region are Muslims.

Under Soviet Rule Europeans soon learned that there were faster ways to trade with China than to use the Silk Road. Ships began carrying goods between China and the seaports of Europe and the Americas. When this happened, trade declined in Central Asia.

This, however, did not stop foreign powers from wanting to control the region. In the 1800s, both Russia and Britain tried to expand their empires into Central Asia. Russia got there first. It captured the city of Tashkent, Uzbekistan, in 1865.

Russia built railroads, factories, and large farms in Central Asia. Some Russians moved into the region, bringing new ways of life. But most people continued to live as they always had. They practiced Islam and lived as nomadic herders.

The outside world, however, was closing in on Central Asia. In 1922, Russian Communists formed the Soviet Union. The Soviets extended communist power over wide areas of Central Asia. The Communists forced people to stop living as nomads. They had to work on **collectives**.

These were farms that were created when the government took over groups of small farms and combined them into large units. Collectives are owned by a country's national government. Soviet collectives did not always produce enough food for people to eat. At least one million Central Asians starved to death during the 1930s.

The Soviets also outlawed the practice of religion. They banned the practice of Islam and tried to stamp out Muslim culture. Many mosques—places of Islamic worship—were torn down. People were expected to celebrate communism, not Islam.

While the Soviets built new industries, schools, and hospitals in Central Asia, they allowed people few freedoms. Critics were jailed, even executed.

The Challenges of Independence

The Soviet Union ruled Central Asia for almost 70 years. In 1991, the Soviet Union broke up. Then Central Asia in turn broke into five independent countries. Since then, the people of these countries have had to learn to govern themselves.

Each country of Central Asia faces unique challenges. The region's industries are old. Some of these industries pollute the environment. Many people do not have jobs. Health care is poor and hard to get.

▼ After the collapse of the Soviet Union, Muslims in Uzbekistan were again free to worship at their blue-domed mosque in the ancient Silk Road city of Samarkand.

Economies of Central Asian Countries

Chart Study Since gaining political independence from the Soviet Union, the countries of Central Asia are working to become economically independent of their former ruler. **Critical Thinking** What is one product produced by all five nations? How do you think each country might be trying to strengthen its economy?

Country	Economic Activity
Kazakstan	Mining, steel production, and farm machine manufacturing are important industries. Grain and cotton are major crops. Kazakstan is also starting to develop its large oil and natural gas supplies.
Kyrgyzstan	Livestock raising and farming are central to the economy. Cotton, tobacco, fruits, and grains are the major crops. Industries include tanning and textile production.
Tajikistan	Tajikistan's economy is mainly agricultural. Cotton is its most important crop. Its major industries are textile and knitware manufacture and some mining.
Turkmenistan	Turkmenistan has large supplies of natural gas. It is working to export more of this valuable resource. Cotton and sheep production are also important.
Uzbekistan	Although it is a poor country, Uzbekistan is one of the world's largest exporters of cotton. It is also a major producer of gold and natural gas.

However, all the countries of Central Asia now proudly celebrate their culture and Islam. Mosques that had fallen into ruin are being rebuilt. The people of Central Asia are teaching their children about their religion. Neighboring Muslim countries are helping. For example, Saudi Arabia donated one million copies of the Quran, the Muslim holy book, to the nations of Central Asia. The people of Central Asia are working hard to make new lives for themselves since independence.

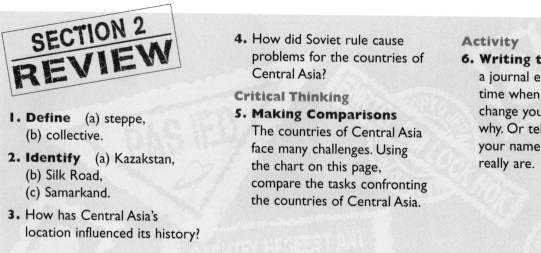

SECTION 2 REVIEW

1. **Define** (a) steppe, (b) collective.

2. **Identify** (a) Kazakstan, (b) Silk Road, (c) Samarkand.

3. How has Central Asia's location influenced its history?

4. How did Soviet rule cause problems for the countries of Central Asia?

Critical Thinking

5. **Making Comparisons** The countries of Central Asia face many challenges. Using the chart on this page, compare the tasks confronting the countries of Central Asia.

Activity

6. **Writing to Learn** Write a journal entry telling about a time when you wanted to change your name. Explain why. Or tell why you think your name reflects who you really are.

SECTION 3

Israel

BUILDING ITS ECONOMY

BEFORE YOU READ

Reach Into Your Background

Think of a time when you were faced with a nearly impossible challenge. How did you react? What strategies did you use to meet the challenge?

Questions to Explore

1. What are Israel's main economic activities?
2. How do geography and politics affect Israel's economy?

Key Terms

desalination
moshavim
kibbutz

Key Places

Negev Desert
Galilee
Jordan River

Picture a land of rock and sand that is the lowest point on the Earth—1,200 feet (366 m) below sea level. Three to four inches of rain (seven to ten cm) fall each year. Daytime temperatures can exceed 120°F (49°C). This is the Negev Desert, which makes up the southern two thirds of the country of Israel. In this uninviting landscape, Kalman Eisenmann makes a living growing tomatoes, peppers, and melons.

▼ With the sands of Israel's Negev Desert rising behind them, workers harvest strawberries. This crop is grown under protective plastic sheeting, which keeps water from evaporating into the hot desert air.

Making the Desert Bloom

Israel is one of the countries of Southwest Asia. Israel's geography is similar to that of the whole region. Two thirds of Southwest Asia is covered by desert. Throughout history, people in desert regions have made a living by herding animals across the desert, not by farming. In Israel, that has changed.

The people of Israel have used technology, new ideas, and hard work to make it possible to farm in the desert. Today, fruits and vegetables grown here are sold around the world. Agriculture has become an important part of Israel's economy.

Technology to the Rescue Kalman Eisenmann grows fruits and vegetables on Negev land that was once barren and dry. He uses an irrigation system that is controlled by a computer.

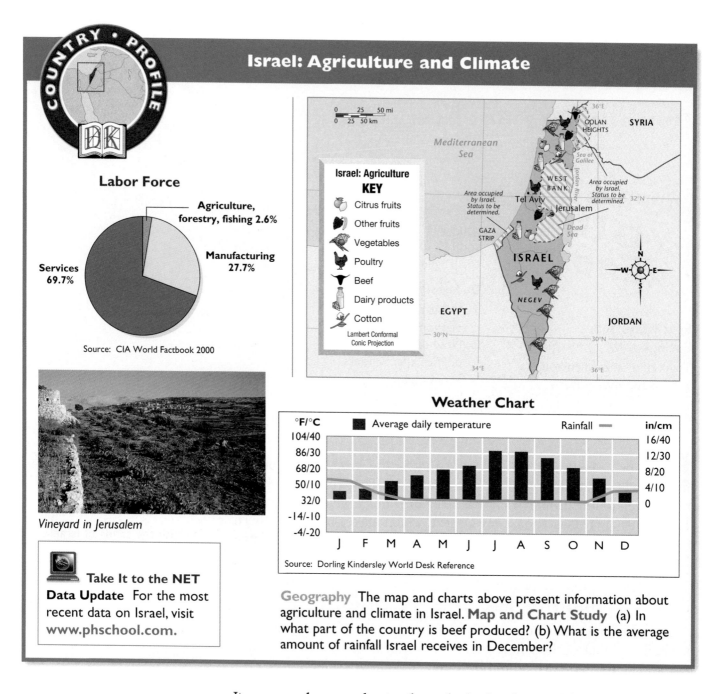

Israel: Agriculture and Climate

Labor Force

Agriculture, forestry, fishing 2.6%

Manufacturing 27.7%

Services 69.7%

Source: CIA World Factbook 2000

Vineyard in Jerusalem

Take It to the NET
Data Update For the most recent data on Israel, visit **www.phschool.com.**

Israel: Agriculture KEY
- Citrus fruits
- Other fruits
- Vegetables
- Poultry
- Beef
- Dairy products
- Cotton

Lambert Conformal Conic Projection

Weather Chart

°F/°C — Average daily temperature — Rainfall — in/cm

Source: Dorling Kindersley World Desk Reference

Geography The map and charts above present information about agriculture and climate in Israel. **Map and Chart Study** (a) In what part of the country is beef produced? (b) What is the average amount of rainfall Israel receives in December?

READ ACTIVELY

Visualize Visualize a desert filled with fruit orchards and vegetable plants. What would be your first reaction?

It moves underground water through plastic tubes straight to the roots of the plants. This way of irrigating crops was invented in Israel. When it was developed, few people lived in this desert. But now half a million people live here.

Irrigation, however, could not be used in the Negev without other advances. The water pumped through the system is brackish, too salty to support growth. The Israelis tried **desalination,** or taking the salt out of the water. But that proved too expensive. So the Israelis developed new plants that soak up the water, but not the salt.

Developing new plants is not easy. Many crops were ruined. "I've buried, salted, sunburned, drowned, and otherwise punished thousands of crop varieties," Kalman Eisenmann says.

Even after developing the right kinds of plants, there is more work to be done before desert turns into farmland. Trees must be planted to prevent erosion. Tractors and other equipment must level the surface of the land. But all of this effort pays off. One farmer cuts open a ripe cantaloupe grown on her farm. "Sweet as ice cream," she tells a visitor, handing him a slice.

Working Together   Israel became a country in 1948. Since then, it has almost doubled the amount of farmland within its borders. One reason for this success has been cooperation among farmworkers. In Israel, most people who do not live in cities live in **moshavim** (moh shah VEEM), small farming villages. The workers here cooperate. They combine their money to buy equipment. They tell each other about new methods of farming. They also pool their crops to get a better price.

The **kibbutz** (kih BOOTS) is another kind of cooperative settlement found in Israel. People who live on a kibbutz cooperate in all parts of life. They eat together, work together, and share profits equally. The people on a kibbutz do not earn any money while they work there. But the kibbutz provides their housing, meals, education, and health care.

On a kibbutz, people do more than farm. They may also work in factories. Some of these factories make products such as electronic equipment and clothing. Manufacturing is an important part of Israel's economy. The country exports its products to many nations.

LINKS ACROSS TIME

Western Wall In A.D. 70, Romans destroyed the Second Temple of Jerusalem, considered most holy by the Jews. Today, a section of the temple still stands. It is part of a larger wall that surrounds a Muslim mosque. The old temple wall, called the Western Wall, is about 160 feet (49 m) long and 60 feet (18 m) high. Long ago, people renamed it the Wailing Wall when they saw Jews praying and mourning near it.

Life on a Kibbutz

On an Israeli kibbutz, all able-bodied adults work. While some adults tend crops such as oranges (left), others are busy cooking, doing the laundry, or teaching school. Children on a kibbutz may live with their parents, or they may stay in a Children's House, where they eat, sleep, and attend school. This kibbutz kindergarten class (above) is learning how to bake bread. **Critical Thinking** How is life for children on a kibbutz similar to your life? How is it different?

Predict How might a nation's use of the Jordan River affect the lives of people living along the river?

Israel and Its Neighbors

Israel has succeeded in making its dry lands come to life. However, like all countries in Southwest Asia, it must continue to manage its water carefully. To do this, Israel must cooperate with its neighbors.

Sharing the Jordan River Galilee, in northern Israel, is a land of rolling green hills and valleys covered with wildflowers. Farmers pick bananas for market. Picnickers sit near the Sea of Galilee and toss scraps of bread to seagulls. Tourists who come to this fertile region may forget that Israel is a dry land. They may also find it hard to believe that Galilee has been the site of conflict between Israel and its Arab neighbors. The Jordan River, which runs through Galilee, is important both to Israel and to its Arab neighbors.

The Jordan River runs along Israel's borders with Syria and Jordan. It flows into the Dead Sea. In many places, this river is small and muddy. However, in Southwest Asia, the Jordan River is a vital resource. Israel, Syria, and Jordan each irrigate their crops with water from the Jordan. For example, Israel uses water from this river to irrigate part of the Negev Desert.

Each country's use of Jordan River water affects its neighbors. The long conflict between Israel and the Arab states makes it hard for these neighbors to trust each other. Therefore, they watch each other's use of the Jordan River closely. When Israel began building a national irrigation system in the 1950s, Syria tried to stop the project. In the 1960s, Israel tried to stop Syria from channeling some of the river's waters. Today, the country of Jordan worries that it does not have enough water to meet its needs. It plans to build a dam near the Sea of Galilee. No building has begun, because if Jordan starts without Israel's approval, war could result.

▼ All young Israelis—men and women—are required to serve in the armed forces. Here, a woman soldier shows how to put together a gun.

The Price of War After becoming a nation, the Israelis dreamed of enriching their new country. They hoped to provide a home for Jews from around the world. In many ways, this dream came true. The economy developed rapidly. Immigrants came to Israel hoping to find a new life. But Israel's changes cost a great deal of money. Israel received help from the United States and other nations. However, the Israelis have not always had enough money to meet the needs of their growing country.

One expense is the military. Israel maintains a large army. It

Israel has occupied the West Bank area since the late 1960s. Recently, however, Israel has turned over control of parts of the West Bank to the Palestinians. Not all Israelis are happy with this plan. They want the Israeli army to remain in the area. In this picture, Israeli soldiers in the West Bank town of Hebron watch as two mothers, one Israeli (on the left), one Palestinian, walk with their children.

uses its army in conflicts with Arab nations. These conflicts have taken a toll on all of the countries involved.

Fortunately, Israel and its neighbors are now taking steps that may lead to a lasting peace. In addition, Israel, Syria, and Jordan are starting to cooperate on the issue of water. They have discussed projects that will benefit them all, such as building dams.

Some Arabs and Jews have not waited for Israel and its neighbors to come to an agreement. Mustafa Zuabi is Arab. His friend Palti Sella is Jewish. They live in Galilee, and they have been close friends for years. According to Zuabi, "Thirty-five years ago, I told Palti that peace would come to this land. Because if one Arab and one Jew can be friends, there's hope for all of us."

SECTION 3 REVIEW

1. **Define** (a) desalination, (b) moshavim, (c) kibbutz.

2. **Identify** (a) Negev Desert, (b) Galilee, (c) Jordan River.

3. What geographic problems has Israel overcome to build a healthy nation?

4. How have Israelis used technology to overcome obstacles?

Critical Thinking

5. **Expressing Problems Clearly** Why have Israel's relations with its neighbors slowed its economic development?

6. **Drawing Conclusions** Would you enjoy working on a kibbutz? Why or why not?

Activity

7. **Writing to Learn** Israel's economy has benefited from farmers working together. Think about a challenge that has faced your community. Then write a paragraph describing how people can work together to solve it.

Saudi Arabia
OIL AND ISLAM

Reach Into Your Background

In the modern world, gasoline and oil have many uses. What petroleum products do you depend on every day?

Questions to Explore

1. How has oil wealth changed Saudi Arabia?
2. How does Islam affect women in Saudi Arabia?

Key Terms

hajj
diversify

Key Places

Mecca
Riyadh

▼ Each year, over two million Muslims make the hajj to Mecca. Here, huge crowds worship at the Kabah, the holiest site in all of Islam. The Kabah is the cube-shaped structure to the left in the picture.

For more than a thousand years, Muslims from all over the world have been making pilgrimages to Mecca, Saudi Arabia. By going to Mecca, they honor the memory of Abraham, who is said to have built the first house of worship here. The pilgrimage is called the **hajj** (hahj). Muslims must make the hajj once in their lifetime if they can. The hajj used to be long, hard, and dangerous. Muslims traveled across mountains and deserts by foot, horse, or camel to reach Mecca. But in recent years, Saudi Arabia has spent billions of dollars to make the journey safer and more comfortable. Today, many pilgrims travel to Mecca by airplane. Modern hotels line the streets of Mecca.

Oil Wealth

In 1900, Mecca was a small and very poor town. Saudi Arabia was one of the poorest countries in the world. Many of its people made a living by herding livestock through the desert. Like most of the countries of Southwest Asia, Saudi Arabia is mostly desert.

But in the 1930s, everything changed. People discovered oil in Southwest Asia. Oil reserves changed the fortunes of Saudi Arabia and several other countries in the region. It made them rich.

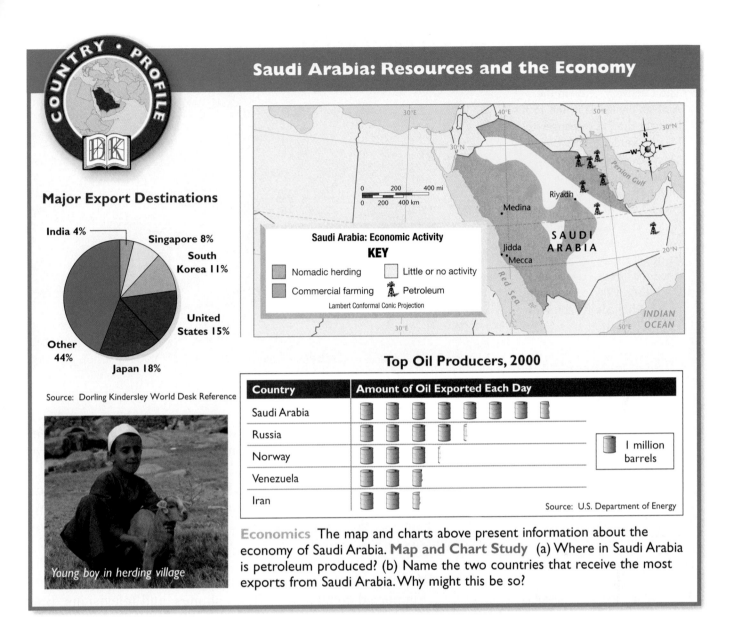

Saudi Arabia: Resources and the Economy

COUNTRY · PROFILE
DK

Major Export Destinations

India 4%
Singapore 8%
South Korea 11%
United States 15%
Other 44%
Japan 18%

Source: Dorling Kindersley World Desk Reference

Young boy in herding village

Saudi Arabia: Economic Activity
KEY
- Nomadic herding
- Commercial farming
- Little or no activity
- Petroleum

Lambert Conformal Conic Projection

SAUDI ARABIA

Riyadh
Medina
Jidda
Mecca
Persian Gulf
Red Sea
INDIAN OCEAN

0 200 400 mi
0 200 400 km

Top Oil Producers, 2000

Country	Amount of Oil Exported Each Day
Saudi Arabia	🛢️🛢️🛢️🛢️🛢️🛢️🛢️🛢️
Russia	🛢️🛢️🛢️🛢️🛢️
Norway	🛢️🛢️🛢️
Venezuela	🛢️🛢️🛢️
Iran	🛢️🛢️🛢️

= 1 million barrels

Source: U.S. Department of Energy

Economics The map and charts above present information about the economy of Saudi Arabia. **Map and Chart Study** (a) Where in Saudi Arabia is petroleum produced? (b) Name the two countries that receive the most exports from Saudi Arabia. Why might this be so?

New Developments When night falls in Riyadh (ree AHD), Saudi Arabia's capital, the skyline begins to glow. The lights of the many apartment and office buildings flicker on. Large buildings line the city streets. When oil prices are high, buildings go up at a rapid pace. Money pours in, allowing communities like Riyadh to modernize. But when oil prices are down, the economy of the entire country is shaken. Many large building projects grind to a stop.

Saudi Arabia has the most important oil economy in the world. Under its deserts lie more than 250 billion barrels of oil. Saudi Arabia has about one fourth of the world's oil. No other country on the Earth exports more petroleum.

Many Saudi leaders think that Saudi Arabia depends too much on oil. The Saudis are trying to **diversify,** or increase the variety of, their economy. They want to create many different ways for the country to earn money. But today, oil exports are still Saudi Arabia's main source of income.

Meanwhile, projects paid for with oil money have changed the lives of all Saudi Arabians. Before the oil boom, there were few roads in Saudi

Take It to the NET
Data Update For the most recent data on Saudi Arabia, visit **www.phschool.com**.

The discovery of oil in the Arabian peninsula in the 1930s brought dramatic changes to Riyadh, Saudi Arabia's capital. Once a small country town, today Riyadh is a modern city with broad highways and skyscrapers of steel and glass. Riyadh ranks as one of the world's fastest-growing cities. Its population has tripled in size since the 1960s. **Critical Thinking** Why do you think oil wealth made Riyadh grow?

READ ACTIVELY

Predict How do modern technology and traditional values exist together in Saudi Arabia?

▼ Growing fruits and vegetables is becoming an important economic activity in Saudi Arabia.

Arabia. Now roads link all parts of the country. In the past, people often lived without electricity and telephones. Now these luxuries are common in Saudi Arabia.

The nation's wealth has also made it possible to build a good school system. Saudi Arabia has built thousands of schools. In 1900, many Saudi Arabians could not read or write. But today, Saudi students are becoming doctors, scientists, and teachers.

Traditional Values Using their oil wealth, Saudis have imported computers, cellular phones, and televisions. But before a new gadget is used, the nation's religious leaders study it. They decide whether each import can be used by Muslims. Only imports that they believe do not violate Muslim values can be used in daily life. In Saudi Arabia, Islam regulates most people's lives.

For example, cities like Riyadh contain department stores, hotels, and universities. But they have no movie theaters or night clubs. The Sunni branch of Islam, which most Saudi Arabians follow, forbids this kind of entertainment.

Alcohol and pork are illegal in Saudi Arabia. All shops must close during the five times a day when Muslims pray. Saudi Arabians use Western inventions to improve their lives. But they make sure these inventions do not interfere with their traditions.

The Role of Women in Saudi Arabia

Many laws in Saudi Arabia deal with the role of women. Women are protected in certain ways. They are also forbidden to do some things. The role of women is changing, but traditional values remain strong.

Old Ways and New Professions In Riyadh, women who go out in public cover themselves with a full-length black cloak. Even their faces are usually covered. This is one of the rules of the country. Another rule is that women may not drive cars. At home, women stay in the female part of the house if guests are visiting.

◀▲This children's doctor in Riyadh (above) wears western-style clothes in her office. In the street, she wears a traditional full-length black cloak similar to the ones worn by these women in the Saudi city of Jidda (left).

Samira Al Tuwaijri (suh MIH ruh at tuh WAY zhree), a young woman who lives in Riyadh, follows these rules. Tuwaijri is also a doctor in the King Fahd Hospital. She is studying to become a surgeon. "Traditionally, women have always . . . stayed at home to cook and look after the family. Working for a living was just not done," says Tuwaijri.

But when Saudi Arabia built new schools, women became better educated. "Women are no longer content to just stay at home. . . . We are able to compete in a man's world," Tuwaijri says.

Despite the changes, women and men usually still remain separate. Boys and girls go to different schools. They do not socialize with one another. Women choose careers where they will not have to work closely with men. Tuwaijri's patients are all women. "I could have entered general medicine, but I have been brought up strictly and it was difficult to adjust to examining male patients," she says.

The Influence of the Quran   Most of the rules governing women's behavior in Saudi Arabia come from the Quran, the holy book of Islam. It requires fair treatment of women. Muslim women could own property long before Western women had that right. However, not all Muslims agree on how to apply the Quran to modern life.

"I suppose it is difficult for those who live in the West to understand why I am not allowed to be photographed," Tuwaijri says. "In Islam, the family is very important and a family decision is accepted by all members without question. . . . Even if I disagreed with it, I would still abide by it."

Like many Saudi women, Tuwaijri is content with her role in a Muslim society. She does not want to live as Western women live. "There are many things in our culture which limit our freedom, but I would not want change overnight," she says. "It is important that we move into the future slowly and with care."

SECTION 4 REVIEW

1. **Define**   (a) hajj, (b) diversify.

2. **Identify**   (a) Mecca, (b) Riyadh.

3. Name three changes that occurred in Saudi Arabia as the country grew wealthy from oil.

4. What happens in Saudi Arabia when oil prices go up? When they go down? Why do many Saudi leaders think their country depends too much on oil?

5. How do Saudi Arabians keep a traditional Muslim way of life even with the changes brought by their oil wealth?

Critical Thinking

6. **Understanding Points of View**   What is Samira Al Tuwaijri's point of view about the place of women in her culture?

Activity

7. **Writing to Learn**   Saudi Arabians have used their wealth to make changes, but have also maintained traditional ways. Write a paragraph about how your life would change if you became rich. What things about your life would you want to remain the same?

Kazakstan

BEYOND INDEPENDENCE

BEFORE YOU READ

Reach Into Your Background

"The United States is a free country." Think about the meaning of this statement. What does freedom mean to you? What does it mean for a country to be free?

Questions to Explore

1. What unites and divides the people of Kazakstan?
2. What challenges does Kazakstan face now that it is independent?

Key Terms
radiation poisoning

Key Places
Semey
Aral Sea

Who is a Kazak? "If a man cannot name his ancestors for seven generations, he is not Kazak," says one man. He can trace his family history back to the nomads who roamed the steppes. Long ago, nomads recited their family histories to each other when they met on the plains. Kazaks still follow this tradition today.

Today, fewer than half of the people in Kazakstan could pass the count-the-generations test. Until recently, the Soviet Union controlled the country. Members of many ethnic groups moved to the area. Many still live here. Now these citizens are working to fit into the new Kazakstan. Some ask whether they can be citizens of Kazakstan if they can never be true Kazaks.

◀ A group of students gather in a school playground in the western Kazakstan city of Beyneu. Kazak children are required to attend school from ages 7 to 18.

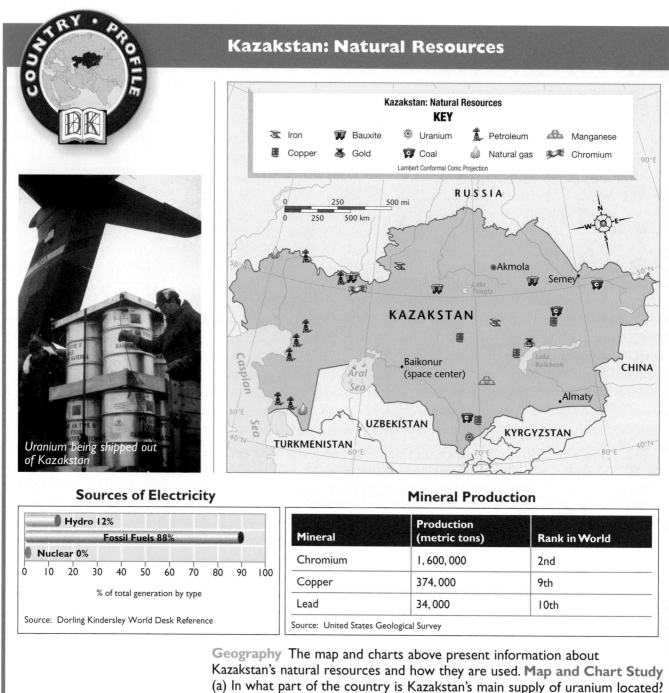

COUNTRY · PROFILE

DK

Kazakstan: Natural Resources

KEY

- Iron
- Copper
- Bauxite
- Gold
- Uranium
- Coal
- Petroleum
- Natural gas
- Manganese
- Chromium

Lambert Conformal Conic Projection

RUSSIA

Akmola · Semey

KAZAKSTAN

Lake Tengiz

Baikonur (space center)

Aral Sea

Lake Bolkhash

CHINA

Almaty

Caspian Sea

UZBEKISTAN

KYRGYZSTAN

TURKMENISTAN

Uranium being shipped out of Kazakstan

Sources of Electricity

- Hydro 12%
- Fossil Fuels 88%
- Nuclear 0%

0 10 20 30 40 50 60 70 80 90 100

% of total generation by type

Source: Dorling Kindersley World Desk Reference

Mineral Production

Mineral	Production (metric tons)	Rank in World
Chromium	1,600,000	2nd
Copper	374,000	9th
Lead	34,000	10th

Source: United States Geological Survey

Geography The map and charts above present information about Kazakstan's natural resources and how they are used. **Map and Chart Study** (a) In what part of the country is Kazakstan's main supply of uranium located? (b) What are Kazakstan's main sources of electricity?

Take It to the NET
Data Update For the most recent data on Kazakstan, visit **www.phschool.com**.

Forces Uniting; Forces Dividing

Kazakstan borders Russia in Central Asia. Look at the map above. What country borders Kazakstan to the east? What countries lie along Kazakstan's southern border? The culture of Kazakstan reflects its location between Asia and Europe, to the northwest.

Kazaks in Kazakstan High up on a lonely plateau, Marat Imashev steps out of his tent, which is made of felt carpets. He looks out over his 650 sheep. He, the sheep, a horse, and two camels have been on the move for a month. They are heading toward a place where his flock can nibble on sweet mountain grass. "I know the way without a map," he says. "Kazaks have been grazing sheep on this plateau for centuries."

When Kazakstan became independent, members of the Kazak ethnic group rejoiced. They began to celebrate their heritage. Kazaks designed a symbol for their new country that shows the wooden wheel that holds together a shepherd's tent. They replaced Russian with Kazak as the official state language. They also built mosques around the country so that Kazaks could again practice Islam. These moves frightened many Russians who live in Kazakstan.

Russians and Kazaks In 1991, almost as many Russians as Kazaks lived in Kazakstan. Most had migrated there since the 1930s to farm. Then Kazakstan became independent. Russians living there worried about what would happen to them.

Today, Russians work at many important jobs in Kazakstan. They speak Russian and have their own schools, theaters, and clubs. Because Russians have some of the best jobs in a land of high unemployment, many Kazaks resent them.

Russian Viktor Mikhailov came to Kazakstan in the 1950s. His job was to turn 60 million acres (24 million hectares) of grazing land into wheat fields. When he arrived in Kazakstan he was surprised to find that the Kazaks bitterly opposed plowing their grazing land under for crops. "We thought we were bringing the future to this country," he says. "And the people say now, 'Why did you come here? You spoiled our pastures. We had a lot of sheep. Now we have no place to herd them.'"

Forging Unity Tensions run high between Russians and Kazaks. The new leadership must forge a united country out of these hostile groups. Kazaks are not the majority of the population, but they control the government. This worries the Russians, who do not speak Kazak and are not Muslim.

One Russian leader thinks that both Russian and Kazak should be the official languages. Otherwise, he says, "Russian speakers will not be involved in the government, and all documents will be in Kazak." A Kazak leader does not want Russians in the government. "We do not want them to interfere with the revival of Kazakstan."

Meanwhile, some leaders worry about Russians leaving the country. If they go, they will take their technical skills with them. This nation needs the help of all its citizens.

Kazakstan's Challenges

During Soviet rule, the Soviets used Kazakstan and its resources for their own ends. This is one of the reasons for the tension between Russians and Kazaks today. Many other challenges facing Kazakstan can also be traced to the Soviet period. One of these problems is the damage to the environment.

Predict What effects have the Russians had in Kazakstan?

A-OK, Baikonur! Kazakstan will long be remembered for its role in the conquest of outer space. Baikonur (by kuh NOOR), a space center in south-central Kazakstan, was the site of several historic Soviet space flights. In 1957, the first human-made satellite was launched from Baikonur. The earliest manned spacecraft to orbit the Earth blasted off from there in 1961. The first woman in space also began her journey in Baikonur.

Ask Questions What would you like to know about the challenges Kazakstan faces today?

Nuclear Fallout Semey is a city in northeastern Kazakstan. Before independence, it was known as Semipalatinsk. During the 1950s and 1960s, the skies around it sometimes lit up with a fierce, blinding flash. Giant mushroom-shaped clouds would appear on the horizon. The earth would shake so hard that the walls of houses 50 miles (80 km) from the flashes and clouds would shudder and crack. The Soviet Union was testing nuclear bombs.

The Soviets had a nuclear testing site nearby. In the 1960s, above-ground nuclear explosions were banned. At this point, the Soviets began exploding their nuclear bombs underground. They exploded 600 bombs in about 40 years. Eventually, protests from local people forced the Soviets to stop the explosions.

However, the region is still polluted with nuclear fallout, radioactive particles that fall from nuclear bombs. The pollution from all these explosions will take years to clean up. This pollution has caused problems for the people around Semey. Many babies in the region are born with serious illnesses. Some will never be able to see, hear, or speak. Many people have **radiation poisoning,** a sickness caused by exposure to radiation produced by nuclear explosions. Others have cancer.

Kazakstan also has to clean up after another Soviet experiment. The Soviets tried to grow cotton on land that was not suited to it. Irrigation systems built to water the cotton diverted a great deal of water from the

▲▶ Ships left high and dry (right) and even wandering turkeys (above) now share land that once was at the bottom of the Aral Sea.

Market Day in Almaty

The Kazak city of Almaty is located on the old Silk Road trade route. For centuries, the city's markets rang with the shouts of merchants buying and selling goods. Today, the city still has busy markets. However, people visit them to buy local goods, not products from foreign lands. At this market, farmers from the area around Almaty sell their produce.

Aral Sea. As a result, the sea has shrunk in size and its water has become very salty. Some experts believe it may take 30 years to repair the damage done to the Aral Sea.

Discovering Strengths   Kazakstan is the largest country in Central Asia. Like all of the new countries of Central Asia, it faces many challenges. But it has some advantages that other nations do not. Kazakstan has many industries. It has the factories and skilled work force it needs to produce manufactured goods. Other countries in the region will need to develop these industries.

Kazakstan is also rich in natural resources. It has coal, lead, zinc, and copper, among other minerals. Most important, it has oil. Kazakstan has already signed an agreement with an American company to start developing the Tengiz oil field. Tengiz is one of the largest oil fields in the world. Resources like this could make the country rich. Oil wealth may help Kazakstan pay the costs of cleaning its environment.

SECTION 5 REVIEW

1. **Define**   radiation poisoning.
2. **Identify**   (a) Semey, (b) Aral Sea.
3. Describe some of the differences between Kazaks and Russians in Kazakstan.

4. What strengths does Kazakstan have in solving its major problems?

Critical Thinking
5. **Recognizing Cause and Effect**   How did the years of Soviet rule affect Kazakstan?
6. **Making Comparisons**   What are some advantages that Kazakstan has over other nations in the region?

Activity
7. **Explorer's Journal**   Write a journal entry explaining how you would feel about Russians living in Kazakstan if you were a Kazak. Then write another journal entry explaining how you would feel about living in Kazakstan if you were a Russian.

Locating Information

Daniel asked Alison, "Do you know what the next concert at the Zip will be?" Alison looked up from her computer screen.

"No, but I can tell you in a few minutes," she said.

"How are you going to do that?" Daniel asked.

"I'll check the Internet," she said.

"Hey, can you show me how?" said Daniel. "I've always wanted to use the Internet, but I don't really understand it."

Get Ready

The Internet is a worldwide network of computers. It is made up of thousands of computers around the globe that communicate over a very complicated network of telephone cables, fiber optic lines, and satellite links. The computers are owned by individuals, schools, businesses, and governments.

People use the Internet to exchange information about nearly every topic. They use it to send words and pictures back and forth to people all over the globe. For example, doctors in the United States use the Internet to share medical information with doctors in China. Music fans share their thoughts about their favorite groups with fans in other countries by sending messages over the Internet.

The World Wide Web is an important part of the Internet. The Web makes information on the Internet easy to find and use. It is made of "Web pages," or individual documents stored in computers on the Internet.

Web pages show information about almost anything at all. For example, many Web pages are set up by stores. By calling up a store's Web page, you can look at the products, read descriptions, and even order items. People have created Web pages about rock groups, families, and whole countries.

As you can imagine, the information on the Internet could fill dozens of libraries. You can use this information for your schoolwork and just for fun. But how can you sort through the pools of information on the Internet to find just what you are looking for?

To start looking, you use special computer programs that will search the Internet for you. These programs are often called search engines.

▶ This is a NASA Web page. An Internet user can find more information about any topic named by "clicking" on one of the boxes.

► After you type in your topic, this search engine will find references to that topic for you.

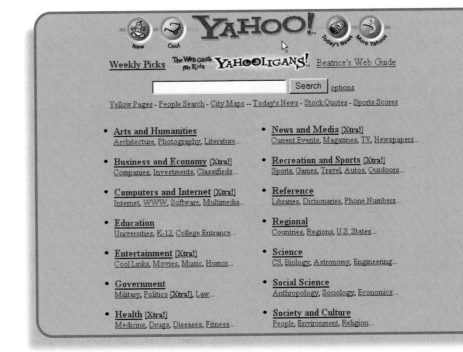

Search engines work like the index of a book. In a book index, you locate the topic you want to read about and then turn to the listed pages. On the Internet, you enter your topic and the search engine looks through the Internet for you, listing all of the Internet sites with information about your topic.

Try It Out

The trick to using a search engine is the same as the trick to using a book index—you have to identify the key words for your topic. A key word is a word or phrase that serves as the key to your topic idea. For example, if your topic is "the greatest ballerinas of all time," your key-words might be "ballerina" or "ballet." These words are more specific than "dance," and will probably give better results. Specific key words usually work better than more general ones. Many search engines have useful tips on searching with key words.

A. Identify your key words. What key words would you use to search the Internet and the World Wide Web for information about these topics?
- Your favorite musical group
- Your favorite sports team
- Your home state
- A hobby or interest of yours

B. Begin your search. If you have Internet access, use the search engines to look for your information. Many schools have Internet connections, as do many public libraries. The search engine will respond to your key words with the names of articles or Web pages.

C. Make a selection. Choose the articles or Web pages that look most interesting to you. The network will show you your selection.

D. Read or print out your selection. You can read the information on the screen, or you can print it out to have on paper.

Apply the Skill

Now prepare for an Internet search for information about Central and Southwest Asia. Follow the same steps as in Try It Out, but research the following topics, in addition to any other ideas you have:

- Typical food in Kazakstan
- History of Israel
- Architecture in Saudi Arabia

Review and Activities

Reviewing Main Ideas

1. What were the accomplishments of the early Mesopotamians?

2. List two conflicts that trouble Southwest Asia.

3. How did Central Asia's location affect its history and cultures?

4. Identify two challenges that the countries of Central Asia face today.

5. How is Israel's agriculture affected by its geography?

6. Explain how Israel's relationship with its neighbors affects its economy.

7. List two ways in which Saudi Arabia has spent some of its oil money.

8. How have the lives of Saudi Arabian women remained the same since the oil boom? How are they different?

9. Explain why there is tension between the Kazaks and the Russians living in Kazakstan.

10. What strengths will help Kazakstan face the challenges of independence?

Reviewing Key Terms

Use each key term below in a sentence that shows the meaning of the term.

1. deity
2. muezzin
3. steppe
4. collective
5. desalination
6. moshavim
7. kibbutz
8. hajj
9. diversify
10. radiation poisoning

Critical Thinking

1. **Identifying Central Issues** Each country in Southwest and Central Asia is unique. However, all these countries have certain similarities. What characteristics do most of the countries in this region share?

2. **Making Comparisons** Israel and Kazakstan are both very young countries. In what ways are these countries alike? In what ways are they different?

Graphic Organizer

Copy the diagram onto a sheet of paper, then fill in the empty boxes to complete the chart.

	Israel	Saudi Arabia	Kazakstan
Traditional Way of Making a Living			
Modern Changes to How People Make a Living			

Map Activity

Southwest and Central Asia

For each place below, write the letter from the map that shows its location. Use the maps in the Activity Atlas at the front of the book to help you.

1. Israel

2. Saudi Arabia

3. Kazakstan

4. Silk Road

5. Negev Desert

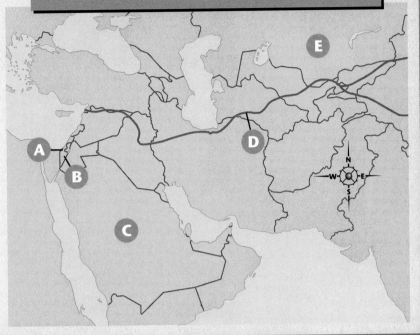

Writing Activity

Writing a Progress Report

All of the countries in Southwest and Central Asia face challenges as they enter the future. Choose one of the countries covered in this chapter and write a progress report about it. Remember to address the problems the nation faces and the solutions being put forward to address those problems.

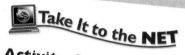

Take It to the NET

Activity Browse the exhibits at the Israel Museum. Which exhibit did you find most interesting? For help in completing this activity, visit www.phschool.com.

Chapter 6 Self-Test To review what you have learned, take the Chapter 6 Self-Test and get instant feedback on your answers. Go to www.phschool.com to take the test.

Skills Review

Turn to the Skills Activity.

Review the way to find information on the Internet. Then complete the following: (a) How is a search engine like an index? (b) Give examples of how you would narrow a topic down to one or more key words.

How Am I Doing?

Answer these questions to help you check your progress.

1. Can I describe the main geographic features of Southwest and Central Asia?

2. Do I understand how cultures in Southwest and Central Asia compare to other Asian cultures I have studied?

3. Can I identify some historic events that have shaped the modern cultures of Southwest and Central Asia?

4. What information from this chapter can I include in my journal?

CHAPTER 7

The Pacific Region

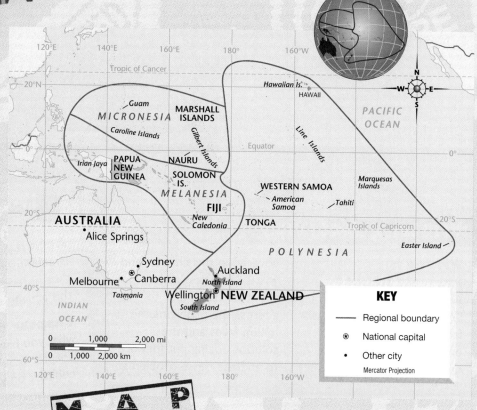

The Pacific region includes the continent of Australia and many islands. The largest islands are those that make up New Guinea and New Zealand, but there are thousands of others. To learn more about the lands and the people of this region, do the following activities.

Study the map

Look at the map scale. What important fact does the map scale tell you about the Pacific region? Name the three large groups of Pacific islands.

Make connections

The Pacific region is one of the largest in the world. But only about 29 million people live here. That is less than 1 percent of the world's population. Why do you think so few people live in this region?

Physical Geography of Australia and New Zealand

Reach Into Your Background

Do you live in a crowded city or in a small town? How close to your neighbors do you live? What are some of the advantages and disadvantages of living in a city? In a small town? Think about these questions as you read about Australia and New Zealand.

Questions to Explore

1. What are the major physical features of Australia and New Zealand?
2. How has physical geography affected the climate, vegetation, and animal life of the region?

Key Terms

marsupial
tectonic plate
geyser
fiord

Key Places

Great Dividing Range
Outback
North Island
South Island
Canterbury Plain

What bird is strange looking, has a long bill, does not fly, and only comes out at night to hunt? If you said a kiwi, you are right. The people of New Zealand are so proud of this unusual bird that they have made it their national symbol. The people even call themselves "Kiwis." The bird is one of many unique animals found in New Zealand and its neighbor to the west, Australia.

Unique Environments

Australia and New Zealand lie between the Pacific Ocean and the Indian Ocean. Both are in the Southern Hemisphere, south of the Equator. This means that their seasons are the opposite of those in the United States. They are far from other landmasses, which has made them unique.

New Zealand and Australia are so far from other large landmasses that many of their animals and plants are found nowhere else on the Earth. Only in New Zealand can you find kiwis and yellow-eyed penguins. Eighty-four percent of the vegetation in New Zealand's forests grows nowhere else. Australia has many unique creatures, such as the kangaroo and the koala. These animals are biologically unique, too.

▼ The Kiwi has no tail. It is the only bird with nostrils at the tip of its beak. These help it sniff out insects and berries.

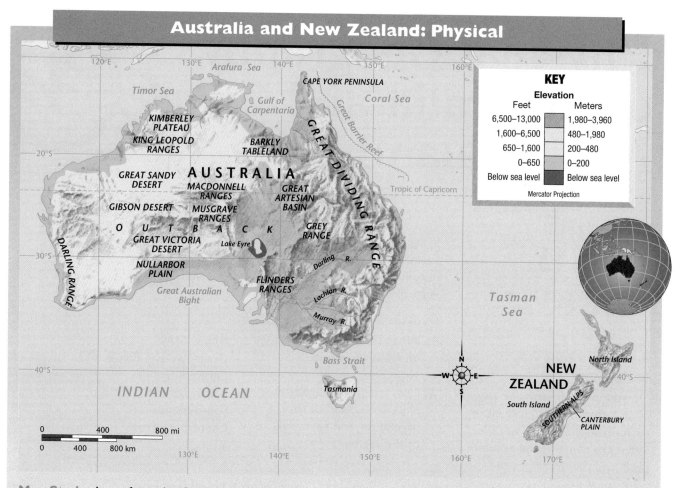

Australia and New Zealand: Physical

KEY

Elevation

Feet		Meters
6,500–13,000		1,980–3,960
1,600–6,500		480–1,980
650–1,600		200–480
0–650		0–200
Below sea level		Below sea level

Mercator Projection

Map Study Apart from the Great Dividing Range, most of Australia is quite flat. The huge area to the west of the Great Dividing Range is made up of plains or low plateaus. In contrast, New Zealand is mountainous or hilly. **Location** Where are most of Australia's deserts located? **Place** Which of New Zealand's two islands is more mountainous?

Ask Questions What would you like to learn about the animals of Australia and New Zealand?

They are **marsupials** (mar soo pea ulz), or animals that carry their young in a body pouch. Marsupials are found elsewhere in the world. The opossum of North America, for instance, is a marsupial. But in Australia, almost all mammals are marsupials. This is not true anywhere else on the Earth.

The uniqueness of New Zealand and Australia is the result of forces beneath the Earth's surface. The outer "skin" of the Earth, or the crust, is broken into huge pieces called **tectonic plates.** Australia, New Zealand, and the Pacific islands are all part of the Indo-Australian plate. Once, it was part of a landmass that included Asia. Then, several hundred million years ago, the plate broke away. Slowly—only an inch or two each year—it moved southeast in the Pacific Ocean.

As the plate moved, the distance between the islands and Asia increased. Over the centuries, small changes occurred naturally in the islands' animals and plants. For instance, many birds have lost the ability to fly, even though they still have small wings. Because of the islands' isolation, these living things did not spread to other regions.

Australia: A Continent and a Country

Australia is the Earth's largest island and smallest continent. It is about as large as the continental United States. That means the part of the United States located between Canada and Mexico. Australia has a much smaller population than the United States. Most Australians live on a narrow plain along Australia's eastern and southeastern coasts. Australia's physical geography explains why.

Find the region along Australia's east coast on the map on the opposite page. This plain has Australia's most fertile farmland and receives ample rain. Winds flowing westward across the Pacific Ocean pick up moisture. As the winds rise to cross the Great Dividing Range—mountains just to the west of the coastal plain—the moisture falls as rain. These winds not only bring rain. They also help make the climate mild and pleasant. Also, Australia's most important rivers, the Murray and Darling, flow through the region. Most Australians live here, in cities.

The rest of Australia is very different. Just west of the Great Dividing Range is a rain shadow. This is a region that gets little precipitation because of a mountain range. This area is made up of semiarid plateaus and desert lands. Since rain seldom falls here, and there are few rivers, people depend on wells for fresh water. Farther west, the huge central plain called the Outback is desert and dry grassland.

▼ The Great Barrier Reef (below) is located off Australia's northeast coast. Measuring about 1,250 miles (2,010 km) in length, it is the largest coral reef in the world. Ayers Rock (below left), is 1.5 miles (2.4 km) long and 1,100 feet (335 m) high. This huge, red rock is a major landmark in Australia's Outback.

Shaped by Volcanoes

Now look at the map and find New Zealand, which lies about 1,200 miles (1,900 km) southeast of Australia. Made up of two islands, New Zealand is much smaller than Australia. The climate is not as hot, because New Zealand is farther from the Equator. Here, the landforms have been shaped by volcanoes. They, in turn, were caused by the movement of tectonic plates. Where plates meet, there often are earthquakes and volcanoes. New Zealand is located where the Pacific plate meets the Indo-Australian plate. Like other island groups, New Zealand's North Island and South Island were formed by volcanoes when these plates collided.

New Zealand is one of the largest countries in the Pacific region—about the size of the state of Colorado. Both its islands have highlands, forests, lakes, and rugged, snowcapped mountains. Although New Zealand is more than 1,000 miles (1,600 km) long, no place is more than 80 miles (129 km) from the sea. The country has a mild climate and plenty of rainfall.

In the middle of North Island lies a volcanic plateau. Three of the volcanoes are active. The volcano called Mount Egmont, however, is inactive. North of the volcanoes, geysers (GY zurz), or hot springs, shoot scalding water over 100 feet (30.5 m) into the air. New Zealanders use this energy to produce electricity.

South Island has a high mountain range called the Southern Alps. Mount Cook, the highest peak in the range, rises to 12,349 feet (3,764 m). Glaciers cover the mountainsides. Below, crystal-clear lakes

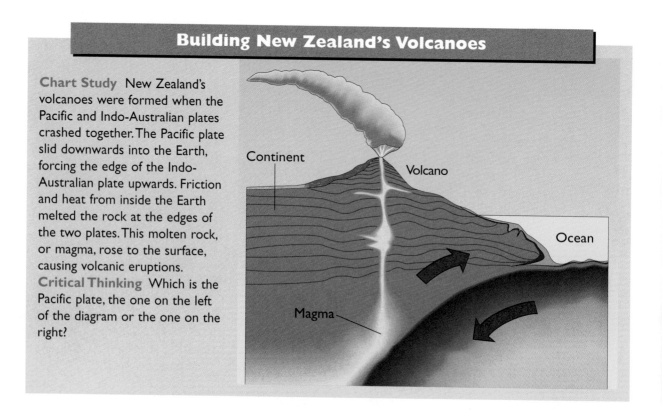

Building New Zealand's Volcanoes

Chart Study New Zealand's volcanoes were formed when the Pacific and Indo-Australian plates crashed together. The Pacific plate slid downwards into the Earth, forcing the edge of the Indo-Australian plate upwards. Friction and heat from inside the Earth melted the rock at the edges of the two plates. This molten rock, or magma, rose to the surface, causing volcanic eruptions.
Critical Thinking Which is the Pacific plate, the one on the left of the diagram or the one on the right?

Continent

Volcano

Ocean

Magma

The picture on the left shows towering Mount Cook on New Zealand's South Island. Sheep, like these grazing in the hills below Mount Cook, far outnumber New Zealand's human inhabitants. Most of the country's people live in harbor cities, like Auckland on New Zealand's North Island (below).

dot the landscape. **Fiords** (fyordz), or narrow inlets, slice the southwest coastline. Here, the mountains reach the sea. To the southeast lies a flat, fertile land called the Canterbury Plain. This is where farmers produce most of New Zealand's crops. Ranchers also raise sheep and cattle here.

Comparing Australia and New Zealand

Although much smaller, New Zealand is like Australia in many ways. In both countries, most of the population lives in cities along the coast. In fact, more than four out of five New Zealanders live in towns and cities. Although their climates are different, both Australia and New Zealand have important natural resources. Both also raise sheep and cattle and grow similar crops.

SECTION 1 REVIEW

1. **Define** (a) marsupial, (b) tectonic plate, (c) geyser, (d) fiord.

2. **Identify** (a) Great Dividing Range, (b) Outback, (c) North Island, (d) South Island, (e) Canterbury Plain.

3. How did Australia and New Zealand's isolation affect their plant and animal life?

4. How do the landscapes of Australia and New Zealand differ? How are they similar?

Critical Thinking

5. **Recognizing Cause and Effect** How have Australia's geography and climate affected where people live?

Activity

6. **Writing to Learn** Find out more about the unique plants and animals of Australia and New Zealand. Choose one that interests you. Write and illustrate a report about it.

Physical Geography of the Pacific Islands

BEFORE YOU READ

Reach Into Your Background

Many people dream of living on a tropical island, or at least of visiting one. Do you? Jot down a brief description of your "dream island." Then see how it compares with the real islands in the South Pacific.

Questions to Explore

1. What is the physical geography of the Pacific islands?
2. What is the difference between high islands and low islands?

Key Terms

high island
low island
atoll
coral

Key Places

Melanesia
Micronesia
Polynesia
Papua New Guinea

▼ This picture shows a phosphate mine on Nauru. Phosphate is Nauru's only natural resource.

Luana Bogdan lives in Nauru (nah OO roo), the third-smallest country in the world. Tomorrow, she will be 12 years old. She is very excited, but she is also sad. Luana knows her family may soon have to leave Nauru.

Nauru's economy depended on its phosphate mines. But now the phosphate, used to make fertilizer, is almost gone. Even worse, mining has stripped the tiny island of its trees and vegetation. Nauru's leaders are trying to restore the island's ruined environment. If they fail, the Nauruans will have to find a new homeland.

Melanesia, Micronesia, and Polynesia

The Pacific Ocean covers nearly one third of the Earth's surface. About 25,000 islands similar to Nauru dot the Pacific. The region is divided into three areas. *Melanesia* (mel uh NEE zhuh) means "black islands." *Micronesia* (my kruh NEE zhuh) means "small islands." *Polynesia* (pahl uh NEE zhuh) means "many islands." Any island that falls inside the boundaries of a particular area belongs to that group.

A High Island in Polynesia

Volcanoes created high islands like the Marquesas Islands in Polynesia. The islands' rich volcanic soil is very good for farming. Coconuts, pineapples, bananas, coffee, sugar cane, and rubber are among the many different crops grown by farmers on high islands.

High Islands and Low Islands   Geographers also divide the Pacific islands into high islands and low islands. Volcanoes form **high islands.** They usually have mountains. The soil, which consists of volcanic ash, is very fertile. Because of their size and because people can grow crops here, high islands support more people than low islands.

Low islands are reefs or atolls. An **atoll** (A tawl) is a small coral island in the shape of a ring. The ring encloses a shallow pool of ocean water called a lagoon. Often, the lagoon has at least one opening to the sea. An atoll often rises only a few feet above the Pacific. Low islands have this shape and low elevation because they are built on coral reefs. **Coral** is a rocklike material made up of the skeletons of tiny sea creatures. A reef develops until it nears the surface. Then sand and other debris accumulate on the reef's surface, raising the island above the level of the water.

Far fewer people live on low islands than on high islands. In part, this is because low islands are quite small. Also, low islands have poor, sandy soil and little fresh water, so it is difficult to raise crops. Most low islanders survive by fishing. They may also grow coconuts, yams, and a starchy root called taro.

The Three Regions   The island region with the most people is Melanesia, which is north and east of Australia. Most of Melanesia's large islands are high islands. New Guinea, for example, has two ranges of high

LINKS TO MATH

Navigating the Oceans
Thousands of years ago, Pacific Islanders navigated hundreds of miles across the open ocean. One of their tools was an "*etak* of sighting." It was the distance a canoe traveled from the time it left an island to the time the island disappeared from the horizon—about 10 miles. They also used an "*etak* of birds." It was the distance between an island and the place where its sea birds usually fed—about 20 miles out to sea.

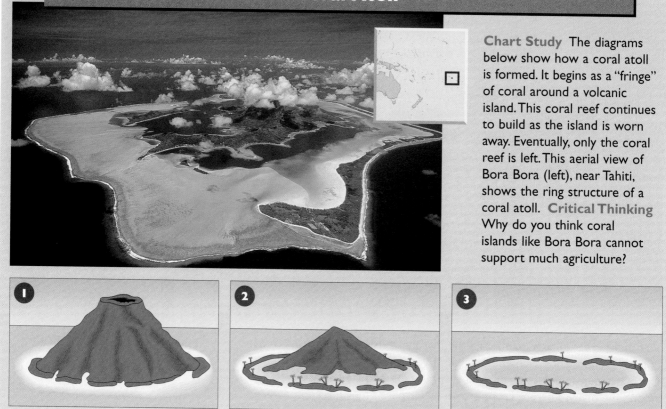

Chart Study The diagrams below show how a coral atoll is formed. It begins as a "fringe" of coral around a volcanic island. This coral reef continues to build as the island is worn away. Eventually, only the coral reef is left. This aerial view of Bora Bora (left), near Tahiti, shows the ring structure of a coral atoll. **Critical Thinking** Why do you think coral islands like Bora Bora cannot support much agriculture?

mountains. It is divided into two countries. The western half of the island is called Irian Jaya (IHR ee ahn JAH yuh). It is part of the country of Indonesia. The eastern half is Papua New Guinea (PAP yuh wuh noo GIN ee), the largest and most populated Melanesian country. Some smaller Melanesian islands are Fiji, the Solomon Islands, and New Caledonia.

Most of the islands of Micronesia lie north of the Equator. Made up largely of low islands, Micronesia covers an area of the Pacific as large as the continental United States. Some of Micronesia's 2,000 islands are less than 1 square mile (2.6 sq km) in area. The largest is Guam, which is just 209 square miles (541 sq km). Most of Micronesia's islands are divided into groups. The largest are the Caroline, Gilbert, Marshall, and Mariana islands. Guam is part of the Marianas.

Polynesia is the largest island region in the Pacific. It includes our fiftieth state, Hawaii. Polynesia consists of a great many high islands, such as Tahiti and Samoa. Dense jungles cover their high volcanic mountains. Along the shores are palm-fringed, sandy beaches. The Tuamotus and Tonga are examples of Polynesia's few low islands and atolls.

Climate and Vegetation of the Pacific

The Pacific islands lie in the tropics. Temperatures are hot year-round. Daytime temperatures reach between the 80s and mid-90s in degrees Fahrenheit (around 32°C). Nighttime temperatures average about 75°F

(24°C). The ocean and the winds keep the temperatures from getting too high. The amount of rainfall marks the change from one season to another.

Some Pacific islands have wet and dry seasons. Most islands, however, receive heavy rainfall all year long. In Hawaii, for example, volcanic peaks such as Mauna Kea (MOW nuh KAY uh) receive 100 inches of rain each year. Usually the rain falls in brief, heavy downpours. Some low islands, however, receive only scattered rainfall.

Because of high temperatures, much rainfall, and fertile soil, high islands like Papua New Guinea and the Hawaiian Islands have rich vegetation. Tropical rain forests cover the hills. Savanna grasses grow in the lowlands. Low islands, on the other hand, have little vegetation. The poor soil supports only palm trees, grasses, and small shrubs.

The Pacific island region has few natural resources. The coconut palm is the most important resource. It provides food, clothing, and shelter. Islanders export dried coconut meat, which is used in margarine, cooking oils, and luxury soaps. Some low islands, like Nauru, have phosphate deposits that can be exported. But the Pacific islands' most valuable resource may be their beauty. Tourism is gaining importance in the region and providing a new source of income.

▲ The wet season in the Pacific often brings violent weather. Here, high winds and driving rain bend the coconut palms on Palmerston Atoll in the Cook Islands.

SECTION 2 REVIEW

1. **Define** (a) high island, (b) low island, (c) atoll, (d) coral.

2. **Identify** (a) Melanesia, (b) Micronesia, (c) Polynesia, (d) Papua New Guinea.

3. Name three large island groups of Micronesia.

4. High islands often have a better standard of living than low islands. Explain why this might be so.

Critical Thinking

5. **Drawing Conclusions** Most Pacific islands have few natural resources. How might this affect trade between these islands and other, more industrial nations around the world?

Activity

6. **Writing to Learn** Suppose you have decided to live on one of the Pacific islands. Write a paragraph explaining why you have decided to move. How will you handle the challenges of island life?

Cultures of Australia, New Zealand, and the Pacific Islands

BEFORE YOU READ

Reach Into Your Background

What if you had to go on a long trip to a place you knew nothing about? How would you get ready? List the things you would take with you. The people who settled in the Pacific island region had to make similar decisions. What do you think they decided to do?

Questions to Explore

1. How did people settle Australia and New Zealand?

2. What groups shaped the cultures of Australia and New Zealand?

3. How have the Pacific island nations been influenced by other cultures?

Key Terms

penal colony
station

Key People and Places

Aborigine
Maori
Easter Island
Auckland

Hundreds of giant stone statues dot the landscape of Easter Island. Made of solid volcanic rock, each statue stands 10 to 40 feet (3 to 12 m) tall. Some weigh more than 50 tons (46 metric tons). A European who saw them in 1722 was astonished:

▼ Tourists gaze awestruck at the eyeless giants that dot Easter Island. No one knows for sure how the ancient islanders carved and erected these statues.

“**T**he stone images . . . caused us to be struck with astonishment [amazed us]. We could not comprehend how . . . these people, who have no thick timber for making any machines . . . had been able to erect such images.”

Easter Island's statues still impress people. Scientists also wonder how people first came to this faraway island and to the other parts of the Pacific region.

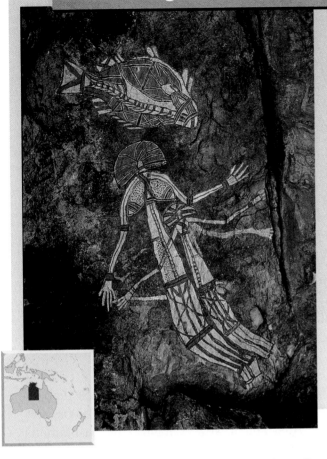

According to Aborigine tradition, in the "Dreamtime" before humans walked the Earth, mythical ancestors formed the world's mountains, rivers, plants, and animals. Aborigines passed their traditions on from generation to generation by word of mouth. Aborigine artists also recorded tales in carvings and rock paintings like this ancient one in northern Australia. Aborigines still use such ancient practices to keep their traditions alive. **Critical Thinking** Why do you think Aborigines used carvings and paintings to pass on their traditions?

Early Settlers in Australia and New Zealand

Scientists think that the Aborigines (ab uh RIJ uh neez), the earliest settlers in Australia, came from Asia about 40,000 years ago. For thousands of years, they hunted and gathered food along the coasts and river valleys. Some learned to live in the harsh Outback.

For thousands of years, the Aboriginal population stayed at a stable, even level. People lived in small family groups that moved from place to place in search of food and water. All had strong religious beliefs about nature and the land. Such beliefs played a key role in their way of life.

The Maori of New Zealand The earliest people in New Zealand were the Maori (MAH oh ree). Their ancestors first traveled from Asia to Polynesia. Then, about 1,000 years ago, the Maori traveled across the ocean to New Zealand. According to Maori legend, seven groups set out in long canoes to find a new homeland. A storm tossed their boats ashore on New Zealand. The Maori quickly adapted to their new home. They settled in villages, making a living as hunters and farmers. But the Maori also prized fighting and conquering their enemies. They often fought other groups of Maori over the possession of land. The Maori used storytelling to pass on their beliefs and tales of their adventures.

Maori Canoes The Maori showed their standing in society by the works of art they owned. For instance, a person might own elaborately carved and painted war canoes. Some were up to 100 feet (30 m) long. Human figures were carved along the hull and into the prow, which is the front part of the boat. The figures often had eyes made of mother-of-pearl. Canoes were painted red and decorated with feather streamers.

These students from Sydney (right) illustrate Australia's ethnic mix—95 percent European. The sports Australians play also illustrate the country's European heritage. Rugby, for example, originated in Great Britain (below).

READ ACTIVELY

Predict How might the discovery of a resource like gold affect the population of a country?

The Arrival of Europeans   European explorers heard about a mysterious continent that lay to the south of Asia. In the 1600s, several ships touched on either Australia or New Zealand. The most famous of these explorers was the Dutch sea captain Abel Janszoon Tasman. The Australian island of Tasmania is named after him. But no one established settlements during Tasman's time. Then, in 1769, British captain James Cook explored New Zealand. The next year, Cook explored the east coast of Australia. He claimed both lands for Britain.

In 1788, the British founded the first colony in Australia as a **penal colony.** This is a place settled by convicts, or prisoners. Soon, other colonists settled in Australia. Some worked for the prison facilities. Others went to find new land. Then, in 1851, gold was discovered. The population soared. Not long after, Britain stopped sending convicts to Australia. Some 50 years later, in 1901, Australia gained independence.

New Zealand was settled by Europeans at about the same time as Australia. In 1840, the British took control of New Zealand. The colony, with its fine harbors and fertile soil, attracted many British settlers. New Zealand gained independence in 1947.

The Cultures of Australia and New Zealand

Today, most Australians and New Zealanders are descendants of British settlers. Some maintain close ties with relatives in Great Britain. They share British culture, holidays, and customs. Most express pride in their British heritage, especially their parliamentary system of government and belief in freedom and democracy.

However, Australia and New Zealand are not exactly alike. Each has its own unique culture. For example, Australians have added many new words to the language. These include *mate,* or "close friend," and *fair go,* or "equal opportunity." New Zealanders are deeply opposed to nuclear warfare. No ships carrying nuclear arms are allowed to use New Zealand harbors.

Most Australians and New Zealanders enjoy a high standard of living. Farming, mining, and manufacturing have made people prosperous. Most families have cars and good housing. Most earn a good income. They spend much of their free time outdoors—camping, on picnics, or relaxing on the beach.

The Aborigines Today   Today, about 200,000 Aborigines live in Australia. Since the arrival of Europeans, the Aborigines have suffered great hardships. In the colonial period, settlers forced these native peoples off their lands. Tens of thousands died of European diseases. Others were forced to work on sheep and cattle **stations,** which are extremely large ranches. The settlers demanded that the Aborigines adopt European ways. As a result, they began to lose their own customs and traditions. Recently, however, life for Aborigines has begun to improve a little.

Other Peoples of Australia
People other than the British settled in Australia. During the gold rush of the 1850s, many people came, including the Chinese. These immigrants hoped to find riches. Although few succeeded, most remained. Many of Australia's large cities have Chinese communities.

After World War II, many Europeans immigrated to Australia. They came from Italy, Yugoslavia, Greece, and Germany. In the 1970s, people fleeing the war in Vietnam took refuge in Australia. And today, immigrants from all over the world continue to arrive.

The Maori Way of Life   When New Zealand became a British colony, Britain promised to protect Maori land. Settlers, however, broke that promise. For many years, the settlers and the Maori clashed violently. The settlers finally defeated the Maori in 1872.

After their defeat, the Maori were forced to adopt English ways. Maori culture seemed in danger of being

▼ The Asian population in Australia has grown in recent years. Here, dancers perform a dance from the Philippines at a folk fair in Sydney.

destroyed. Slowly, however, Maori leaders gained more power. They recovered some traditional lands. New laws now allow the Maori to practice their customs and ceremonies.

Today, there are more than 300,000 Maori in New Zealand. They make up about 9 percent of the country's population. Many Maori now live in cities. They work in businesses, factories, and offices. But they still honor their Maori heritage. Many speak both Maori and English. Thanks to their artists, writers, and singers, Maori culture is an important part of the lives of all New Zealanders.

Other Peoples of New Zealand At the end of World War II, many Europeans migrated to New Zealand. Recently, Vietnamese and Cambodian refugees have looked to New Zealand for safety. And many people from the Polynesian islands have settled here. Today, more Polynesians live in New Zealand's largest city, Auckland, than in any other city in the world.

The Cultures of the Pacific Islands

Scientists believe that the first people to inhabit the Pacific islands came from Southeast Asia more than 30,000 years ago. First, these people settled on New Guinea, Melanesia's largest island. Then, over thousands of years, they traveled across the Pacific by canoe to Micronesia and later Polynesia.

A Variety of Cultures As people settled the Pacific region, they developed many different cultures. Because of the distances between islands, groups could not communicate with each other. Therefore, each group developed its own language, customs, and religious beliefs. However, the island people did have many things in common. Their ocean environment shaped their lives. It fed them and was their main means of transportation and trade. Most built their lives around their small villages. Many also farmed.

From Colonies to Independence The arrival of Europeans in the 1800s had a great impact on the Pacific islands. Britain, France, and Germany set up trading posts and naval bases on many islands. Japan and the United States soon joined the race for control of the Pacific region. In the late 1800s, these nations turned the islands into colonies. For the next 100 years, foreign nations ruled the people of the Pacific.

Ask Questions What would you like to learn about the culture and history of the Pacific islands?

▼ At Rotorua, where many Maori people live, a woman in traditional dress heats her food in the sizzling hot springs.

Life in the Pacific Islands

Life in the Pacific islands presents vivid contrasts. In cities like Papeete, the capital of Tahiti (left), modern apartment buildings and automobiles are a common sight. In contrast, most of Papua New Guinea's four million residents still farm, fish, and build their houses in the traditional way (below).

After World War II, most Pacific islands gained independence. By then, traditional island cultures had blended with cultures from Europe, America, and other countries. Most governments were democratic. Most churches were Christian. Many Pacific Islanders read and spoke English. Foreign companies operated businesses and large farms here. Since independence, the lives of most island people have improved. But incomes are still low. Many depend on fishing or on growing such crops as taro and yams to make a living.

SECTION 3 REVIEW

1. **Define** (a) penal colony, (b) station.

2. **Identify** (a) Aborigine, (b) Maori, (c) Easter Island, (d) Auckland.

3. Where do scientists believe the native peoples of Australia, New Zealand, and the Pacific islands come from?

4. What happened to native peoples when Europeans arrived in Australia, New Zealand, and the Pacific islands?

Critical Thinking

5. **Making Comparisons** In what ways are the histories of the Aborigines and the Maori similar? In what ways are they different?

6. **Drawing Conclusions** Why might people who live on an island be able to preserve their culture for a long period without change?

Activity

7. **Writing to Learn** Write 10 brief entries for a time line that shows the history of Australia, New Zealand, and the Pacific islands.

Australia

THREE WAYS OF LIFE

BEFORE YOU READ

Reach Into Your Background

Think about what you know about American history. When settlers moved west in the United States, what happened to Native American lands and ways of life? European settlers in Australia moved into Aboriginal lands in the 1800s. Make a list of what you think happened to the Aborigines.

Questions to Explore

1. Why is Australia developing close ties with Pacific Rim nations?

2. Why are cattle and sheep ranches important to Australia?

3. How is the Australian government changing the way it deals with Aborigines?

Key Term
artesian well

Key Places
Sydney
Alice Springs

Michael Chang owns a successful trading company in Sydney, Australia's largest city. From his office in a modern glass skyscraper, he sometimes watches Sydney's busy harbor. What interests him most are the large cargo ships.

John Koeyers and his family own a huge cattle ranch in northwest Australia. He uses a Jeep to round up the herds on his ranch. The Koeyers sell most of their cattle to companies that supply fast-food restaurants in Asian nations.

Lyle Sansbury is chairman of the Board of Directors of the Nurungga Farming Company. He is very proud of the farm. It produces barley, wheat, cattle, and sheep. Lyle is full of plans for expanding the company into other activities, such as fish farming. The Nurungga Farm is one of the successful businesses owned and run by Aborigines.

▼ The Sydney Opera House was completed in 1973. The building's white concrete arches look like the sails of a huge ship.

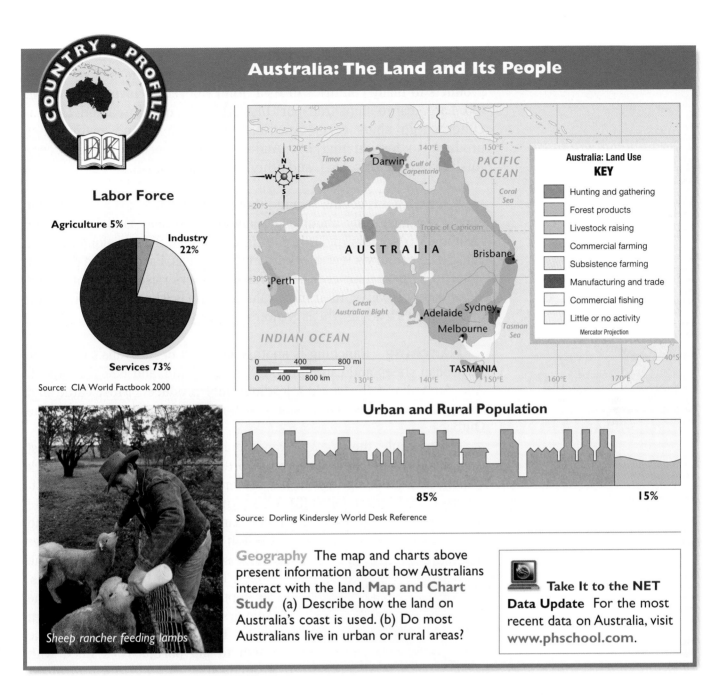

COUNTRY · PROFILE

Labor Force

Agriculture 5%
Industry 22%
Services 73%

Source: CIA World Factbook 2000

Australia: Land Use
KEY

- Hunting and gathering
- Forest products
- Livestock raising
- Commercial farming
- Subsistence farming
- Manufacturing and trade
- Commercial fishing
- Little or no activity

Mercator Projection

Urban and Rural Population

85%   15%

Source: Dorling Kindersley World Desk Reference

Sheep rancher feeding lambs

Geography The map and charts above present information about how Australians interact with the land. **Map and Chart Study** (a) Describe how the land on Australia's coast is used. (b) Do most Australians live in urban or rural areas?

Take It to the NET Data Update For the most recent data on Australia, visit **www.phschool.com**.

A Trading Economy

Michael Chang, the Koeyers, and Lyle Sansbury are all Australians. The definition of *Australian* has changed since Australia achieved independence. It is no longer "British." It now reflects the diversity of Australia's people. Today, Australia has close ties with other nations of the Pacific Rim. These nations border the Pacific Ocean. They include Japan, South Korea, China, and Taiwan. The United States is another major Pacific Rim nation. It is one of Australia's key trading partners.

Japan, the United States, and other Pacific Rim nations have invested large amounts of money in Australia's economy. They also have set up banks, insurance companies, and other businesses in Australia. More and more, Australia's economy depends on trade with these Pacific Rim countries.

READ ACTIVELY

Predict What do all three people have in common? How do they contribute to Australia's economy?

Michael Chang's trading company is just one of hundreds of companies that do business with Pacific Rim countries. He sends various products to many countries in Asia. John Koeyers is involved in trade, too. Large cargo ships transport his cattle to South Korea and Taiwan. Other cargo ships carry Australian wool, meat, and many other products to foreign markets. And even larger ocean tankers carry Australia's coal, zinc, lead, and other minerals to Japan.

Farming It seems strange that farm products are an important export, because only about 6 percent of Australia's land is good for farming. Most of this land is in southeastern Australia and along the east coast. The country's few rivers are in those areas. Farmers use the river water to irrigate their crops. Australian farmers raise barley, oats, and sugar cane. However, their most valuable crop is wheat. Australia is one of the world's leading wheat growers and exporters.

Ranching Ranching is another key part of Australia's economy. Australian sheep and cattle provide lamb, mutton, and beef for export. And Australia is the world's leading wool producer. Most cattle and sheep are raised on large stations. Some of the largest are in the Outback.

For example, the Koeyers' ranch is in a hot, dry area in northwest Australia. It covers 680,000 acres (275,196 hectares). Another Outback station, near Alice Springs in the center of Australia, is even larger. It covers 12,000 square miles (31,080 sq km)—about as much as the state of Maryland. Even with this much land, the cattle can barely find enough grass for grazing. Fresh water also is scarce. Rain falls rarely, and the region has only a few small streams. To supply water for their cattle, the Koeyers use underground **artesian wells.** These are drilled deep into the Earth to tap porous rock filled with groundwater.

Visualize Visualize a large sheep or cattle station in the Outback.

Cattle Round-Up

In Australia's hot, dry Outback, ranchers graze sheep and cattle on huge ranches. Some of these ranches, or stations, are bigger than some American states. At round-up time, ranchers often use helicopters to locate stray cattle.

Aborigines: Seeking Respect

Lyle Sansbury is like many young Aborigines. They are working hard to make sure the people and governments of Australia treat them with respect. They are trying to preserve their culture. And they are having a growing role in the economic life of the country.

Aboriginal leaders have worked to improve the lives of their people. Their schools now teach Aboriginal

◀ An Aborigine artist makes a traditional bark painting of a kangaroo, Australia's best-known marsupial.

Early Human Circle Art In northwestern Australia is a giant sandstone rock. At its base, archaeologists discovered circles—thousands of them—carved into it. More were found on boulders nearby. Each circle is about 1.2 inches (3 cm) in diameter. Tests showed that ancient people carved the rings about 75,000 years ago. That is 25,000 years before archaeologists had thought humans migrated to Australia! Everyone's theories had to be revised.

languages. Aborigines again celebrate important events with ancestral songs and dances. And artists have strengthened Aboriginal culture by creating traditional rock paintings and tree bark paintings.

Aborigine leaders like Lyle Sansbury have helped their people in another important way, too. They have influenced the government of Australia. The government has begun to return Aboriginal land to them. The government has built schools and hospitals on their land. It has also set aside some of their sacred places.

Aborigines have gained more rights. But their main goal is to regain their ancestral lands. Australia's courts have helped. However, many ranchers and farmers now live on those lands. These people strongly oppose giving the land back. This struggle may take many years to resolve. But Aborigines believe they will win.

SECTION 4 REVIEW

1. **Define** artesian well.

2. **Identify** (a) Sydney, (b) Alice Springs.

3. In what area are Australia's major trading partners located?

4. What are some of the key aspects of Australia's economy?

Critical Thinking

5. **Drawing Conclusions** In American history, Native Americans were forced from their homelands and moved to reservations. For years, Native Americans have been fighting to regain their original homelands. How does this compare with the history and struggle of the Aborigines?

Activity

6. **Writing to Learn** Pretend that you and your family live on the huge cattle station near Alice Springs. Write a description of what you think your life would be like. Include ideas about your special school, your tasks, and your free time.

Drawing Conclusions

Ms. Lee walked into the classroom. Tim looked up at her.

"Uh-oh," he whispered. "Looks like a pop quiz!" Tim flipped open his textbook and started to quickly review the chapter.

Sheila heard Tim. Why did he think there would be a pop quiz?

"How can you tell?" she whispered.

"Look at Ms. Lee!" said Tim, still studying. "Do you see that little yellow notebook in her hand?" Sheila saw it.

"She uses that notebook to write test questions. Whenever she pulls it out, we have a quiz."

That was enough for Sheila. She opened her textbook to review last night's homework. Just then, Ms. Lee said. "Good morning class. Please close your books for a pop quiz!"

Get Ready

Tim was prepared for the pop quiz because he drew a conclusion about Ms. Lee. Drawing conclusions means adding clues, or evidence, that you read or see to what you already know. Drawing conclusions is a skill that will help you get the most out of what you read for school or outside of school.

When you read, you often find information that you already know something about. For example, if you read about a person from Australia, you might remember something you already know—that Australians speak English. You then think to yourself that this Australian person probably speaks English. You have just drawn a conclusion.

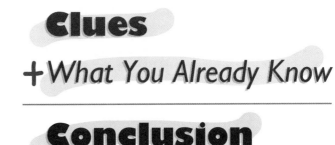

Clues

+ What You Already Know

Conclusion

Try It Out

Practice drawing conclusions from the following sentences by answering the questions.

> About 1,000 years ago, the Maori people traveled across the ocean to the large islands of New Zealand.

A. What clues about the Maori are included in this quotation?

B. What do you already know about people who live on islands?

C. What conclusion can you draw about the role of the sea in Maori life?

> Pacific Islanders read and speak English.

D. What clue about the people of the Pacific islands is in this quotation?

E. What do you already know about the countries where English is the official language?

F. What conclusion can you draw about the history of the Pacific islands?

Apply the Skill

Practice drawing conclusions by reading the section in this chapter called "Australia: A Continent and a Country." After you first read the paragraph, answer the following questions.

1 What clues about human use of Australian land are in the "Lands of Australia" paragraph?

2 What do you already know about the relationship between geography, climate and human settlement?

3 What conclusions might you draw about where Australians farm and the locations of their cities?

Review and Activities

Reviewing Main Ideas

1. How do scientists explain the unique plant and animal life of Australia and New Zealand?

2. Where do most people in Australia live? Why?

3. How does New Zealand's shape affect its climate?

4. (a) What are two differences between high islands and low islands? (b) What is one similarity?

5. What are the three main groups of Pacific islands?

6. Where do scientists think the first settlers in Australia and New Zealand came from?

7. (a) How did the Europeans' arrival in Australia and New Zealand affect the Aborigines and the Maori? (b) How did it affect the people who lived on the Pacific islands?

8. (a) What rights have Aborigines gained in recent years? (b) What is their chief goal?

Reviewing Key Terms

Match the definitions in Column I with the key terms in Column II.

Column I

1. a ring-shaped coral island surrounding a lagoon

2. a rocklike substance made from the skeletons of tiny sea creatures

3. a place settled by prisoners

4. a large ranch in Australia

5. a narrow valley or inlet from the sea

6. a large section of the Earth's crust

Column II

a. tectonic plate

b. coral

c. fiord

d. atoll

e. penal colony

f. station

Critical Thinking

1. **Making Comparisons** European arrival greatly affected the cultures of Australia, New Zealand, and the Pacific islands. Compare the European influences on these places. How were they similar? How were they different? Draw a chart to show similarities and differences.

2. **Drawing Conclusions** Why is British culture so influential in Australia and New Zealand? How might immigration from Asia and other areas affect culture in these two countries? Explain.

Graphic Organizer

Copy the web onto a sheet of paper. Then fill in the empty ovals. Add some ovals to each group of Pacific islands for the names of islands within that group. Fill them in to complete the web.

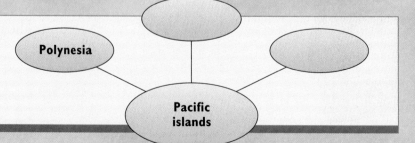

Polynesia

Pacific islands

Map Activity

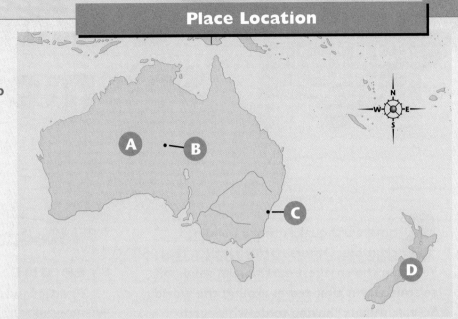

Australia and New Zealand

For each place listed below, write the letter from the map that shows its location.

1. New Zealand

2. Sydney

3. Australia

4. Alice Springs

Writing Activity

Writing a Sight-seeing Plan

Choose one country that you read about in this chapter. Then do some research to learn more about it. If you spent a week there, what would you see? Write a list describing the things you would most want to see and do in a week. Then organize your list into a day-by-day plan.

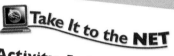

Take It to the NET

Activity Explore several Web sites on the Pacific island nations. How is Australia similar to the other Pacific island nations? How is it different? For help in completing this activity, visit www.phschool.com.

Chapter 7 Self-Test To review what you have learned, take the Chapter 7 Self-Test and get instant feedback on your answers. Go to www.phschool.com to take the test.

Skills Review

Turn to the Skills Activity.

Review the three-part process of drawing a conclusion. Then answer the following questions: (a) If you conclude that this is the last chapter in your Asia book, what clues tell you so? (b) How can you use what you already know about books?

How Am I Doing?

Answer these questions to help you check your progress.

1. Can I locate Australia, New Zealand, and the Pacific region on a map?

2. Can I describe the history and culture of the region?

3. Do I understand how Europeans affected native cultures in the region?

4. What information from this chapter can I include in my journal?

Building a Seismograph

Some earthquakes make buildings crumble. Others hardly rattle a teacup. Yet even the smallest earthquake sends off seismic waves that travel around the world. *Seismic* means "having to do with earthquakes." To tell an earthquake's strength and size, scientists measure these waves with an instrument called a seismograph.

Purpose

Building a model seismograph can help you understand how scientists measure an earthquake's size. This instrument detects motion and can be built with a few simple materials.

Materials

- two stacks of books, each about 10 inches high
- table or desk
- roll of adding-machine tape
- fine-line marker
- paper cup
- about 30 inches of string
- dozen or so marbles
- ruler
- pencil

Procedure

STEP ONE

Predict what a seismograph does. A seismograph draws lines on a piece of paper to make a seismogram. What do you think a seismogram for a large earthquake might look like? For a small earthquake? Sketch your predictions.

STEP TWO

Begin building your seismograph.

A. Place two stacks of books, each about 10 inches high, on a desk or table. Place the books less than one pencil-length apart.

B. With the pencil, poke a small hole in the center of the bottom of the paper cup. Poke one hole each on two opposite sides of the cup, just under the rim.

C. Slip the fine-line marker, with the point down, through the bottom of the cup. Tie the ends of the string to the holes under the cup's rim.

STEP THREE

STEP FOUR

STEP THREE

Complete your seismograph.

A. Place the ruler across the two stacks of books. Hang the cup from the ruler by the string.

B. As shown in the photo, slide the pencil through the roll of adding machine tape. Place the pencil sideways behind the gap between the stacks of books, so that the tape can be pulled through evenly. Pull the tape through the gap.

C. Fill the cup with marbles, to weight the cup and to hold the marker in place. Now push the marker down until it touches the tape. Adjust the length of string so that the tip of the marker is just touching the paper.

STEP FOUR

Pull the tape through the seismograph. Have two partners stand on opposite sides of the desk. One partner should pull the end of the tape slowly. Notice the line the seismograph makes on your seismogram.

STEP FIVE

Create an earthquake. The second partner shakes the table slowly while the first pulls the adding machine tape under the marker. The moving desk represents the motion of seismic waves inside the Earth. Now shake the desk harder. How does the line change?

Observations

1 How does the motion of the desk change the appearance of the line on your seismogram?

2 How do these lines compare with your predictions in Step 1?

ANALYSIS AND CONCLUSION

1. How do you think scientists measure the size of an earthquake from looking at a seismogram? How might they tell from the seismogram how long an earthquake lasted?

2. Unlike your model, a seismograph can measure seismic waves from earthquakes too far away to be seen or felt. Why might it be useful to have a machine able to measure earthquakes from far away?

ASIA AND THE PACIFIC
PROJECT POSSIBILITIES

As you study Asia and the Pacific, you will be reading and thinking about these important questions.

☛ **GEOGRAPHY** What are the main physical features of Asia and the Pacific?

☛ **HISTORY** How have ancient civilizations of Asia and the Pacific influenced the world today?

☛ **CULTURE** What are the main characteristics of the cultures of Asia and the Pacific?

☛ **GOVERNMENT** What types of government exist in Asia and the Pacific today?

☛ **ECONOMICS** How do the people of this region make a living?

What do you know about Asia and the Pacific? It's time to show it!

GEO CLEO

Project Menu

The chapters in this book hold some answers to these questions. Now you can find your own answers as you do projects on your own or with your classmates. Make your own discoveries about Asia and the Pacific!

Agriculture Center
Build an information center about agriculture in Asia and the Pacific. Draw a large map of the region and hang it on your classroom wall. Then, as you read about different kinds of farming, mark them on the appropriate region of your map. Design a small poster for each major type of agriculture. On your poster, write about the location of this type of agriculture, the land, climate, products, and how the farms work. Find or draw a picture for each poster.

From Questions to Careers

ENGINEER

Many of the countries in Asia export great numbers of electronic, mechanical, and consumer goods. Americans buy many of these products and sell goods to Asian countries as well. American engineers and technicians work on both continents. They design and produce goods such as autos, televisions, and household tools. Engineers use scientific knowledge to design and build these goods. Engineers and some technicians have college degrees, and other technicians learn their skills by working directly with machinery.

People also design and build the factory equipment used to make these products. What is the best way to run a company? How do you make a factory work well? Many Asian and American business managers and engineers share ideas to answer these questions.

▼ American and Japanese engineers plan a new project.

Independence Biography Choose an Asian or Pacific country that was once ruled by colonists from another country. Find a person who played a major role in this country's struggle for independence. Write a biography of this person and his or her part in the end of colonialism. Include a description of some of the problems of the country's struggle for independence, as well as a paragraph or two about its history since independence was gained.

Asian Trade Fair With your class, plan a trade fair for the countries of Asia and the Pacific. As you read this book, choose a country to research. Find out about its major products, factories, and trade partners. Set up a booth to show and tell visitors about trade in your country. Bring books about the country and make posters, pamphlets, and charts for your booth.

Travel Log As you read this book, keep a diary of experiences of a journey through Asia and the Pacific islands. Write an entry for each country you read about. Focus on a part of the country or culture that most interests you. Think about the sights, smells, and sounds of that country. Write about your reaction to things that are new or strange to you. Display your travel log for the class to read.

Reference

TABLE OF CONTENTS

MAP AND Handbook GLOBE

This Map and Globe Handbook is designed to help you develop some of the skills you need to be a world explorer. These can help you whether you explore from the top of an elephant in India or from a computer at school.

You can use the information in this handbook to improve your map and globe skills. But the best way to sharpen your skills is to practice. The more you practice, the better you'll get.

GEO CLEO and GEO LEO

Table of Contents

Five Themes of Geography

Studying the geography of the entire world can be a huge task. You can make that task easier by using the five themes of geography: location, place, human-environment interaction, movement, and regions. The themes are tools you can use to organize information and to answer the where, why, and how of geography.

1 Location answers the question, "Where is it?" You can think of the location of a continent or a country as its address. You might give an absolute location such as "22 South Lake Street" or "40°N and 80°W." You might also use a relative address, telling where one place is by referring to another place. "Between school and the mall" and "eight miles east of Pleasant City" are examples of relative locations.

2 Place identifies the natural and human features that make one place different from every other place. You can identify a specific place by its landforms, climate, plants, animals, people, or cultures. You might even think of place as a geographic signature. Use the signature to help you understand the natural and human features that make one place different from every other place.

I. Location
Chicago, Illinois, occupies one location on the Earth. No other place has exactly the same absolute location.

2. Place
Ancient cultures in Egypt built distinctive pyramids. Use the theme of place to help you remember features that exist only in Egypt.

3 Human-Environment Interaction focuses on the relationship between people and the environment. As people live in an area, they often begin to make changes to it, usually to make their lives easier. For example, they might build a dam to control flooding during rainy seasons. Also, the environment can affect how people live, work, dress, travel, and communicate.

4 Movement answers the question "How do people, goods, and ideas move from place to place?" Remember that, often, what happens in one place can affect what happens in another. Use the theme of movement to help you trace the spread of goods, people, and ideas from one location to the next.

5 Regions is the last geographic theme. A region is a group of places that share common features. Geographers divide the world into many types of regions. For example, countries, states, and cities are political regions. The people in these places live under the same type of government. Other features can be used to define regions. Places that have the same climate belong to a particular climate region. Places that share the same culture belong to a cultural region. The same place can be found in more than one region. The state of Hawaii is in the political region of the United States. Because it has a tropical climate, Hawaii is also part of a tropical climate region.

PRACTICE YOUR WORLD EXPLORER SKILLS

1. What is the absolute location of your school? What is one way to describe its relative location?

2. What might be a "geographic signature" of the town or city you live in?

3. Give an example of human-environment interaction where you live.

4. Name at least one thing that comes into your town or city and one that goes out. How is each moved? Where does it come from? Where does it go?

5. What are several regions you think your town or city belongs in?

3. Human-Environment Interaction
Peruvians have changed steep mountain slopes into terraces suitable for farming. Think how this environment looked before people made changes.

4. Movement
Arab traders brought not only goods to Kuala Lumpur, Malaysia, but also Arab building styles and the Islamic religion.

5. Regions
Wheat farming is an important activity in Kansas. This means that Kansas is part of a farming region.

Understanding Movements of the Earth

Planet Earth is part of our solar system. The Earth revolves around the sun in a nearly circular path called an orbit. A revolution, or one complete orbit around the sun, takes 365 1/4 days, or a year. As the Earth revolves around the sun, it is also spinning around in space. This movement is called a rotation. The Earth rotates on its axis—an invisible line through the center of the Earth from the North Pole to the South Pole. The Earth makes one full rotation about every 24 hours. As the Earth rotates, it is daytime on the side facing the sun. It is night on the side away from the sun.

The Earth's axis is tilted at an angle. Because of this tilt, sunlight strikes different parts of the Earth at certain points in the year, creating different seasons.

Earth's Revolution and the Seasons

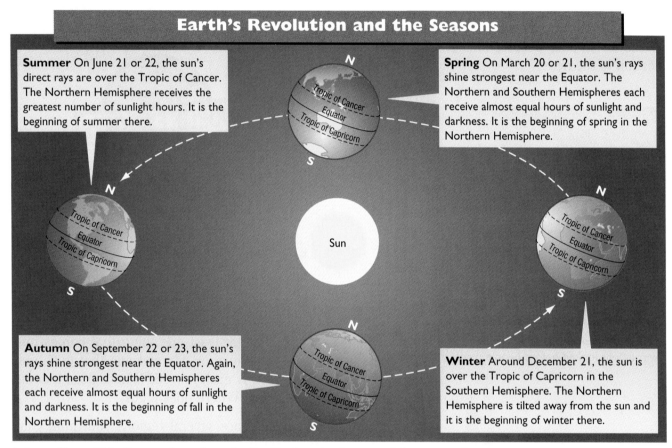

Summer On June 21 or 22, the sun's direct rays are over the Tropic of Cancer. The Northern Hemisphere receives the greatest number of sunlight hours. It is the beginning of summer there.

Spring On March 20 or 21, the sun's rays shine strongest near the Equator. The Northern and Southern Hemispheres each receive almost equal hours of sunlight and darkness. It is the beginning of spring in the Northern Hemisphere.

Autumn On September 22 or 23, the sun's rays shine strongest near the Equator. Again, the Northern and Southern Hemispheres each receive almost equal hours of sunlight and darkness. It is the beginning of fall in the Northern Hemisphere.

Winter Around December 21, the sun is over the Tropic of Capricorn in the Southern Hemisphere. The Northern Hemisphere is tilted away from the sun and it is the beginning of winter there.

▲ **Location** This diagram shows how the Earth's tilt and orbit around the sun combine to create the seasons. Remember, in the Southern Hemisphere the seasons are reversed.

1 What causes the seasons in the Northern Hemisphere to be the opposite of those in the Southern Hemisphere?

2 During which two months of the year do the Northern and Southern Hemispheres have about equal hours of daylight and darkness?

Maps and Globes Represent the Earth

Globes

A globe is a scale model of the Earth. It shows the actual shapes, sizes, and locations of all the Earth's landmasses and bodies of water. Features on the surface of the Earth are drawn to scale on a globe. This means a smaller unit of measure on the globe stands for a larger unit of measure on the Earth.

Because a globe is made in the true shape of the Earth, it offers these advantages for studying the Earth.

- The shape of all land and water bodies are accurate.
- Compass directions from one point to any other point are correct.
- The distance from one location to another is always accurately represented.

However, a globe presents some disadvantages for studying the Earth. Because a globe shows the entire Earth, it cannot show small areas in great detail. Also, a globe is not easily folded and carried from one place to another. For these reasons, geographers often use maps to learn about the Earth.

Maps

A map is a drawing or representation, on a flat surface, of a region. A map can show details too small to be seen on a globe. Floor plans, mall directories, and road maps are among the maps we use most often.

While maps solve some of the problems posed by globes, they have some disadvantages of their own. Maps flatten the real round world. Mapmakers cut, stretch, push, and pull some parts of the Earth to get it all flat on paper. As a result, some locations may be distorted. That is, their size, shape, and relative location may not be accurate. For example, on most maps of the entire world, the size and shape of the Antarctic and Arctic regions are not accurate.

PRACTICE YOUR WORLD EXPLORER SKILLS

1. What is the main difference between a globe and a map?

2. What is one advantage of using a globe instead of a map?

Global Gores

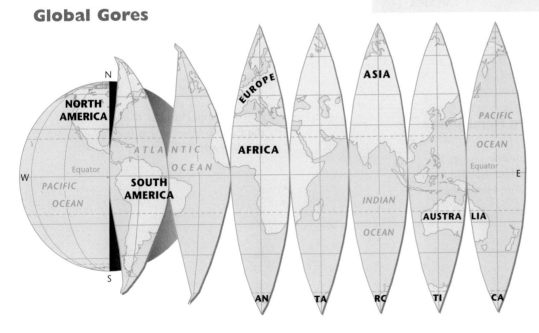

◀ Location
When mapmakers flatten the surface of the Earth, curves become straight lines. As a result, size, shape, and distance are distorted.

The Hemispheres

Another name for a round ball like a globe is a sphere. The Equator, an imaginary line halfway between the North and South Poles, divides the globe into two hemispheres. (The prefix *hemi* means "half.") Land and water south of the Equator are in the Southern Hemisphere. Land and water north of the Equator are in the Northern Hemisphere.

Mapmakers sometimes divide the globe along an imaginary line that runs from North Pole to South Pole. This line, called the Prime Meridian, divides the globe into the Eastern and Western Hemispheres.

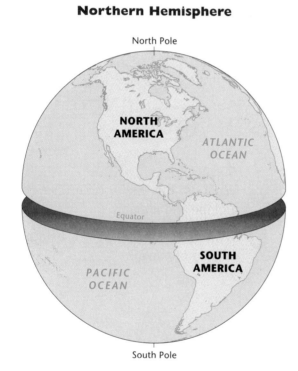

Northern Hemisphere

North Pole

NORTH AMERICA

ATLANTIC OCEAN

Equator

PACIFIC OCEAN

SOUTH AMERICA

South Pole

Southern Hemisphere

▲ The Equator divides the Northern Hemisphere from the Southern Hemisphere.

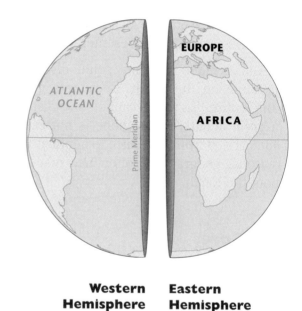

ATLANTIC OCEAN

Prime Meridian

EUROPE

AFRICA

Western Hemisphere   **Eastern Hemisphere**

▲ The Prime Meridian divides the Eastern Hemisphere from the Western Hemisphere.

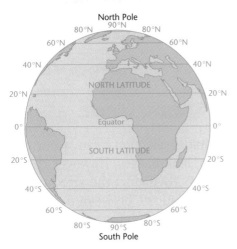

Parallels of Latitude

The Equator, at 0° latitude, is the starting place for measuring latitude or distances north and south. Most globes do not show every parallel of latitude. They may show every 10, 20, or even 30 degrees.

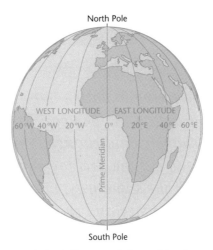

Meridians of Longitude

The Prime Meridian, at 0° longitude, runs from pole to pole through Greenwich, England. It is the starting place for measuring longitude or distances east and west. Each meridian of longitude meets its opposite longitude at the North and South Poles.

The Global Grid

Two sets of lines cover most globes. One set of lines runs parallel to the Equator. These lines, including the Equator, are called *parallels of latitude.* They are measured in degrees (°). One degree of latitude represents a distance of about 70 miles (112 km). The Equator has a location of 0°. The other parallels of latitude tell the direction and distance from the Equator to another location.

The second set of lines runs north and south. These lines are called *meridians of longitude.* Meridians show the degrees of longitude east or west of the Prime Meridian, which is located at 0°. A meridian of longitude tells the direction and distance from the Prime Meridian to another location. Unlike parallels, meridians are not the same distance apart everywhere on the globe.

Together the pattern of parallels of latitude and meridians of longitude is called the global grid. Using the lines of latitude and longitude, you can locate any place on Earth. For example, the location of 30° north latitude and 90° west longitude is usually written as 30°N, 90°W. Only one place on Earth has these coordinates—the city of New Orleans, in the state of Louisiana.

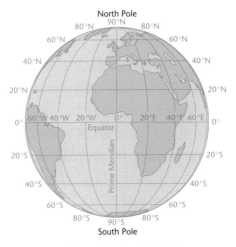

The Global Grid

By using lines of latitude and longitude, you can give the absolute location of any place on the Earth.

1. Which continents lie completely in the Northern Hemisphere? The Western Hemisphere?

2. Is there land or water at 20°S latitude and the Prime Meridian? At the Equator and 60°W longitude?

Map Projections

magine trying to flatten out a complete orange peel. The peel would split. The shape would change. You would have to cut the peel to get it to lie flat. In much the same way, maps cannot show the correct size and shape of every landmass or body of water on the Earth's curved surface. Maps shrink some places and stretch others. This shrinking and stretching is called distortion—*a change made to a shape.*

To make up for this disadvantage, mapmakers use different map projections. Each map projection is a way of showing the round Earth on flat paper. Each type of projection has some distortion. No one projection can accurately show the correct area, shape, distance, and direction for the Earth's surface. Mapmakers use the projection that has the least distortion for the information they are studying.

Same-Shape Maps

Some map projections can accurately show the shapes of landmasses. However, these projections often greatly distort the size of landmasses as well as the distance between them.

One of the most common same-shape maps is a Mercator projection, named for the mapmaker who invented it. The Mercator projection accurately shows shape and direction, but it distorts distance and size. In this projection, the northern and southern areas of the globe appear stretched more than areas near the Equator. Because the projection shows true directions, ships' navigators use it to chart a straight line course between two ports.

Mercator Projection

Equal-Area Maps

Some map projections can show the correct size of landmasses. Maps that use these projections are called equal-area maps. In order to show the correct size of landmasses, these maps usually distort shapes. The distortion is usually greater at the edges of the map and less at the center.

Robinson Maps

Many of the maps in this book use the Robinson projection. This is a compromise between the Mercator and equal-area projections. It gives a useful overall picture of the world. The Robinson projection keeps the size and shape relationships of most continents and oceans but does distort size of the polar regions.

Azimuthal Maps

Another kind of projection shows true compass direction. Maps that use this projection are called azimuthal maps. Such maps are easy to recognize—they are usually circular. Azimuthal maps are often used to show the areas of the North and South Poles. However, azimuthal maps distort scale, area, and shape.

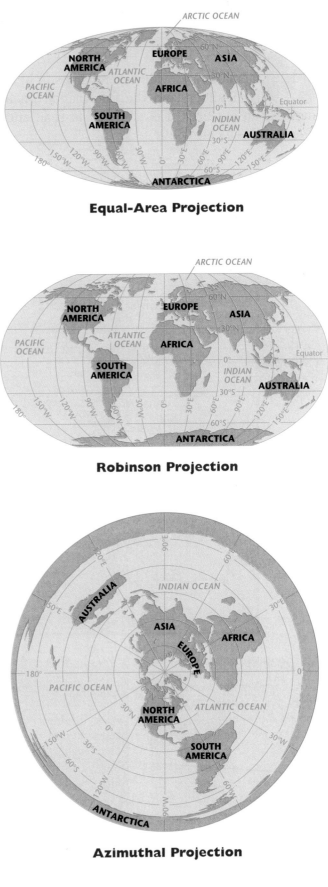

Equal-Area Projection

Robinson Projection

Azimuthal Projection

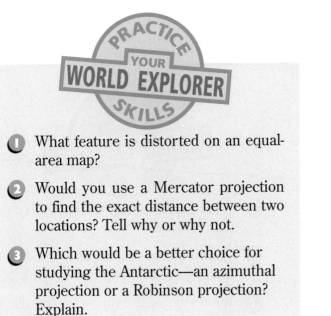

1 What feature is distorted on an equal-area map?

2 Would you use a Mercator projection to find the exact distance between two locations? Tell why or why not.

3 Which would be a better choice for studying the Antarctic—an azimuthal projection or a Robinson projection? Explain.

Parts of a Map

Mapmakers provide several clues to help you understand the information on a map. As an explorer, it is your job to read and interpret these clues.

Compass

Many maps show north at the top of the map. One way to show direction on a map is to use an arrow that points north. There may be an N shown with the arrow. Many maps give more information about direction by displaying a compass showing the directions, north, east, south, and west. The letters N, E, S, and W are placed to indicate these directions.

Title

The title of a map is the most basic clue. It signals what kinds of information you are likely to find on the map. A map titled *West Africa: Population Density* will be most useful for locating information about where people live in West Africa.

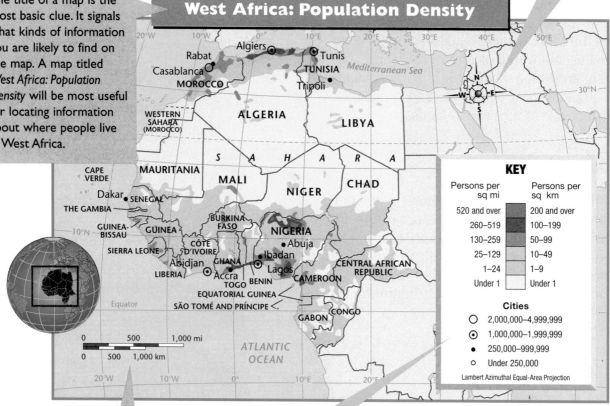

West Africa: Population Density

KEY

Persons per sq mi	Persons per sq km
520 and over	200 and over
260–519	100–199
130–259	50–99
25–129	10–49
1–24	1–9
Under 1	Under 1

Cities
- ◯ 2,000,000–4,999,999
- ◉ 1,000,000–1,999,999
- • 250,000–999,999
- ◦ Under 250,000

Lambert Azimuthal Equal-Area Projection

Scale

A map scale helps you find the actual distances between points shown on the map. You can measure the distance between any two points on the map, compare them to the scale, and find out the actual distance between the points. Most map scales show distances in both miles and kilometers.

Key

Often a map has a key, or legend, that shows the symbols used on the map and what each one means. On some maps, color is used as a symbol. On those maps, the key also tells the meaning of each color.

PRACTICE YOUR WORLD EXPLORER SKILLS

1. What part of a map tells you what the map is about?

2. Where on the map should you look to find out the meaning of this symbol? •

3. What part of the map can you use to find the distance between two cities?

Comparing Maps of Different Scale

ere are three maps drawn to three different scales. The first map shows Moscow's location in the northeastern portion of Russia. This map shows the greatest area—a large section of northern Europe. It has the smallest scale (1 inch = about 900 miles) and shows the fewest details. This map can tell you what direction to travel to reach Moscow from Finland.

Find the red box on Map 1. It shows the whole area covered by Map 2. Study Map 2. It gives a closer look at the city of Moscow. It shows the features around the city, the city's boundary, and the general shape of the city. This map can help you find your way from the airport to the center of town.

Now find the red box on Map 2. This box shows the area shown on Map 3. This map moves you closer into the city. Like the zoom on a computer or camera, Map 3 shows the smallest area but has the greatest detail. This map has the largest scale (1 inch = about 0.8 miles). This is the map to use to explore downtown Moscow.

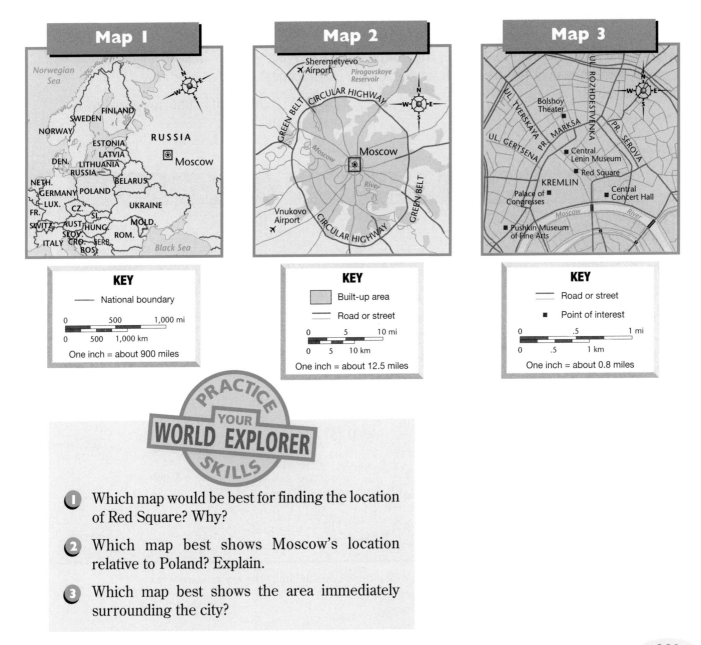

1. Which map would be best for finding the location of Red Square? Why?

2. Which map best shows Moscow's location relative to Poland? Explain.

3. Which map best shows the area immediately surrounding the city?

Political Maps

Mapmakers create maps to show all kinds of information. The kind of information presented affects the way a map looks. One type of map is called a political map. Its main purpose is to show continents, countries, and divisions within countries such as states or provinces. Usually different colors are used to show different countries or divisions within a country. The colors do not have any special meaning. They are used only to make the map easier to read.

Political maps also show where people have built towns and cities. Symbols can help you tell capital cities from other cities and towns. Even though political maps do not give information that shows what the land looks like, they often include some physical features such as oceans, lakes, and rivers.

Political maps usually have many labels. They give country names, and the names of capital and major cities. Bodies of water such as lakes, rivers, oceans, seas, gulfs, and bays are also labeled.

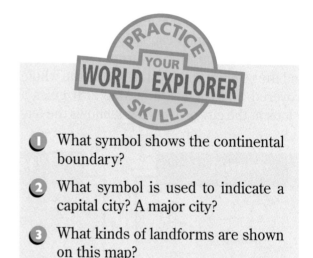

PRACTICE YOUR WORLD EXPLORER SKILLS

1. What symbol shows the continental boundary?

2. What symbol is used to indicate a capital city? A major city?

3. What kinds of landforms are shown on this map?

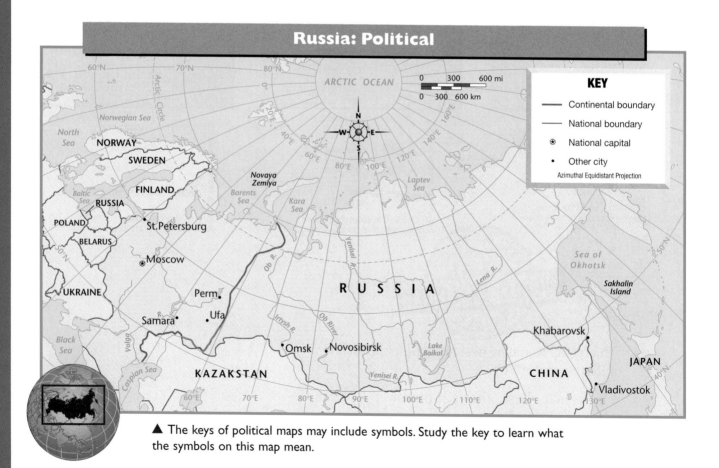

Russia: Political

KEY

— Continental boundary
— National boundary
⊛ National capital
• Other city

Azimuthal Equidistant Projection

▲ The keys of political maps may include symbols. Study the key to learn what the symbols on this map mean.

Physical Maps

Like political maps, physical maps show country labels and labels for capital cities. However, physical maps also show what the land of a region looks like by showing the major physical features such as plains, hills, plateaus, or mountains. Labels give the names of features such as mountain peaks, mountains, plateaus, and river basins.

In order to tell one landform from another, physical maps often show elevation and relief.

Elevation is the height of the land above sea level. Physical maps in this book use color to show elevation. Browns and oranges show higher lands while blues and greens show lands that are at or below sea level.

Relief shows how quickly the land rises or falls. Hills, mountains, and plateaus are shown on relief maps using shades of gray. Level or nearly level land is shown without shading. Darkly shaded areas indicate steeper lands.

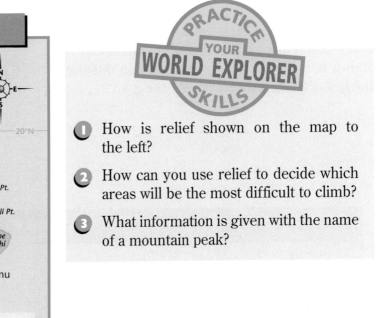

Hawaii: Physical

▲ On a physical map, shading is sometimes used to show relief. Use the shading to locate the mountains in Hawaii.

PRACTICE YOUR WORLD EXPLORER SKILLS

1. How is relief shown on the map to the left?

2. How can you use relief to decide which areas will be the most difficult to climb?

3. What information is given with the name of a mountain peak?

▼ Mauna Kea, an extinct volcano, is the highest peak in the state of Hawaii. Find Mauna Kea on the map.

Special Purpose Maps

As you explore the world, you will encounter many different kinds of special purpose maps. For example, a road map is a special purpose map. The title of each special purpose map tells the purpose and content of the map. Usually a special purpose map highlights only one kind of information. Examples of special purpose maps include land use, population distribution, recreation, transportation, natural resources, or weather.

The key on a special purpose map is very important. Even though a special purpose map shows only one kind of information, it may present many different pieces of data. This data can be shown in symbols, colors, or arrows. In this way, the key acts like a dictionary for the map.

Reading a special purpose map is a skill in itself. Look at the map below. First, try to get an overall sense of what it shows. Then, study the map to identify its main ideas. For example, one main idea of this map is that much of the petroleum production in the region takes place around the Persian Gulf.

1. What part of a special purpose map tells what information is contained on the map?

2. What part of a special purpose map acts like a dictionary for the map?

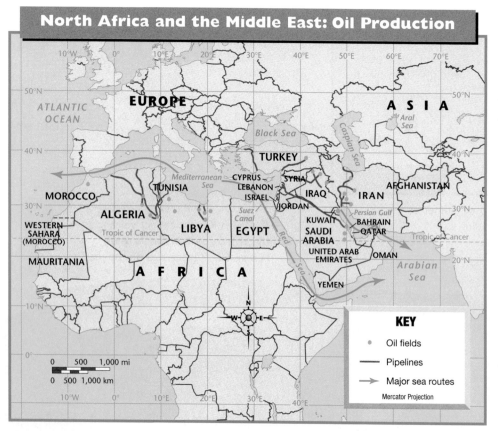

North Africa and the Middle East: Oil Production

◀ The title on a special purpose map indicates what information can be found on the map. The symbols used on the map are explained in the map's key.

KEY
- Oil fields
— Pipelines
→ Major sea routes

Mercator Projection

Landforms, Climate Regions, and Natural Vegetation Regions

Maps that show landforms, climate, and vegetation regions are special purpose maps. Unlike the boundary lines on a political map, the boundary lines on these maps do not separate the land into exact divisions. A tropical wet climate gradually changes to a tropical wet and dry climate. A tundra gradually changes to an ice cap. Even though the boundaries between regions may not be exact, the information on these maps can help you understand the region and the lives of people in it.

Landforms

Understanding how people use the land requires an understanding of the shape of the land itself. The four most important landforms are mountains, hills, plateaus, and plains. Human activity in every region in the world is influenced by these landforms.

- **Mountains** are high and steep. Most are wide at the bottom and rise to a narrow peak or ridge. Most geographers classify a mountain as land that rises at least 2,000 feet (610 m) above sea level. A series of mountains is called a mountain range.

- **Hills** rise above surrounding land and have rounded tops. Hills are lower and usually less steep than mountains. The elevation of surrounding land determines whether a landform is called a mountain or a hill.
- A **plateau** is a large, mostly flat area of land that rises above the surrounding land. At least one side of a plateau has a steep slope.
- **Plains** are large areas of flat or gently rolling land. Plains have few changes in elevation. Many plains areas are located along coasts. Others are located in the interior regions of some continents.

▶ A satellite view of the Earth showing North and South America. What landforms are visible in the photograph?

Climate Regions

Another important influence in the ways people live their lives is the climate of their region. Climate is the weather of a given location over a long period of time. Use the descriptions in the table below to help you visualize the climate regions shown on maps.

Climate	Temperatures	Precipitation
Tropical		
Tropical wet	Hot all year round	Heavy all year round
Tropical wet and dry	Hot all year round	Heavy when sun is overhead, dry other times
Dry		
Semiarid	Hot summers, mild to cold winters	Light
Arid	Hot days, cold nights	Very light
Mild		
Mediterranean	Hot summers, cool winters	Dry summers, wet winters
Humid subtropical	Hot summers, cool winters	Year round, heavier in summer than in winter
Marine west coast	Warm summers, cool winters	Year round, heavier in winter than in summer
Continental		
Humid continental	Hot summers, cold winters	Year round, heavier in summer than in winter
Subarctic	Cool summers, cold winters	Light
Polar		
Tundra	Cool summers, very cold winters	Light
Ice cap	Cold all year round	Light
Highlands	Varies, depending on altitude and direction of prevailing winds	Varies, depending on altitude and direction of prevailing winds

Natural Vegetation Regions

Natural vegetation is the plant life that grows wild without the help of humans. A world vegetation map tells what the vegetation in a place would be if people had not cut down forests or cleared grasslands. The table below provides descriptions of natural vegetation regions shown on maps. Comparing climate and vegetation regions can help you see the close relationship between climate and vegetation.

Vegetation	Description
Tropical rain forest	Tall, close-growing trees forming a canopy over smaller trees, dense growth in general
Deciduous forest	Trees and plants that regularly lose their leaves after each growing season
Mixed forest	Both leaf-losing and cone-bearing trees, no type of tree dominant
Coniferous forest	Cone-bearing trees, evergreen trees and plants
Mediterranean vegetation	Evergreen shrubs and small plants
Tropical savanna	Tall grasses with occasional trees and shrubs
Temperate grassland	Tall grasses with occasional stands of trees
Desert scrub	Low shrubs and bushes, hardy plants
Desert	Little or no vegetation
Tundra	Low shrubs, mosses, lichens; no trees
Ice cap	Little or no vegetation
Highlands	Varies, depending on altitude and direction of prevailing winds

1 How are mountains and hills similar? How are they different?

2 What is the difference between a plateau and a plain?

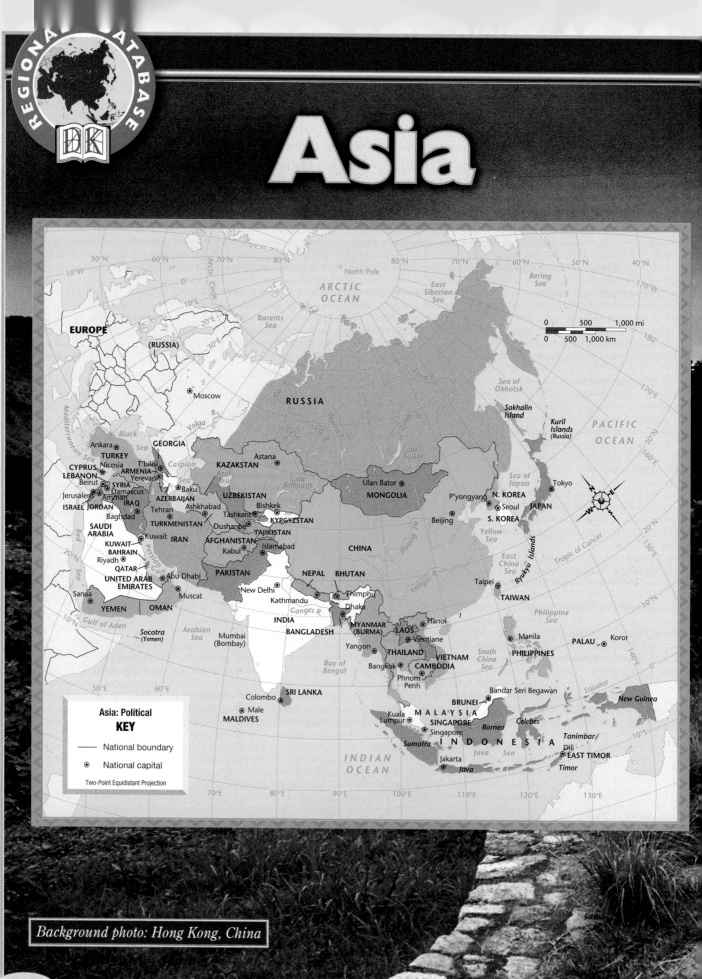

Asia

Asia: Political
KEY

— National boundary

⊛ National capital

Two-Point Equidistant Projection

| 0 | 500 | 1,000 mi |
| 0 | 500 | 1,000 km |

Background photo: Hong Kong, China

GEOFACTS

Asia and the Pacific

Population: 3,679,873,000

Most Populated City: Tokyo, Japan (18.1 million)

Largest Country: Asian Russia (13,119,582 sq mi/ 5,065,471 sq km)

Smallest Country: Maldives (116 sq mi/ 300 sq km)

Highest Point: Mt. Everest (29,035 ft/8,850 m)

Lowest Point: Dead Sea (-1,286 ft/-392 m)

Longest River: Yangzi River (3,965 mi/6,380 km)

Hong Kong, China

Taj Mahal, India

East Asia

Capital: Beijing

Area: 3,600,927 sq mi/
9,326,410 sq km

Population: 1.3 billion

Ethnic Groups: Han, Hui, Zhuang

Religions: traditional beliefs,
Buddhist, Muslim

Government: Communist state

Currency: Yuan

Exports: machinery and equipment,
textiles and clothing, footwear, toys

Official Language: Mandarin

China
(CHY nuh)

Capital: Tokyo

Area: 145,374 sq mi/376,520 sq km

Population: 126.5 million

Ethnic Groups: Japanese, Korean

Religions: Shinto and Buddhist,
Buddhist, Christian

Government: constitutional monarchy

Currency: Yen

Exports: motor vehicles, semicon-
ductors, office machinery, chemicals

Official Language: Japanese

Japan
(juh PAN)

Background photo: Great Wall of China

Capital: Ulan Bator

Area: 604,247 sq mi/1,565,000 sq km

Population: 2.6 million

Ethnic Groups: Mongol, Kazak, Chinese, Russian

Religions: Tibetan Buddhist, Muslim

Government: republic

Currency: Tugrik

Exports: copper, livestock, animal products, cashmere, wool, hides, fluorspar, other nonferrous metals

Official Language: Khalka Mongol

Mongolia
(mong GOH lee uh)

Capital: Seoul

Area: 38,120 sq mi/98,730 sq km

Population: 46.5 million

Ethnic Group: Korean

Religions: Buddhist, Protestant, Roman Catholic, Confucian

Government: republic

Currency: South Korean won

Exports: electronic products, machinery and equipment, motor vehicles, steel, ships, textiles, clothing

Official Language: Korean

South Korea
(sowth kuh REE uh)

Capital: P'yongyang

Area: 46,490 sq mi/120,410 sq km

Population: 23.7 million

Ethnic Group: Korean

Religions: Buddhist, Confucian, Christian, syncretic Chondogyo

Government: authoritarian socialist

Currency: North Korean won

Exports: minerals, metallurgical products, manufactures, agricultural and fishery products

Official Language: Korean

North Korea
(nawrth kuh REE uh)

Capital: Taipei

Area: 12,456 sq mi/32,260 sq km

Population: 21.7 million

Ethnic Groups: indigenous Chinese, mainland Chinese, Aborigine

Religions: Buddhist, Confucian, Taoist, Christian

Government: multiparty democracy

Currency: Taiwan dollar

Exports: electronics, electric and machinery equipment, metals

Official Language: Mandarin

Taiwan
(TEYE wahn)

South Asia

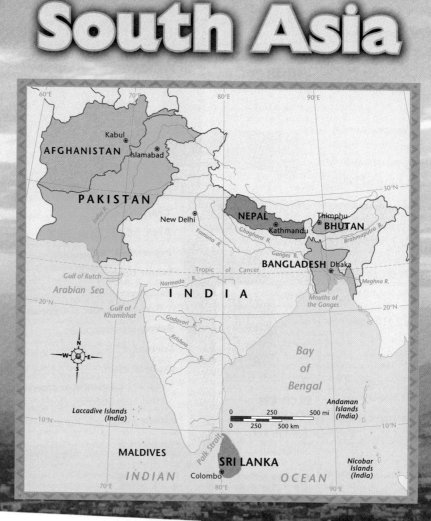

Kabul · Islamabad
AFGHANISTAN
PAKISTAN
New Delhi
NEPAL · Kathmandu · Thimphu · BHUTAN
BANGLADESH · Dhaka
Gulf of Kutch
Arabian Sea
INDIA
Gulf of Khambhat
Mouths of the Ganges
Tropic of Cancer
Laccadive Islands (India)
Bay of Bengal
Andaman Islands (India)
MALDIVES
SRI LANKA
Colombo
INDIAN OCEAN
Nicobar Islands (India)

Capital: Kabul

Area: 251,770 sq mi/652,090 sq km

Population: 21.9 million

Ethnic Groups: Pashto, Tajik, Hazara

Religions: Sunni Muslim, Shi'a Muslim

Government: administered by factions

Currency: Afghani

Exports: fruits, nuts, hand-woven carpets, wool, cotton, hides, pelts

Official Languages: Dari and Pashtu

Afghanistan
(af GAN i stan)

Capital: Dhaka

Area: 51,703 sq mi/133,910 sq km

Population: 126.9 million

Ethnic Groups: Bengali, Biharis

Religions: Muslim, Hindu

Government: republic

Currency: Taka

Exports: garments, jute and jute goods, leather, frozen fish and seafood

Official Language: Bengali

Bangladesh
(ban gluh DESH)

Background photo: Pushker, India

Capital: Thimphu

Area: 18,147 sq mi/47,000 sq km

Population: 2.1 million

Ethnic Groups: Bhote, Nepalese, indigenous tribes

Religions: Mahayana Buddhist, Hindu

Government: monarchy

Currency: Ngultrum

Exports: cardamom, gypsum, timber, handicrafts, cement, fruit, electricity

Official Language: Dzongkha

Bhutan
(boo TAHN)

Capital: Kathmandu

Area: 52,818 sq mi/136,800 sq km

Population: 23.4 million

Ethnic Groups: Newar, Indian, Tibetan, Gurung, Magar, Tamang

Religions: Hindu, Buddhist, Muslim, Christian

Government: parliamentary democracy

Currency: Nepalese rupee

Exports: carpets, clothing, leather

Official Language: Nepali

Nepal
(nuh PAWL)

Capital: New Delhi

Area: 1,147,949 sq mi/2,973,190 sq km

Population: 998 million

Ethnic Groups: Indo-Aryan, Dravidian, Mongoloid

Religions: Hindu, Muslim, Christian, Sikh, Buddhist

Government: federal republic

Currency: Indian rupee

Exports: textile goods, gems

Official Languages: Hindi and English

India
(IN dee uh)

Capital: Islamabad

Area: 297,637 sq mi/770,880 sq km

Population: 152.3 million

Ethnic Groups: Punjabi, Sindhi, Pashtu, Baluch, Muhajir

Religions: Sunni Muslim, Shi'a Muslim, Hindu, Christian

Government: federal republic

Currency: Pakistani rupee

Exports: cotton, fabrics and yarn, rice, other agricultural products

Official Language: Urdu

Pakistan
(PAK i stan)

Capital: Male

Area: 116 sq mi/300 sq km

Population: 278,000

Ethnic Groups: South Indian, Sinhalese, Arab

Religions: Sunni Muslim

Government: republic

Currency: Rufiyaa

Exports: fish, clothing

Official Language: Dhivehi

Maldives
(MAHL dives)

Capital: Colombo

Area: 24,996 sq mi/64,740 sq km

Population: 18.6 million

Ethnic Groups: Sinhalese, Tamil, Moor

Religions: Buddhist, Hindu, Christian, Muslim

Government: republic

Currency: Sri Lanka rupee

Exports: textiles and apparel, tea, diamonds, coconut products

Official Languages: Sinhala, Tamil, English

Sri Lanka
(sree LAHN kuh)

Southeast Asia

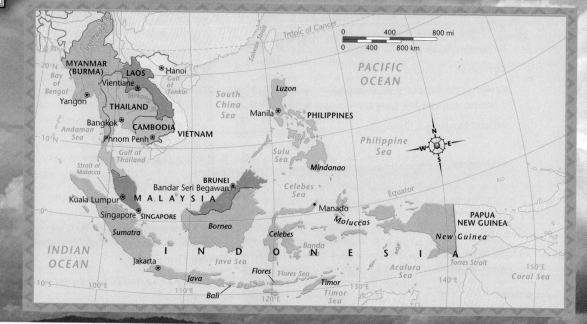

Capital: Bandar Seri Begawan

Area: 2,035 sq mi/5,270 sq km

Population: 322,000

Ethnic Groups: Malay, Chinese, indigenous

Religions: Muslim, Buddhist, Christian, traditional beliefs

Government: constitutional sultanate

Currency: Brunei dollar

Exports: crude oil, liquefied natural gas, petroleum products

Official Language: Malay

Brunei
(broo NEYE)

Capital: Jakarta

Area: 699,447 sq mi/1,811,570 sq km

Population: 209.3 million

Ethnic Groups: Javanese, Sudanese, Madurese, Coastal Malays

Religions: Muslim, Protestant, Roman Catholic, Hindu, Buddhist

Government: republic

Currency: Rupiah

Exports: oil and gas, plywood

Official Language: Bahasa Indonesia

Indonesia
(in duh NEE zhuh)

Capital: Phnom Penh

Area: 68,154 sq mi/176,520 sq km

Population: 10.9 million

Ethnic Groups: Khmer, Chinese, Vietnamese

Religions: Theravada Buddhist

Government: democracy under a constitutional monarchy

Currency: Riel

Exports: timber, garments, rubber, rice, fish

Official Language: Khmer

Cambodia
(kam BOH dee uh)

Capital: Vientiane

Area: 89,112 sq mi/230,800 sq km

Population: 5.3 million

Ethnic Groups: Lao Loum, Lao Theung, Lao Soung

Religions: Buddhist, Animist

Government: Communist state

Currency: New kip

Exports: wood products, garments, electricity, coffee, tin

Official Language: Laotian

Laos
(LAY ohs)

Capital: Kuala Lumpur

Area: 126,853 sq mi/328,550 sq km

Population: 21.8 million

Ethnic Groups: Malay, Chinese, indigenous tribes, Indian

Religions: Muslim, Buddhist, Chinese faiths, Christian, traditional beliefs

Government: constitutional monarchy

Currency: Ringgit

Exports: electronic equipment, petroleum, natural gas, chemicals

Official Languages: English, Bahasa Malay

Malaysia
(muh LAY zhuh)

Capital: Singapore

Area: 236 sq mi/610 sq km

Population: 3.5 million

Ethnic Groups: Chinese, Malay, Indian

Religions: Buddhist, Daoist, Muslim, Christian, Hindu

Government: parliamentary republic

Currency: Singapore dollar

Exports: machinery and equipment, chemicals, mineral fuels

Official Languages: Malay, English, Mandarin Chinese, Tamil

Singapore
(SIN guh pawr)

Capital: Yangon

Area: 253,876 sq mi/657,540 sq km

Population: 45.1 million

Ethnic Groups: Burman, Shan, Karen, Rakhine

Religions: Buddhist, Christian, Muslim, Hindu

Government: military regime

Currency: Kyat

Exports: pulses and beans, prawns, fish, rice, teak

Official Language: Burmese

Myanmar
(myahn mahr)

Capital: Bangkok

Area: 197,255 sq mi/510,890 sq km

Population: 60.9 million

Ethnic Groups: Thai, Chinese, Khmer, Malay

Religions: Theravada Buddhist, Muslim, Christian

Government: constitutional monarchy

Currency: Baht

Exports: computers and parts, textiles, rice

Official Language: Thai

Thailand
(TY lund)

Capital: Manila

Area: 115,830 sq mi/300,000 sq km

Population: 74.5 million

Ethnic Groups: Malay, Indonesian and Polynesian, Chinese, Indian

Religions: Roman Catholic, Protestant, Muslim, Buddhist

Government: republic

Currency: Philippine peso

Exports: electronic equipment, machinery, transport equipment

Official Languages: English and Filipino

Philippines
(FIL uh peenz)

Capital: Hanoi

Area: 125,621 sq. mi/325,360 sq. km

Population: 78.7 million

Ethnic Groups: Vietnamese, Chinese, Thai

Religions: Buddhist, Roman Catholic

Government: Communist state

Currency: Dông

Exports: crude oil, marine products, rice, coffee, rubber, tea, garments

Official Language: Vietnamese

Vietnam
(vee et NAHM)

Background photo: Baracy, Philippines

Southwest and Central Asia

Background photo: Petra, Jordan

Map labels:

20°E 30°E 50°N

⊛ Akmola

KAZAKSTAN

Lake Zaysan

Aral Sea

Lake Balkhash

Black Sea

Ankara •

GEORGIA Tbilisi •

TURKEY

ARMENIA AZERBAIJAN

Yerevan ⊛ Baku ⊛

UZBEKISTAN

⊛ Bishkek

Tashkent • KYRGYZSTAN

CYPRUS Nicosia ⊛

Mediterranean Sea

SYRIA

LEBANON

Beirut ⊛ Damascus •

Jerusalem ⊛ Amman ⊛

ISRAEL JORDAN IRAQ Baghdad ⊛

TURKMENISTAN

Dushanbe ⊛ TAJIKISTAN

Ashkhabad ⊛

Tehran ⊛

IRAN

KUWAIT Kuwait ⊛

SAUDI BAHRAIN

ARABIA Manama ⊛

Riyadh ⊛

Persian Gulf

OMAN

Doha ⊛ Abu Dhabi ⊛

QATAR

UNITED ARAB EMIRATES

Muscat ⊛

OMAN

Tropic of Cancer

Arabian Sea

Red Sea

Sanaa ⊛ YEMEN

Gulf of Aden Socotra (Yemen)

0 250 500 mi

0 250 500 km

N W E S

40°E 50°E 60°E 70°E 10°N

20°N

30°N

40°N

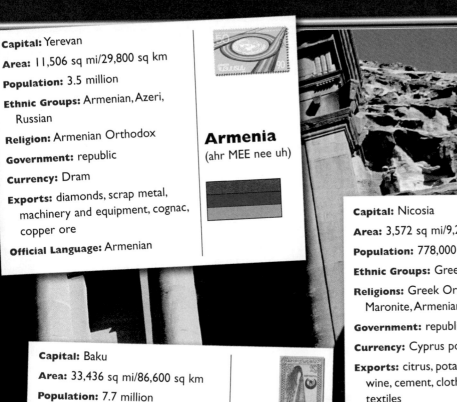

Capital: Yerevan

Area: 11,506 sq mi/29,800 sq km

Population: 3.5 million

Ethnic Groups: Armenian, Azeri, Russian

Religion: Armenian Orthodox

Government: republic

Currency: Dram

Exports: diamonds, scrap metal, machinery and equipment, cognac, copper ore

Official Language: Armenian

Armenia
(ahr MEE nee uh)

Capital: Nicosia

Area: 3,572 sq mi/9,251 sq km

Population: 778,000

Ethnic Groups: Greek, Turkish

Religions: Greek Orthodox, Muslim, Maronite, Armenian Apostolic

Government: republic

Currency: Cyprus pound

Exports: citrus, potatoes, grapes, wine, cement, clothing, shoes, textiles

Official Languages: Greek and Turkish

Cyprus
(SY prus)

Capital: Baku

Area: 33,436 sq mi/86,600 sq km

Population: 7.7 million

Ethnic Groups: Azeri, Armenian, Russian, Daghestani

Religions: Muslim, Russian Orthodox, Armenian Orthodox

Government: republic

Currency: Manat

Exports: oil, gas, machinery, cotton, foodstuffs

Official Language: Azerbaijani

Azerbaijan
(a zur by JAHN)

Capital: Tbilisi

Area: 26,911 sq mi/69,700 sq km

Population: 5 million

Ethnic Groups: Georgian, Armenian, Russian, Azeri

Religions: Georgian Orthodox, Muslim, Russian Orthodox

Government: republic

Currency: Lari

Exports: citrus fruits, tea, wine, other agricultural products

Official Language: Georgian

Georgia
(JAWR ja)

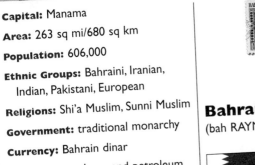

Capital: Manama

Area: 263 sq mi/680 sq km

Population: 606,000

Ethnic Groups: Bahraini, Iranian, Indian, Pakistani, European

Religions: Shi'a Muslim, Sunni Muslim

Government: traditional monarchy

Currency: Bahrain dinar

Exports: petroleum and petroleum products, aluminum

Official Language: Arabic

Bahrain
(bah RAYN)

Capital: Tehran

Area: 3,572 sq mi/9,251 sq km

Population: 66.8 million

Ethnic Groups: Persian, Azeri, Lur and Bakhtiari, Kurd, Arab

Religions: Shi'a Muslim, Sunni Muslim

Government: theocratic republic

Currency: Iranian rial

Exports: petroleum, carpets, fruits, nuts, hides, iron, steel

Official Language: Farsi

Iran
(ih RAN)

Capital: Jerusalem

Area: 7,849 sq mi/20,330 sq km

Population: 6.1 million

Ethnic Groups: Jewish, Arab

Religions: Jewish, Sunni Muslim, Druze, Christian

Government: parliamentary democracy

Currency: New Israeli shekel

Exports: machinery, equipment, software, cut diamonds, chemicals

Official Languages: Hebrew and Arabic

Israel
(IZ ree ul)

Capital: Baghdad

Area: 168,869 sq mi/437,370 sq km

Population: 22.5 million

Ethnic Groups: Arab, Kurdish, Persian, Turkoman

Religions: Shi'a Ithna Muslim, Sunni Muslim, Christian

Government: republic

Currency: Iraqi dinar

Exports: crude oil

Official Language: Arabic

Iraq
(ih RAK)

Capital: Amman

Area: 34,336 sq mi/88,930 sq km

Population: 6.5 million

Ethnic Groups: Arab, Armenian, Circassian

Religions: Sunni Muslim, Christian

Government: constitutional monarchy

Currency: Jordanian dinar

Exports: phosphates, fertilizers, potash, agricultural products, manufactures

Official Language: Arabic

Jordan
(JAWR dun)

Capital: Astana

Area: 1,049,150 sq mi/2,717,300 sq km

Population: 16.3 million

Ethnic Groups: Kazak, Russian, Ukrainian, German, Uzbek, Tatar

Religions: Sunni Muslim, Russian Orthodox, Protestant

Government: republic

Currency: Tenge

Exports: oil, ferrous and nonferrous metals, machinery, chemicals, grain

Official Language: Kazak

Kazakstan
(kah zak STAN)

Capital: Bishkek

Area: 76,640 sq mi/198,500 sq km

Population: 4.7 million

Ethnic Groups: Kyrgyz, Russian, Uzbek, Ukrainian, Tatar

Religions: Muslim, Russian Orthodox

Government: republic

Currency: Som

Exports: cotton, wool, meat, tobacco, gold, mercury, uranium

Official Languages: Kyrgyz and Russian

Kyrgyzstan
(kir gi STAN)

Capital: Kuwait City

Area: 6,880 sq mi/17,820 sq km

Population: 1.9 million

Ethnic Groups: Kuwaiti, Arab, South Asian, Iranian

Religions: Muslim, Christian, Hindu, Parsi

Government: nominal constitutional monarchy

Currency: Kuwaiti dinar

Exports: oil and refined products

Official Language: Arabic

Kuwait
(koo WAYT)

Capital: Beirut

Area: 3950 sq mi/10,230 sq km

Population: 3.2 million

Ethnic Groups: Arab, Armenian

Religions: Muslim, Christian

Government: republic

Currency: Lebanese pound

Exports: foodstuffs and tobacco, textiles, chemicals, metal and metal products, electrical equipment and products, jewelry

Official Language: Arabic

Lebanon
(LEB uh nun)

Capital: Muscat

Area: 82,030 sq mi/212,460 sq km

Population: 2.5 million

Ethnic Groups: Arab, Baluchi, South Asian, African

Religions: Ibadhi Muslim, Sunni Muslim, Shi'a Muslim, Hindu

Government: monarchy

Currency: Omani rial

Exports: petroleum, fish, metals, textiles

Official Language: Arabic

Oman
(oh MAHN)

Capital: Doha

Area: 4,247 sq mi/11,000 sq km

Population: 589,000

Ethnic Groups: Arab, Pakistani, Indian, Iranian

Religion: Muslim

Government: traditional monarchy

Currency: Qatar riyal

Exports: petroleum products, fertilizers, steel

Official Language: Arabic

Qatar
(KAH tar)

Capital: Damascus

Area: 71,060 sq mi/184,060 sq km

Population: 15.7 million

Ethnic Groups: Arab, Kurdish, Armenian, Turkmen, Circassian

Religions: Sunni Muslim, other Muslim, Christian

Government: republic

Currency: Syrian pound

Exports: petroleum, textiles, manufactured goods, fruits and vegetables

Official Language: Arabic

Syria
(SEER ee uh)

Capital: Riyadh

Area: 829,995 sq mi/2,149,690 sq km

Population: 20.9 million

Ethnic Groups: Arab, Afroasian

Religions: Sunni Muslim, Shi'a Muslim

Government: monarchy

Currency: Saudi riyal

Exports: petroleum, petroleum products

Official Language: Arabic

Saudi Arabia
(SOW dee uh
RAY bee uh)

Capital: Dushanbe

Area: 55,251 sq mi/143,100 sq km

Population: 6.1 million

Ethnic Groups: Tajik, Uzbek, Russian

Religions: Sunni Muslim, Shi'a Muslim

Government: republic

Currency: Tajik ruble

Exports: aluminum, electricity, cotton, fruits, vegetable oil, textiles

Official Language: Tajik

Tajikistan
(tah ji ki STAN)

Capital: Ankara

Area: 297,154 sq mi/769,630 sq km

Population: 65.5 million

Ethnic Groups: Turkish, Kurdish, Arab

Religion: Muslim

Government: republican parliamentary democracy

Currency: Turkish lira

Exports: apparel, foodstuffs, textiles, metal manufactures

Official Language: Turkish

Turkey
(TUR kee)

Capital: Tashkent

Area: 172,741 sq mi/447,400 sq km

Population: 23.9 million

Ethnic Groups: Uzbek, Russian, Tajik, Kazak

Religions: Sunni Muslim, Eastern Orthodox

Government: republic

Currency: Som

Exports: cotton, gold, natural gas, mineral fertilizers, ferrous metals

Official Language: Uzbek

Uzbekistan
(ooz BEH ki stan)

Capital: Ashgabat

Area: 188,445 sq mi/488,100 sq km

Population: 4.4 million

Ethnic Groups: Turkmen, Uzbek, Russian

Religions: Sunni Muslim, Eastern Orthodox

Government: republic

Currency: Manat

Exports: oil, gas, cotton

Official Language: Turkmen

Turkmenistan
(turk MEH nuh stan)

Capital: Abu Dhabi

Area: 32,278 sq mi/83,600 sq km

Population: 2.4 million

Ethnic Groups: Asian, Arab, Emirian

Religion: Muslim

Government: federation

Currency: UAE dirham

Exports: crude oil, natural gas, dried fish, dates

Official Language: Arabic

United Arab Emirates
(yoo NEYE tid AYR ub EH muh rayts)

Capital: Sana'a

Area: 203,849 sq mi/527,970 sq km

Population: 17.5 million

Ethnic Groups: Arab, Afro-Arab, Indian, Somali, European

Religions: Shi'a Muslim, Sunni Muslim, Jewish, Christian, Hindu

Government: republic

Currency: Rial and dinar

Exports: crude oil, cotton, coffee, dried and salted fish

Official Language: Arabic

Yemen
(YEM un)

Australia, New Zealand, and the Pacific Islands

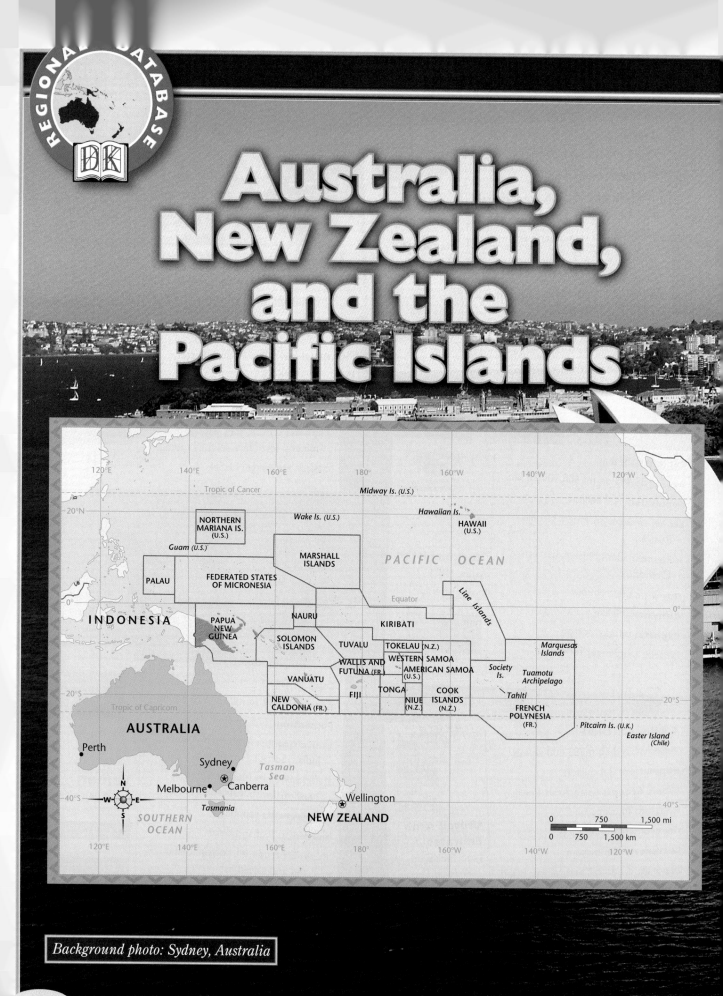

Background photo: Sydney, Australia

GEOFACTS

Australia, New Zealand, and the Pacific Islands

Population: 28,658,000

Most Populated City: Sydney, Australia (3.7 million)

Largest Country: Australia (2,941,283 sq mi/ 7,617,930 sq km)

Smallest Country: Nauru (8 sq mi/21 sq km)

Highest Point: Mt. Wilhelm (14,794 ft/4,509 m)

Lowest Point: Dead Sea (-52 ft/-16 m)

Longest River: Darling River (2,330 mi/ 3,750 km)

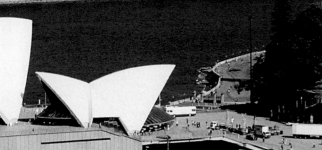

Australia

Australia and New Zealand

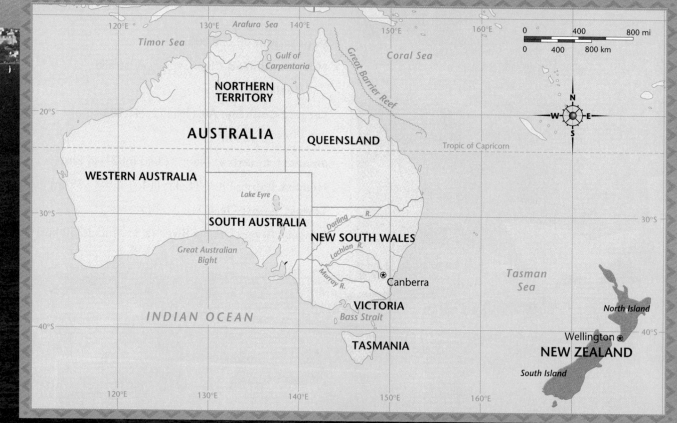

Timor Sea

120°E — 130°E — Arafura Sea — 140°E — 150°E — 160°E

Gulf of Carpentaria

Coral Sea

Great Barrier Reef

NORTHERN TERRITORY

20°S

AUSTRALIA

QUEENSLAND

Tropic of Capricorn

WESTERN AUSTRALIA

Lake Eyre

30°S

SOUTH AUSTRALIA

Darling R.

NEW SOUTH WALES

Lachlan R.

Great Australian Bight

Murray R.

⊛ Canberra

Tasman Sea

North Island

INDIAN OCEAN

40°S

VICTORIA

Bass Strait

Wellington ⊛

40°S

TASMANIA

NEW ZEALAND

South Island

120°E — 130°E — 140°E — 150°E — 160°E

0 — 400 — 800 mi
0 — 400 — 800 km

Capital: Canberra

Area: 2,941,283/7,617,930 sq km

Population: 18.7 million

Ethnic Groups: European, Asian, Aboriginal

Religions: Roman Catholic, Anglican, United Church, Protestant

Government: parliamentary democracy

Currency: Australian dollar

Exports: coal, gold, meat, wool, aluminum, iron ore, wheat

Official Language: English

Australia
(aw STRAYL yuh)

Capital: Wellington

Area: 103,733 sq mi/268,670 sq km

Population: 3.8 million

Ethnic Groups: European, Maori, Chinese, Pacific Islander

Religions: Anglican, Presbyterian, Roman Catholic, Methodist

Government: parliamentary democracy

Currency: New Zealand dollar

Exports: dairy products, meat, fish, wool, forestry products

Official Languages: English and Maori

New Zealand
(noo ZEE lund)

Pacific Island Nations

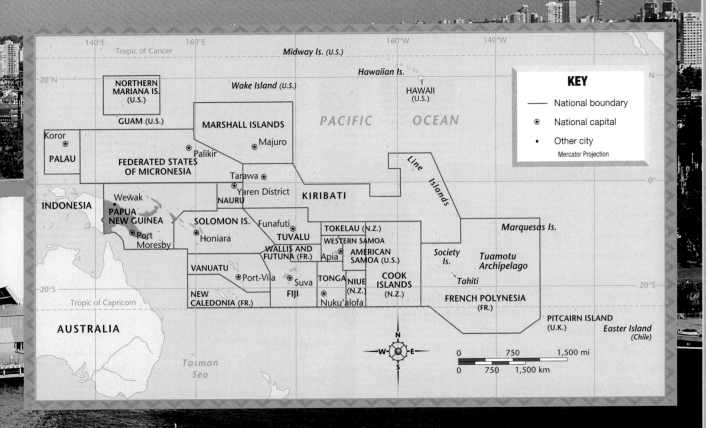

KEY	
——	National boundary
✷	National capital
•	Other city

Mercator Projection

Map labels: 140°E, 160°E, 160°W, 140°W, Tropic of Cancer, Midway Is. (U.S.), 20°N, NORTHERN MARIANA IS. (U.S.), Wake Island (U.S.), Hawaiian Is., HAWAII (U.S.), PACIFIC OCEAN, N, GUAM (U.S.), MARSHALL ISLANDS, Koror, Majuro, Palikir, PALAU, FEDERATED STATES OF MICRONESIA, Tarawa, Line Islands, 0°, INDONESIA, Wewak, Yaren District, KIRIBATI, PAPUA NEW GUINEA, NAURU, Marquesas Is., SOLOMON IS., Funafuti, TOKELAU (N.Z.), Port Moresby, Honiara, TUVALU, WESTERN SAMOA, Society Is., Tuamotu Archipelago, WALLIS AND FUTUNA (FR.), AMERICAN SAMOA (U.S.), Apia, VANUATU, Tahiti, Port-Vila, Suva, TONGA, NIUE (N.Z.), COOK ISLANDS (N.Z.), 20°S, NEW CALEDONIA (FR.), FIJI, Nuku'alofa, FRENCH POLYNESIA (FR.), Tropic of Capricorn, AUSTRALIA, PITCAIRN ISLAND (U.K.), Easter Island (Chile), Tasman Sea, N W E S, 0 750 1,500 mi, 0 750 1,500 km

Capital: Palikir

Area: 271 sq mi/702 sq km

Population: 109,000

Ethnic Groups: Micronesian, Polynesian

Religions: Roman Catholic, Protestant

Government: constitutional government

Currency: United States dollar

Exports: fish, garments, bananas, black pepper

Official Language: English

Federated States of Micronesia
(my kroh NEE zha)

Capital: Suva

Area: 7,054 sq mi/18,270 sq km

Population: 806,000

Ethnic Groups: indigenous Fijian, Indian

Religions: Hindu, Methodist, Roman Catholic, Muslim

Government: republic

Currency: Fiji dollar

Exports: sugar, clothing, gold, processed fish, lumber

Official Language: English

Fiji
(FEE jee)

Capital: Bairiki

Area: 274 sq mi/710 sq km

Population: 78,000

Ethnic Groups: Micronesian

Religions: Roman Catholic, Kiribati Protestant

Government: republic

Currency: Australian dollar

Exports: copra, seaweed, fish

Official Language: English

Kiribati
(kir uh BAH tee)

Capital: Koror

Area: 196 sq mi/508 sq km

Population: 18,000

Ethnic Group: Palavans

Religions: Roman Catholic, Modekngei

Government: constitutional government

Currency: United States dollar

Exports: trochus (type of shellfish), tuna, copra, handicrafts

Official Languages: Belauan and English

Palau
(pah LAH oo)

Capital: Delap district

Area: 70 sq mi/181 sq km

Population: 59,000

Ethnic Group: Micronesian

Religion: Christian

Government: constitutional government in free association with the U.S.

Currency: United States dollar

Exports: fish, coconut oil, trochus shells

Official Languages: Marshallese and English

Marshall Islands
(MAHR shul EYE lunds)

Capital: Port Moresby

Area: 174,849 sq mi/452,860

Population: 4.7 million

Ethnic Groups: Melanesian, Papuan, Negrito, Micronesian, Polynesian

Religions: traditional beliefs, Roman Catholic, Lutheran, Anglican

Government: parliamentary democracy

Currency: Kina

Exports: oil, gold, copper ore, logs, palm oil, coffee

Official Language: English

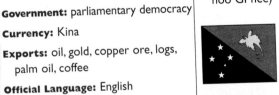

Papua New Guinea
(PAP yoo uh noo GI nee)

Capital: none

Area: 8.2 sq mi/21.2 sq km

Population: 11,000

Ethnic Groups: Nauruan, other Pacific Islanders, Chinese, Vietnamese, European

Religion: Christian

Government: republic

Currency: Australian dollar

Export: phosphates

Official Language: Nauruan

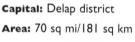

Nauru
(nah OO roo)

Capital: Apia

Area: 1,093 sq mi/2,830 sq km

Population: 177,000

Ethnic Groups: Samoan, Euronesian

Religion: Christian

Government: constitutional monarchy

Currency: Tala

Exports: coconut oil and cream, copra, fish

Official Languages: English and Samoan

Samoa
(suh MOH uh)

Capital: Fongafale

Area: 10 sq mi/26 sq km

Population: 10,000

Ethnic Groups: Polynesian

Religions: Church of Tuvalu, Seventh Day Adventist, Baha'i

Government: constitutional monarchy

Currency: Australian dollar and Tuvaluan dollar

Exports: copra

Official Language: English

Tuvalu
(too vuh LOO)

Capital: Honiara

Area: 10,639 sq mi/27,556 sq km

Population: 430,000

Ethnic Groups: Melanesian, Polynesian, Micronesian, European

Religions: Anglican, Roman Catholic, South Seas Evangelical

Government: parliamentary democracy

Currency: Solomon Islands dollar

Exports: timber, fish, palm oil

Official Language: English

Solomon Islands
(SAHL uh mun EYE lunds)

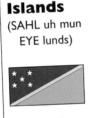

Capital: Port-Vila

Area: 4,707 sq mi/12,190 sq km

Population: 200,000

Ethnic Groups: Melanesian, French

Religions: Presbyterian, Anglican, Roman Catholic, traditional beliefs

Government: republic

Currency: Vatu

Exports: copra, beef, cocoa, timber

Official Languages: Bislama, English, French

Vanuatu
(vahn wah TOO)

Capital: Nuku'alofa

Area: 278 sq mi/720 sq km

Population: 97,000

Ethnic Groups: Polynesian, other Pacific groups, European

Religions: Free Wesleyan, Roman Catholic

Government: constitutional monarchy

Currency: Pa'anga

Exports: squash, fish, vanilla beans

Official Languages: English and Tongan

Tonga
(TAHNG guh)

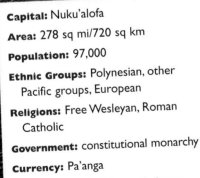

Atlas

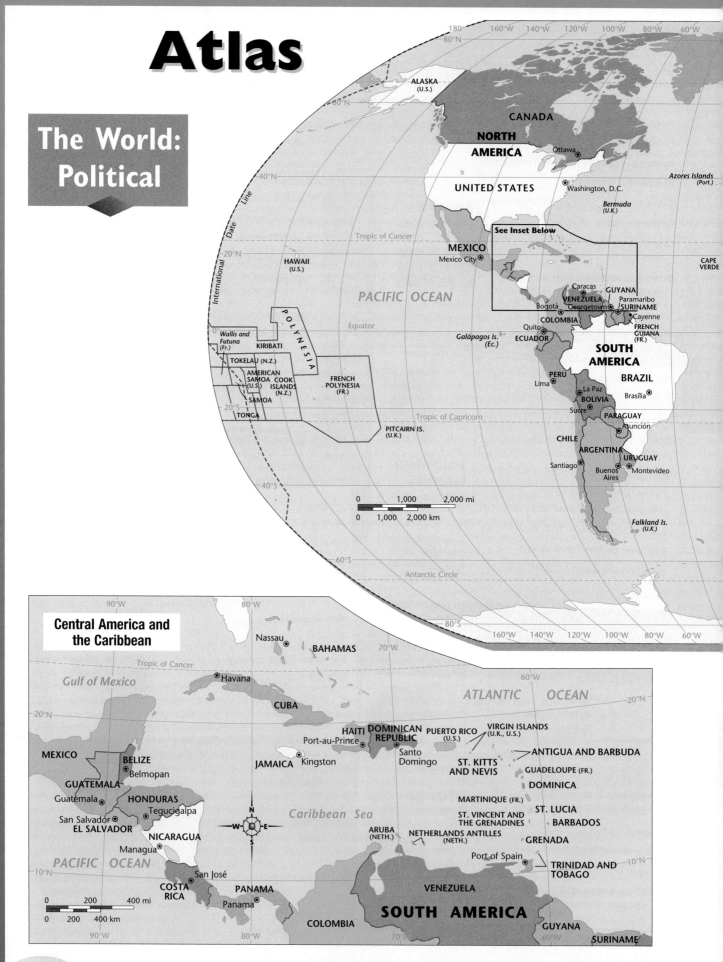

Central America and the Caribbean

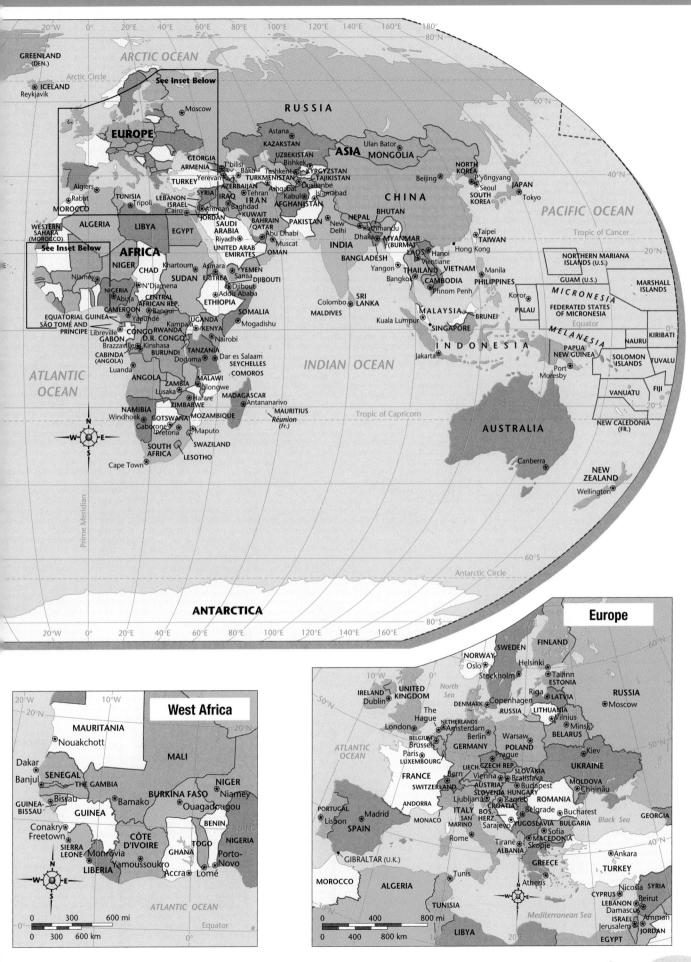

ARCTIC OCEAN

GREENLAND (DEN.)

ICELAND
Reykjavik

Arctic Circle

See Inset Below

EUROPE

Moscow

RUSSIA

ASIA

Astana
KAZAKSTAN

Ulan Bator

MONGOLIA

GEORGIA
ARMENIA
T'bilisi
Yerevan
TURKEY
Baku
AZERBAIJAN

UZBEKISTAN
Bishkek
Tashkent
KYRGYZSTAN
TAJIKISTAN
Ashgabat
Dushanbe
TURKMENISTAN

Beijing

CHINA

NORTH
KOREA
P'yŏngyang
Seoul
SOUTH
KOREA

JAPAN

Tokyo

PACIFIC OCEAN

Algiers

Rabat

MOROCCO

TUNISIA
Tripoli

LEBANON
ISRAEL
Cairo

SYRIA
IRAQ
Amman
JORDAN

Baghdad

IRAN
Tehran

Kabul
AFGHANISTAN

Islamabad

Tropic of Cancer

40°N

WESTERN
SAHARA
(MOROCCO)

ALGERIA

LIBYA

EGYPT

KUWAIT
BAHRAIN
SAUDI
ARABIA
QATAR
Riyadh
Abu Dhabi
UNITED ARAB
EMIRATES
OMAN
Muscat

PAKISTAN

New
Delhi

NEPAL
Kathmandu

BHUTAN

Dhaka

Taipei
Hong Kong
TAIWAN

20°N

See Inset Below

AFRICA

NIGER

CHAD

Niamey

Khartoum

SUDAN

Asmara
ERITREA

YEMEN
Sanaa

DJIBOUTI

INDIA

BANGLADESH

Colombo

MYANMAR
(BURMA)
Yangon
LAOS
Hanoi
Vientiane
THAILAND
Bangkok
CAMBODIA
Phnom Penh
VIETNAM

Manila

PHILIPPINES

NORTHERN MARIANA
ISLANDS (U.S.)

GUAM (U.S.)

MICRONESIA

MARSHALL
ISLANDS

MALDIVES

SRI
LANKA

FEDERATED STATES
OF MICRONESIA

PALAU

NAURU

KIRIBATI

NIGERIA
Abuja
CENTRAL
AFRICAN REP.
Bangui

N'Djamena

CAMEROON
Yaoundé

ETHIOPIA
Addis Ababa

SOMALIA

Mogadishu

MALAYSIA

Kuala Lumpur

BRUNEI

SINGAPORE

MELANESIA

EQUATORIAL GUINEA
SÃO TOMÉ AND
PRÍNCIPE
Libreville
GABON
Brazzaville
CABINDA
(ANGOLA)

CONGO
D.R. CONGO
Kinshasa

Kampala
UGANDA
RWANDA
KENYA
Nairobi
BURUNDI

TANZANIA
Dodoma
Dar es Salaam
SEYCHELLES

INDONESIA

Jakarta

INDIAN OCEAN

PAPUA
NEW GUINEA
Port
Moresby

SOLOMON
ISLANDS

TUVALU

ATLANTIC
OCEAN

Luanda

ANGOLA

ZAMBIA
Lusaka

MALAWI
Lilongwe

COMOROS

MADAGASCAR
Antananarivo

MAURITIUS
Réunion
(Fr.)

Tropic of Capricorn

AUSTRALIA

VANUATU

FIJI

NAMIBIA
Windhoek

ZIMBABWE
Harare

BOTSWANA
Gaborone
Pretoria
Maputo

MOZAMBIQUE

SWAZILAND

20°S

NEW CALEDONIA
(FR.)

SOUTH
AFRICA
Cape Town

LESOTHO

Canberra

NEW
ZEALAND

Wellington

60°S

Antarctic Circle

ANTARCTICA

80°S

West Africa

MAURITANIA
Nouakchott

MALI

Dakar
SENEGAL
Banjul
THE GAMBIA
GUINEA-
BISSAU
Bissau
GUINEA
Bamako
BURKINA FASO
Ouagadougou
NIGER
Niamey

Conakry
Freetown
SIERRA
LEONE
Monrovia
LIBERIA
Yamoussoukro
CÔTE
D'IVOIRE
GHANA
Accra
BENIN
TOGO
Lomé
NIGERIA
Porto-
Novo

ATLANTIC OCEAN

Equator

0   300   600 mi
0   300   600 km

Europe

SWEDEN
FINLAND
NORWAY
Oslo
Helsinki
Stockholm
Tallinn
ESTONIA
IRELAND
UNITED
KINGDOM
Dublin
North
Sea
DENMARK
Copenhagen
Riga
LATVIA
RUSSIA
Moscow
LITHUANIA
Vilnius
The
Hague
NETHERLANDS
Amsterdam
Minsk
BELARUS
London
BELGIUM
Brussels
Berlin
Warsaw
Kiev
GERMANY
POLAND
Paris
LUXEMBOURG
Prague
UKRAINE
CZECH REP.
SLOVAKIA
FRANCE
Bern
Vienna
Bratislava
Budapest
MOLDOVA
Chişinău
SWITZERLAND
LIECH.
AUSTRIA
SLOVENIA HUNGARY
Ljubljana
Zagreb
ROMANIA
GEORGIA
ANDORRA
CROATIA
Belgrade
Bucharest
PORTUGAL
Madrid
ITALY
BOS.
HERZ.
YUGOSLAVIA
BULGARIA
Lisbon
MONACO
SAN
MARINO
Sarajevo
Sofia
Black Sea
SPAIN
Rome
Tiranë
MACEDONIA
Skopje
Ankara
ALBANIA
GIBRALTAR (U.K.)
GREECE
TURKEY
MOROCCO
ALGERIA
Tunis
Athens
Nicosia
SYRIA
CYPRUS
LEBANON
Beirut
Damascus
TUNISIA
Mediterranean Sea
ISRAEL
Jerusalem
Amman
JORDAN
LIBYA
EGYPT

0   400   800 mi
0   400   800 km

The World: Physical

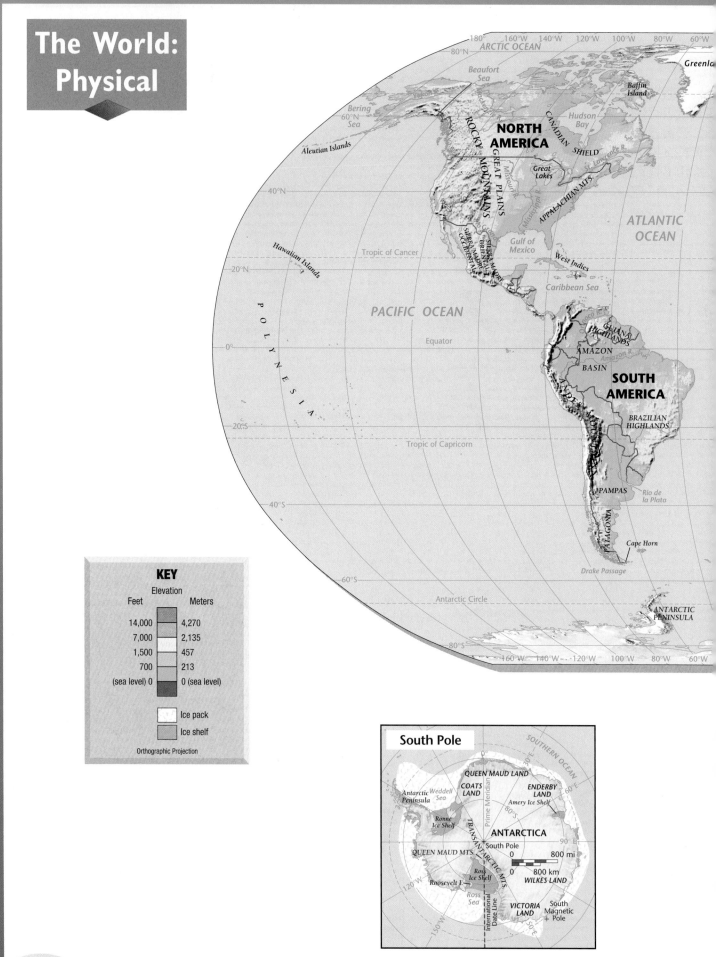

ARCTIC OCEAN
Greenla

Beaufort
Sea

Baffin
Island

Yukon

Bering
60°N
Sea

NORTH
AMERICA

Hudson
Bay

CANADIAN SHIELD

St. Lawrence R.

Aleutian Islands

ROCKY MOUNTAINS

GREAT PLAINS

Missouri R.

Great
Lakes

APPALACHIAN MTS.

ATLANTIC
OCEAN

40°N

Mississippi R.

Hawaiian Islands

Tropic of Cancer

20°N

SIERRA MADRE
OCCIDENTAL

SIERRA MADRE
ORIENTAL

Gulf of
Mexico

West Indies

Caribbean Sea

P
O
L
Y
N
E
S
I
A

PACIFIC OCEAN

Orinoco R.

GUIANA
HIGHLANDS

AMAZON
BASIN

Equator

0°

Amazon R.

SOUTH
AMERICA

ANDES MTS.

BRAZILIAN
HIGHLANDS

20°S

Tropic of Capricorn

PAMPAS

Rio de
la Plata

40°S

PATAGONIA

Cape Horn

Drake Passage

60°S

Antarctic Circle

ANTARCTIC
PENINSULA

80°S

KEY

Elevation

Feet		Meters
14,000		4,270
7,000		2,135
1,500		457
700		213
(sea level) 0		0 (sea level)

Ice pack

Ice shelf

Orthographic Projection

South Pole

SOUTHERN OCEAN

QUEEN MAUD LAND

COATS
LAND

ENDERBY
LAND

Antarctic
Peninsula

Weddell
Sea

Amery Ice Shelf

Ronne
Ice Shelf

ANTARCTICA

TRANSANTARCTIC MTS.

South Pole

90°E

QUEEN MAUD MTS.

Ross
Ice Shelf

0   800 mi

0   800 km

Roosevelt I.

WILKES LAND

Ross
Sea

VICTORIA
LAND

South
Magnetic
+ Pole

Prime Meridian

International
Date Line

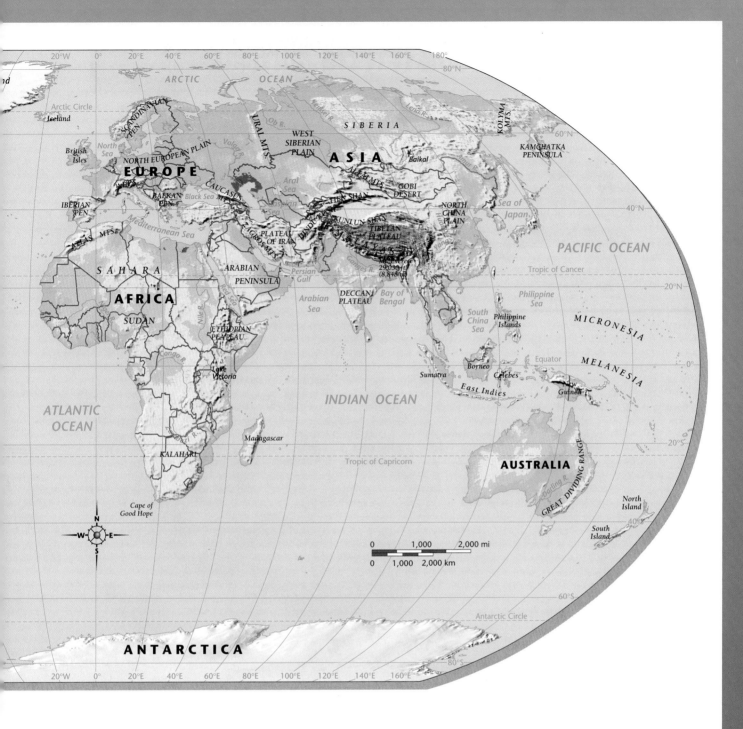

20°W 0° 20°E 40°E 60°E 80°E 100°E 120°E 140°E 160°E 180°

ARCTIC OCEAN

80°N

Arctic Circle

Iceland

SCANDINAVIAN PEN.

URAL MTS.

Ob R.

Yenisey R.

SIBERIA

Lena R.

KOLYMA MTS.

60°N

British Isles

North Sea

NORTH EUROPEAN PLAIN

Volga R.

WEST SIBERIAN PLAIN

A S I A

L. Baikal

KAMCHATKA PENINSULA

EUROPE

ALPS

BALKAN PEN.

Black Sea

CAUCASUS MTS.

Aral Sea

Caspian Sea

ALTAI MTS.

TIEN SHAN

GOBI DESERT

NORTH CHINA PLAIN

Sea of Japan

40°N

IBERIAN PEN.

Mediterranean Sea

ATLAS MTS.

ZAGROS MTS.

PLATEAU OF IRAN

HINDU KUSH

KUNLUN SHAN

TIBETAN PLATEAU

HIMALAYAS

Mt. Everest 29,035 ft (8,848 m)

Huang R.

PACIFIC OCEAN

Tropic of Cancer

20°N

SAHARA

AFRICA

SUDAN

Nile R.

Red Sea

ARABIAN PENINSULA

Persian Gulf

Arabian Sea

DECCAN PLATEAU

Ganges R.

Bay of Bengal

South China Sea

Philippine Islands

Philippine Sea

MICRONESIA

ETHIOPIAN PLATEAU

Congo R.

Lake Victoria

Sumatra

Borneo

Celebes

East Indies

Equator

New Guinea

MELANESIA

0°

ATLANTIC OCEAN

INDIAN OCEAN

KALAHARI

Zambezi R.

Madagascar

20°S

Tropic of Capricorn

AUSTRALIA

GREAT DIVIDING RANGE

Darling R.

North Island

Cape of Good Hope

N
W E
S

0   1,000   2,000 mi
0   1,000   2,000 km

South Island

40°S

60°S

Antarctic Circle

A N T A R C T I C A

80°S

20°W 0° 20°E 40°E 60°E 80°E 100°E 120°E 140°E 160°E

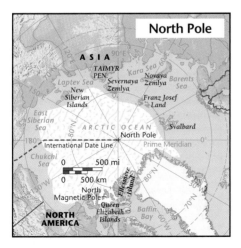

North Pole

A S I A

TAIMYR PEN.

Kara Sea

Laptev Sea

Severnaya Zemlya

Novaya Zemlya

Barents Sea

New Siberian Islands

Franz Josef Land

East Siberian Sea

ARCTIC OCEAN

Svalbard

North Pole

Prime Meridian

International Date Line

Chukchi Sea

0   500 mi
0   500 km

North Magnetic Pole

Ellesmere Island

Queen Elizabeth Islands

Baffin Bay

NORTH AMERICA

United States: Political

ARCTIC OCEAN

RUSSIA

ALASKA

CANADA

Bering Strait

Arctic Circle

70°N

70°N

60°N

Yukon River

Anchorage

Bering Sea

Gulf of Alaska

Juneau

160°W

140°W

0   250   500 mi

0   250   500 km

50°N

120°W

110°W

Seattle

Olympia

WASHINGTON

Spokane

Columbia

Portland

Salem

OREGON

Klamath Falls

Eureka

40°N

Winnemucca

Sacramento

San Francisco

Carson City

NEVADA

CALIFORNIA

Los Angeles

PACIFIC

OCEAN

San Diego

Las Vegas

Cedar City

Snake River

Boise

IDAHO

Twin Falls

Helena

MONTANA

Billings

Missouri River

Minc

Bismar

Sheridan

Jackson

WYOMING

Pi

Rapid C

NEBRAS

Cheyenne

Great Salt Lake

Salt Lake City

UTAH

Colorado River

Grand Junction

Denver

COLORADO

Pueblo

Ark

ARIZONA

Phoenix

Tucson

Albuquerque

NEW MEXICO

Santa Fe

Rio Grande

Roswell

El Paso

MEXICO

160°W

155°W

Honolulu

PACIFIC OCEAN

HAWAII

20°N

20°N

Hilo

155°W

0   50   100 mi

0   50   100 km

Tropic of Cancer

120°W

110°W

CANADA

Lake Superior

Duluth

Sault Ste. Marie

Lake Huron

NORTH DAKOTA

MINNESOTA

Minneapolis • St. Paul

MICHIGAN

Lake Michigan

Lake Ontario

Presque Isle

MAINE

• Augusta

• Portland

Montpelier

VERMONT

NEW HAMPSHIRE

• Concord

• Boston

SOUTH DAKOTA

WISCONSIN

Milwaukee

Madison

Lansing

Detroit

NEW YORK

Albany

Buffalo

MASSACHUSETTS

• Providence

Hartford

New Haven

RHODE ISLAND

CONNECTICUT

40°N

Missouri

Chicago

IOWA

Cedar Rapids

Des Moines

Omaha

Lincoln

ILLINOIS

Springfield

INDIANA

Indianapolis

Lake Erie

Cleveland

OHIO

Columbus

Cincinnati

PENNSYLVANIA

Harrisburg

Pittsburgh

New York City

Trenton

NEW JERSEY

Philadelphia

Dover

Baltimore

Annapolis

DELAWARE

Washington, D.C.

MARYLAND

WEST VIRGINIA

Richmond

Charleston

VIRGINIA

Norfolk

KANSAS

Topeka

Kansas City

Jefferson City

MISSOURI

St. Louis

Louisville

Frankfort

KENTUCKY

Ohio River

Tennessee River

Raleigh

NORTH CAROLINA

• Charlotte

Wichita

River

Nashville

TENNESSEE

Memphis

Columbia

SOUTH CAROLINA

Charleston

OKLAHOMA

Tulsa

Oklahoma City

ARKANSAS

Little Rock

Pine Bluff

Red River

Mississippi River

Birmingham

Atlanta

GEORGIA

Columbus

Savannah

ATLANTIC OCEAN

Dallas

MISSISSIPPI

ALABAMA

Jackson

Montgomery

Columbus

Jacksonville

Shreveport

Hattiesburg

TEXAS

Austin

Tallahassee

30°N

San Antonio

Houston

Baton Rouge

LOUISIANA

New Orleans

FLORIDA

Tampa

Lake Okeechobee

Rio Grande

Gulf of Mexico

Miami

N
W E
S

0   150   300 mi
0   150   300 km

KEY

—— National boundary
—— State boundary
⊛ National capital
⊙ State capital
• Other city

Transverse Mercator Projection

90°W   80°W   70°W

90°W   80°W

ATLAS   233

North and South America: Political

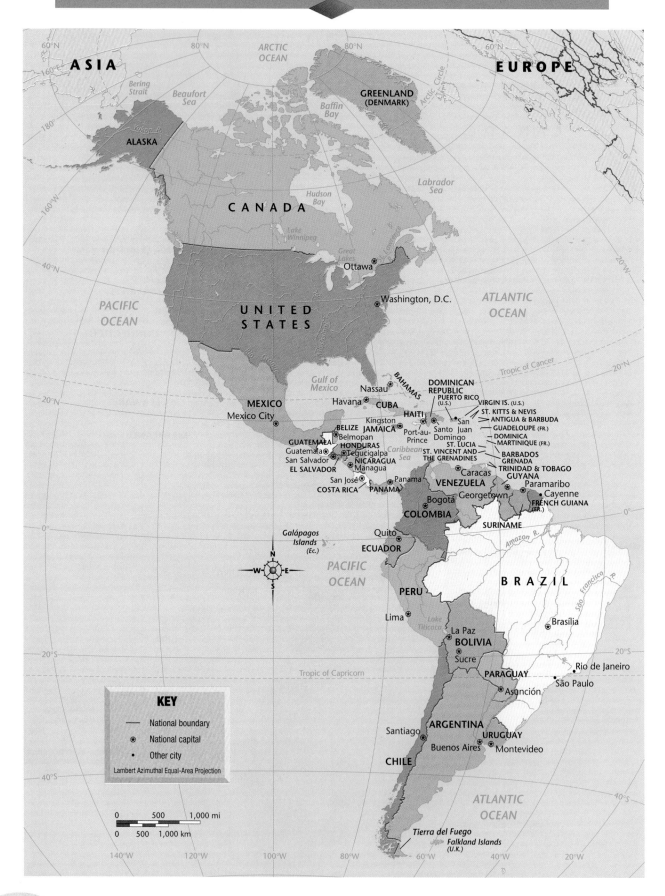

ASIA

ARCTIC OCEAN

Bering Strait

Beaufort Sea

EUROPE

60°N

80°N

80°N

60°N

160°W

180°

GREENLAND (DENMARK)

Arctic Circle

ALASKA

Yukon R.

Baffin Bay

20°W

0°

Labrador Sea

CANADA

40°N

Hudson Bay

Lake Winnipeg

St. Lawrence R.

Great Lakes

Ottawa

PACIFIC OCEAN

UNITED STATES

Washington, D.C.

ATLANTIC OCEAN

20°W

Mississippi R.

Rio Grande

Tropic of Cancer

20°N

Gulf of Mexico

BAHAMAS

Nassau

DOMINICAN REPUBLIC

PUERTO RICO (U.S.)

VIRGIN IS. (U.S.)

20°N

MEXICO

Havana

CUBA

HAITI

ST. KITTS & NEVIS

Mexico City

Kingston

Port-au-Prince

Santo Domingo

San Juan

ANTIGUA & BARBUDA

GUADELOUPE (FR.)

BELIZE

JAMAICA

DOMINICA

GUATEMALA

Belmopan

MARTINIQUE (FR.)

Guatemala

HONDURAS

Tegucigalpa

Caribbean Sea

ST. LUCIA

BARBADOS

San Salvador

NICARAGUA

ST. VINCENT AND THE GRENADINES

GRENADA

EL SALVADOR

Managua

TRINIDAD & TOBAGO

San José

Caracas

GUYANA

COSTA RICA

PANAMA

Panama

VENEZUELA

Georgetown

Paramaribo

Cayenne

Galápagos Islands (Ec.)

Bogotá

SURINAME

FRENCH GUIANA (FR.)

0°

COLOMBIA

0°

Quito

ECUADOR

Amazon R.

PACIFIC OCEAN

BRAZIL

São Francisco R.

PERU

Lima

Lake Titicaca

Brasília

La Paz

BOLIVIA

Rio de Janeiro

Sucre

20°S

Tropic of Capricorn

PARAGUAY

São Paulo

20°S

Asunción

KEY

ARGENTINA

URUGUAY

Santiago

Buenos Aires

Montevideo

— National boundary

⊛ National capital

• Other city

Lambert Azimuthal Equal-Area Projection

CHILE

40°S

0   500   1,000 mi

0   500   1,000 km

ATLANTIC OCEAN

40°S

Tierra del Fuego

Falkland Islands (U.K.)

140°W

120°W

100°W

80°W

60°W

40°W

20°W

North and South America: Physical

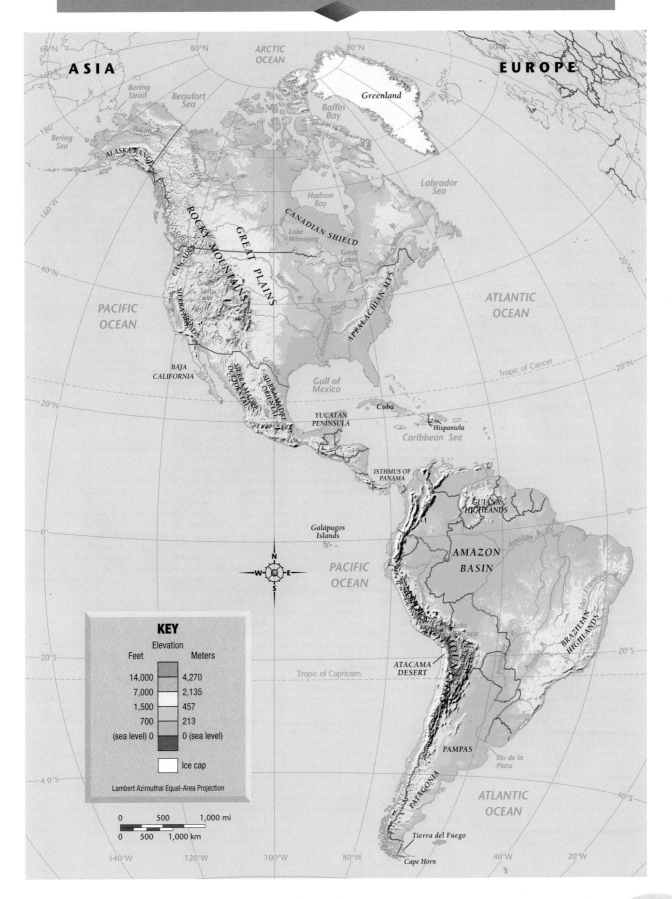

KEY

Elevation

Feet		Meters
14,000		4,270
7,000		2,135
1,500		457
700		213
(sea level) 0		0 (sea level)
	Ice cap	

Lambert Azimuthal Equal-Area Projection

0   500   1,000 mi

0   500   1,000 km

ASIA

EUROPE

ARCTIC
OCEAN

Greenland

Bering
Strait

Beaufort
Sea

Baffin
Bay

Bering
Sea

ALASKA RANGE

Yukon R.

Arctic Circle

Labrador
Sea

Hudson
Bay

CANADIAN SHIELD

Lake
Winnipeg

ROCKY MOUNTAINS

GREAT PLAINS

Great
Lakes

Missouri R.

Ohio

APPALACHIAN MTS.

ATLANTIC
OCEAN

PACIFIC
OCEAN

CASCADES

SIERRA NEVADA

Great
Salt
Lake

Mississippi R.

Rio Grande

BAJA
CALIFORNIA

SIERRA MADRE
OCCIDENTAL

SIERRA MADRE
ORIENTAL

Tropic of Cancer

Gulf of
Mexico

YUCATÁN
PENINSULA

Cuba

Hispaniola

Caribbean Sea

ISTHMUS OF
PANAMA

Orinoco R.

GUIANA
HIGHLANDS

Galápagos
Islands

AMAZON
BASIN

Amazon R.

PACIFIC
OCEAN

N
W   E
S

Lake
Titicaca

São Francisco R.

BRAZILIAN
HIGHLANDS

ANDES MOUNTAINS

Tropic of Capricorn

ATACAMA
DESERT

Paraná R.

20°S

PAMPAS

Rio de la
Plata

Paraguay R.

PATAGONIA

ATLANTIC
OCEAN

Tierra del Fuego

Cape Horn

Europe: Political

KEY

—— National boundary

⊛ National capital

• Other city

Lambert Azimuthal Equal-Area Projection

ARCTIC OCEAN

Arctic Circle

Reykjavik ⊛ **ICELAND**

Faeroe Is. (Den.)

Shetland Is. (U.K.)

ATLANTIC OCEAN

FINLAND

Gulf of Bothnia

SWEDEN

NORWAY
Lillehammer •

Turku • • Helsinki • St. Petersburg

Tallinn

Oslo ⊛   Stockholm ⊛   **ESTONIA**   **RUSSIA**

Moscow ⊛

• Göteborg   Riga ⊛   **LATVIA**

North Sea   Baltic Sea

DENMARK   **LITHUANIA**
Copenhagen ⊛   Vilnius ⊛   **BELARUS**

RUSSIA   Minsk ⊛

IRELAND   **UNITED KINGDOM**   Gdańsk •
Dublin ⊛   **POLAND**
• Manchester   Warsaw ⊛   Kiev ⊛

Berlin ⊛   Łódź •   **UKRAINE**
Amsterdam   **GERMANY**
The Hague ⊛ ⊛   Katowice •
London ⊛   **NETHERLANDS**   • Kraków
English Channel   • Cologne   Prague ⊛   **CZECH**
Brussels ⊛   • Bonn   **REPUBLIC**   **SLOVAKIA**   **MOLDOVA**
BELGIUM   • Frankfurt   Brno •   Chişinău ⊛
LUXEMBOURG   Danube R.   Bratislava ⊛
⊛ Luxembourg   • Munich   Vienna ⊛   • Budapest   • Cluj-Napoca
⊛ Paris   **LIECHTENSTEIN**   **AUSTRIA**   **HUNGARY**   **ROMANIA**
Bay of Biscay   Bern ⊛   Ljubljana ⊛
FRANCE   **SWITZERLAND**   **SLOVENIA**   Zagreb ⊛   Bucharest ⊛   Black Sea
Milan •   **CROATIA**
SAN MARINO   **BOSNIA-**   • Belgrade
Marseille •   **MONACO**   **HERZEGOVINA**
PORTUGAL   **ANDORRA**   Corsica   **ITALY**   Sarajevo ⊛   **YUGOSLAVIA**   **BULGARIA**
• Madrid   • Barcelona   **VATICAN**   Podgorica •   Sofia ⊛
Lisbon ⊛   **CITY**   ⊛ Rome   **ALBANIA**   Skopje ⊛
SPAIN   Sardinia   **MACEDONIA**
Balearic Is.   • Naples   Tiranë •   Aegean Sea
Tyrrhenian Sea   **GREECE**
Strait of Gibraltar   **GIBRALTAR** (U.K.)   Mediterranean Sea   Ionian Sea
Athens ⊛
Sicily   Crete

AFRICA   **MALTA**

0   250   500 mi
0   250   500 km

N W E S

Europe: Physical

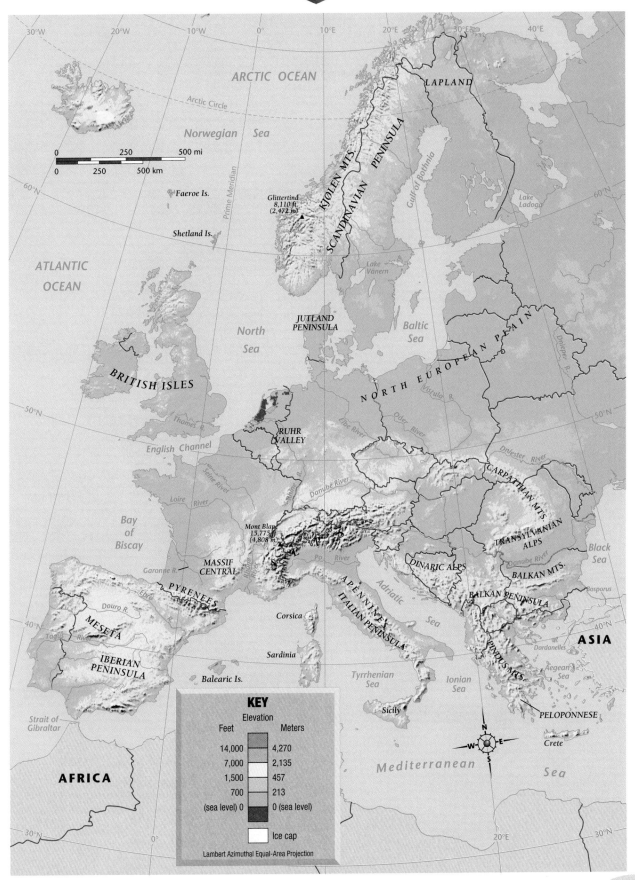

ARCTIC OCEAN

LAPLAND

Arctic Circle

Norwegian Sea

0 — 250 — 500 mi
0 — 250 — 500 km

Faeroe Is.

Glittertind
8,110 ft.
(2,472 m)

KJØLEN MTS.

SCANDINAVIAN PENINSULA

Gulf of Bothnia

Lake Ladoga

Shetland Is.

ATLANTIC OCEAN

60°N

Lake Vänern

JUTLAND PENINSULA

Baltic Sea

North Sea

BRITISH ISLES

NORTH EUROPEAN PLAIN

50°N

Thames R.

Vistula R.

Dnieper R.

Elbe River

Oder River

English Channel

RUHR VALLEY

Seine River

Danube River

Dniester River

CARPATHIAN MTS.

Loire River

Bay of Biscay

Mont Blanc
15,775 ft.
(4,808 m)

Po River

TRANSYLVANIAN ALPS

Black Sea

MASSIF CENTRAL

Garonne R.

DINARIC ALPS

Danube River

BALKAN MTS.

PYRENEES

Ebro R.

APENNINES

Adriatic Sea

BALKAN PENINSULA

Bosporus

MESETA

Douro R.

ITALIAN PENINSULA

Corsica

40°N

Dardanelles

ASIA

Tagus River

IBERIAN PENINSULA

Sardinia

Tyrrhenian Sea

Aegean Sea

PINDUS MTS.

Balearic Is.

Ionian Sea

PELOPONNESE

Sicily

Crete

Strait of Gibraltar

KEY
Elevation

Feet	Meters
14,000	4,270
7,000	2,135
1,500	457
700	213
(sea level) 0	0 (sea level)

Ice cap

Lambert Azimuthal Equal-Area Projection

AFRICA

Mediterranean Sea

30°N

Africa: Political

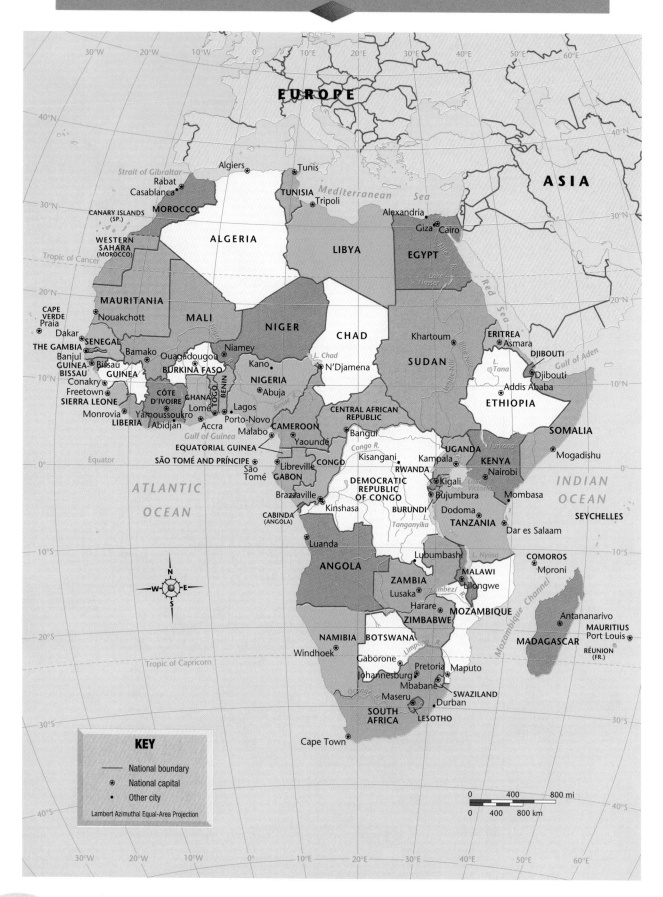

EUROPE

ASIA

Strait of Gibraltar

Algiers · Tunis

Rabat
Casablanca ·
MOROCCO
TUNISIA
· Tripoli

Mediterranean Sea

Alexandria ·

CANARY ISLANDS
(SP.)

**WESTERN
SAHARA
(MOROCCO)**

ALGERIA

LIBYA

EGYPT

Giza · Cairo

Tropic of Cancer

Lake Nasser

MAURITANIA

MALI

NIGER

CHAD

Khartoum ·

Red Sea

ERITREA
· Asmara

DJIBOUTI

Gulf of Aden

**CAPE
VERDE**
Praia
· Dakar
Nouakchott ·

Niamey
Kano ·

NIGERIA

SUDAN

SENEGAL
Bamako · Ouagadougou
THE GAMBIA
Banjul
GUINEA
BISSAU · Bissau
BURKINA FASO

L. Chad

N'Djamena

White Nile

Blue Nile

L. Tana

Djibouti ·

Addis Ababa ·

ETHIOPIA

Conakry
Freetown ·
SIERRA LEONE
Monrovia ·
LIBERIA
GUINEA
**CÔTE
D'IVOIRE**
GHANA
Yamoussoukro ·
Abidjan
Lomé ·
TOGO
BENIN
· Abuja
Lagos
Accra · Porto-Novo
Malabo ·

**CENTRAL AFRICAN
REPUBLIC**
Bangui ·

SOMALIA

· Mogadishu

CAMEROON
Yaoundé ·

UGANDA
Kampala ·

L. Turkana

KENYA
Nairobi ·

Gulf of Guinea

EQUATORIAL GUINEA

SÃO TOMÉ AND PRÍNCIPE
São
Tomé ·

Equator

Kisangani ·

RWANDA
Kigali ·

L. Victoria

**INDIAN
OCEAN**

Libreville ·
CONGO
GABON

Congo R.

Mombasa ·

Brazzaville ·

**DEMOCRATIC
REPUBLIC
OF CONGO**

BURUNDI
Bujumbura ·
Dodoma ·
L. Tanganyika

SEYCHELLES

**ATLANTIC
OCEAN**

Kinshasa ·
**CABINDA
(ANGOLA)**

Luanda ·

ANGOLA

Lubumbashi ·

ZAMBIA
Lusaka ·

Harare ·

TANZANIA
Dar es Salaam ·

L. Nyasa

MALAWI
Lilongwe ·

COMOROS
· Moroni

Zambezi

Mozambique Channel

Antananarivo ·

MAURITIUS
Port Louis ·

MADAGASCAR

NAMIBIA
BOTSWANA
Windhoek ·

ZIMBABWE
MOZAMBIQUE

Limpopo

**RÉUNION
(FR.)**

Tropic of Capricorn

Gaborone ·
Johannesburg ·
Pretoria ·
Maputo

SWAZILAND
Mbabane ·

Orange

Maseru · Durban ·

**SOUTH
AFRICA**

LESOTHO

Cape Town ·

KEY

— National boundary

⊛ National capital

· Other city

Lambert Azimuthal Equal-Area Projection

| 0 | 400 | 800 mi |
| 0 | 400 | 800 km |

Africa: Physical

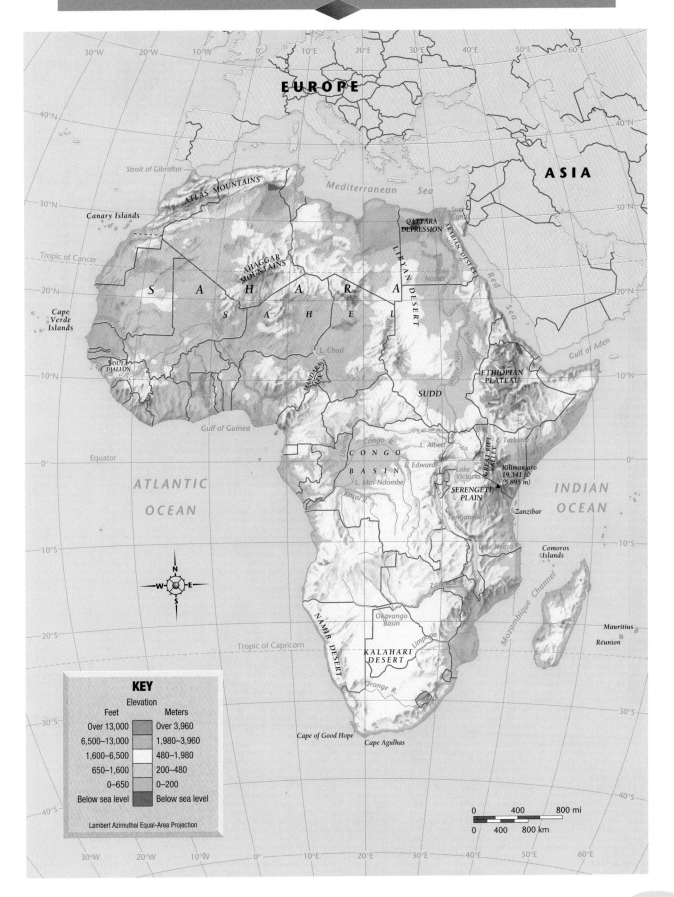

EUROPE

ASIA

Strait of Gibraltar

ATLAS MOUNTAINS

Mediterranean Sea

Canary Islands

Suez Canal

QATTARA DEPRESSION

Tropic of Cancer

AHAGGAR MOUNTAINS

ARABIAN DESERT

Lake Nasser

S A H A R A

Cape Verde Islands

S A H E L

LIBYAN DESERT

Red Sea

FOUTA DJALLON

L. Chad

MANDARA MTS.

White Nile

Blue Nile

Gulf of Aden

ETHIOPIAN PLATEAU

SUDD

Gulf of Guinea

Congo R.

Ubangi

L. Albert

L. Turkana

Equator

C O N G O

B A S I N

L. Edward

GREAT RIFT VALLEY

Kilimanjaro 19,341 ft. (5,895 m)

ATLANTIC OCEAN

L. Mai-Ndombe

Lake Victoria

INDIAN OCEAN

Kasai R.

SERENGETI PLAIN

Zanzibar

Tanganyika

Lake Nyasa

Comoros Islands

Zambezi

Mozambique Channel

Mauritius

Réunion

NAMIB DESERT

Okavango Basin

Limpopo R.

Tropic of Capricorn

KALAHARI DESERT

Orange R.

Cape of Good Hope

Cape Agulhas

KEY

Elevation

Feet		Meters
Over 13,000		Over 3,960
6,500–13,000		1,980–3,960
1,600–6,500		480–1,980
650–1,600		200–480
0–650		0–200
Below sea level		Below sea level

Lambert Azimuthal Equal-Area Projection

N
W E
S

0   400   800 mi
0   400   800 km

Asia: Political

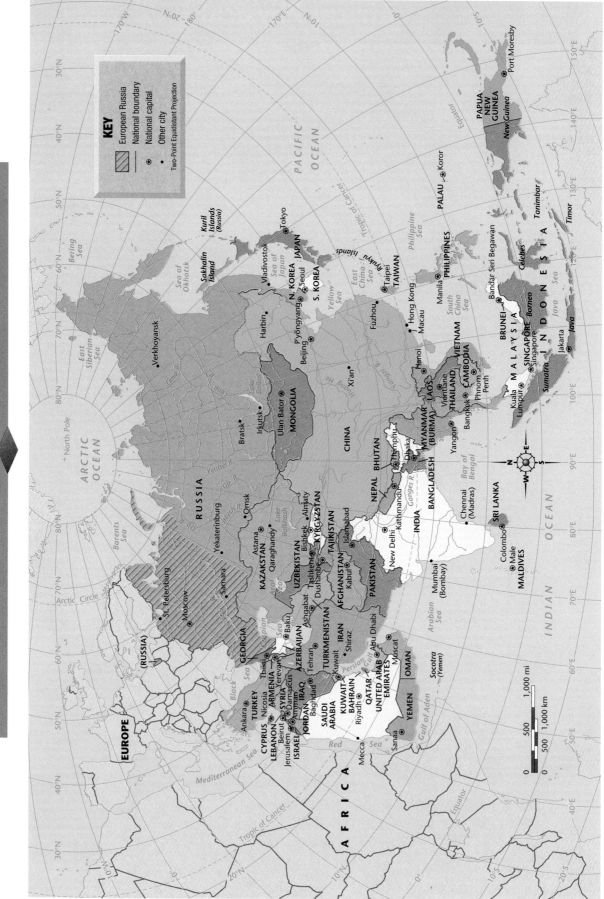

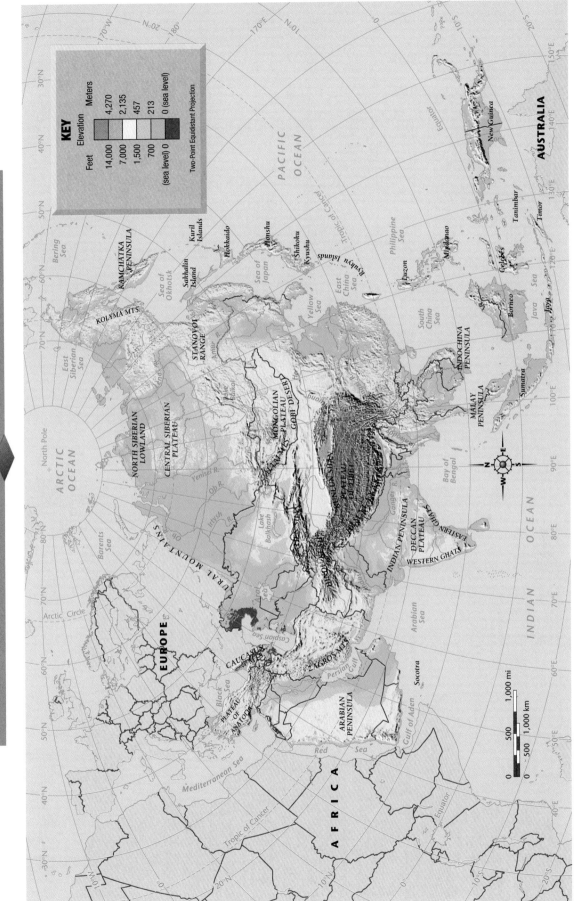

Asia: Physical

KEY

Feet	Meters
14,000	4,270
7,000	2,135
1,500	457
700	213
(sea level) 0	0 (sea level)

Elevation

Two-Point Equidistant Projection

ARCTIC OCEAN

North Pole

Arctic Circle

EUROPE

URAL MOUNTAINS

Barents Sea

NORTH SIBERIAN LOWLAND

CENTRAL SIBERIAN PLATEAU

East Siberian Sea

KOLYMA MTS.

STANOVOI RANGE

KAMCHATKA PENINSULA

Bering Sea

Sea of Okhotsk

Sakhalin Island

Kuril Islands

Hokkaido

Honshu

Sea of Japan

Shikoku

Kyushu

Yellow Sea

East China Sea

Ryukyu Islands

PACIFIC OCEAN

Lake Baikal

Yenisei R.

Ob R.

Irtysh

Lake Balkhash

MONGOLIAN PLATEAU

GOBI DESERT

ALTAI

HIMALAYAS

PLATEAU OF TIBET

Ganges R.

INDIAN PENINSULA

DECCAN PLATEAU

WESTERN GHATS

EASTERN GHATS

Bay of Bengal

INDOCHINA PENINSULA

South China Sea

Philippine Sea

Luzon

Mindanao

Celebes

MALAY PENINSULA

Sumatra

Borneo

Java Sea

Java

Timor

Tanimbar

New Guinea

AUSTRALIA

Equator

Tropic of Cancer

INDIAN OCEAN

Arabian Sea

Socotra

ARABIAN PENINSULA

Gulf of Aden

Red Sea

ZAGROS MTS.

Persian Gulf

Caspian Sea

Aral Sea

CAUCASUS MTS.

Black Sea

PLATEAU OF ANATOLIA

Mediterranean Sea

AFRICA

Tropic of Cancer

Equator

1,000 mi

500   1,000 km

0   500

0

Australia, New Zealand, and the Pacific Islands: Physical–Political

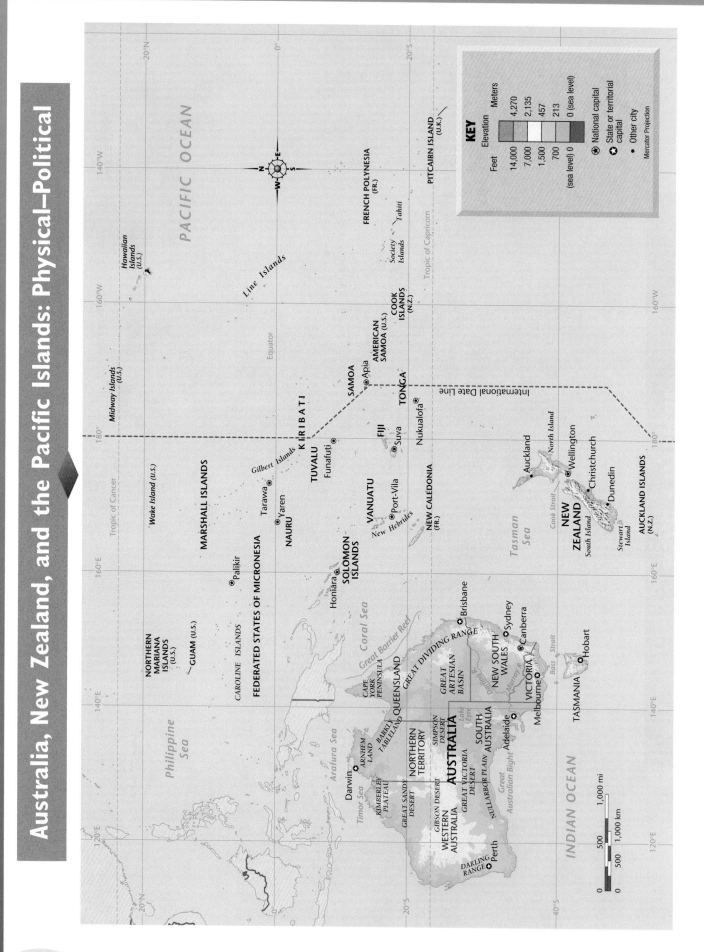

PACIFIC OCEAN

INDIAN OCEAN

Philippine Sea

Arafura Sea

Coral Sea

Timor Sea

Tasman Sea

KEY

Elevation

Feet	Meters
14,000	4,270
7,000	2,135
1,500	457
700	213
(sea level) 0	0 (sea level)

⊛ National capital
✪ State or territorial capital
• Other city

Mercator Projection

Hawaiian Islands (U.S.)

Midway Islands (U.S.)

Line Islands

FRENCH POLYNESIA (FR.)

Society Islands — Tahiti

Tropic of Capricorn

PITCAIRN ISLAND (U.K.)

Wake Island (U.S.)

Tropic of Cancer

MARSHALL ISLANDS

COOK ISLANDS (N.Z.)

AMERICAN SAMOA (U.S.)

SAMOA
• Apia

TONGA
⊛ Nukualofa

KIRIBATI

TUVALU
⊛ Funafuti

Equator

Gilbert Islands

Tarawa ⊛

NAURU
⊛ Yaren

FIJI
• Suva

VANUATU
• Port-Vila

New Hebrides

NEW CALEDONIA (FR.)

International Date Line

NORTHERN MARIANA ISLANDS (U.S.)

GUAM (U.S.)

CAROLINE ISLANDS

FEDERATED STATES OF MICRONESIA

Palikir •

SOLOMON ISLANDS
⊛ Honiara

Auckland •

North Island

⊛ Wellington
• Christchurch

NEW ZEALAND
South Island

• Dunedin

Cook Strait

Stewart Island

AUCKLAND ISLANDS (N.Z.)

Great Barrier Reef

Brisbane •

GREAT DIVIDING RANGE

NEW SOUTH WALES
• Sydney
✪ Canberra

GREAT ARTESIAN BASIN

Darling R.

Murray R.

VICTORIA
✪ Melbourne

Bass Strait

TASMANIA
⊛ Hobart

CAPE YORK PENINSULA

BARKLY TABLELAND

QUEENSLAND

ARNHEM LAND

Darwin •

NORTHERN TERRITORY

SIMPSON DESERT

Lake Eyre

SOUTH AUSTRALIA

Adelaide ✪

AUSTRALIA

KIMBERLEY PLATEAU

GREAT SANDY DESERT

GIBSON DESERT

GREAT VICTORIA DESERT

NULLARBOR PLAIN

Great Australian Bight

WESTERN AUSTRALIA

DARLING RANGE
Perth ✪

Scale

0 500 1,000 mi

0 500 1,000 km

The Arctic

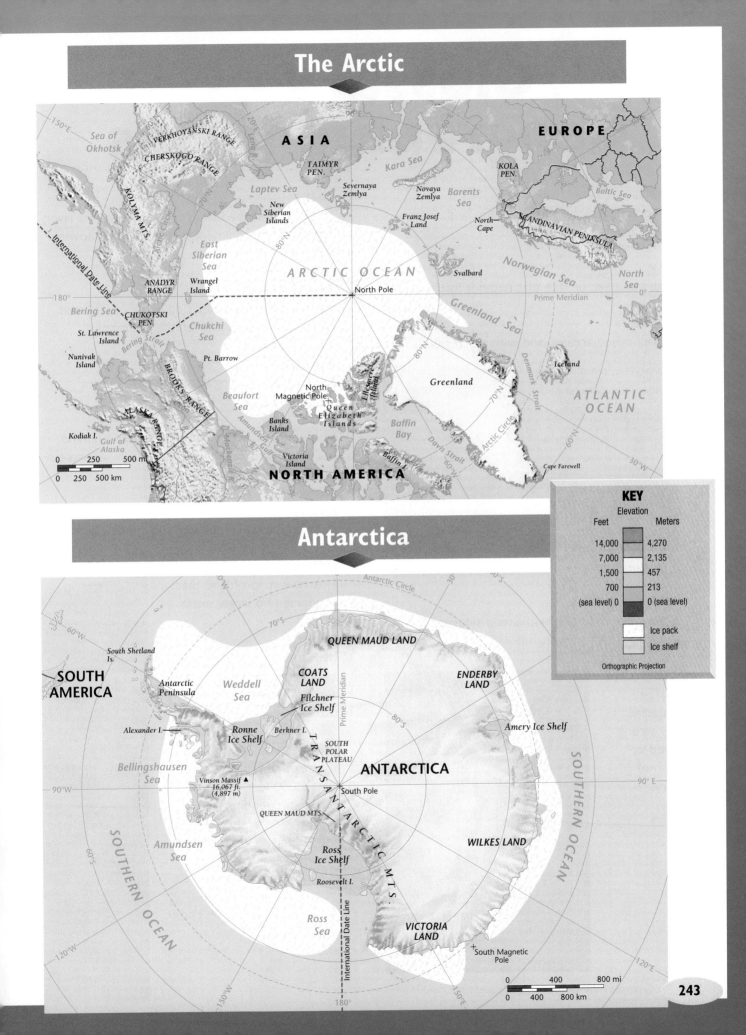

Sea of Okhotsk

VERKHOYANSKI RANGE
CHERSKOGO RANGE
KOLYMA MTS.

ASIA

TAIMYR PEN.

Laptev Sea

Severnaya Zemlya

New Siberian Islands

East Siberian Sea

Novaya Zemlya

Kara Sea

Franz Josef Land

North Cape

KOLA PEN.

EUROPE

Barents Sea

Baltic Sea

SCANDINAVIAN PENINSULA

International Date Line

Arctic Circle

ANADYR RANGE

Wrangel Island

ARCTIC OCEAN

North Pole

Svalbard

Norwegian Sea

North Sea

Prime Meridian

Greenland Sea

Denmark Strait

Iceland

ATLANTIC OCEAN

KOLYMA MTS.

Bering Sea

CHUKOTSKI PEN.

Chukchi Sea

St. Lawrence Island

Bering Strait

Pt. Barrow

Nunivak Island

BROOKS RANGE

Beaufort Sea

North Magnetic Pole

Queen Elizabeth Islands

Ellesmere Island

Greenland

ALASKA RANGE

Banks Island

Amundsen Gulf

Baffin Bay

Kodiak I.

Gulf of Alaska

Victoria Island

Mackenzie R.

Baffin I.

Davis Strait

Arctic Circle

Cape Farewell

NORTH AMERICA

0   250   500 mi
0   250   500 km

Antarctica

Antarctic Circle

QUEEN MAUD LAND

South Shetland Is.

SOUTH AMERICA

Antarctic Peninsula

Weddell Sea

COATS LAND

Filchner Ice Shelf

ENDERBY LAND

Alexander I.

Ronne Ice Shelf

Berkner I.

SOUTH POLAR PLATEAU

Amery Ice Shelf

Bellingshausen Sea

Vinson Massif ▲ 16,067 ft. (4,897 m)

TRANSANTARCTIC MTS.

ANTARCTICA

South Pole

SOUTHERN OCEAN

Amundsen Sea

QUEEN MAUD MTS.

Ross Ice Shelf

WILKES LAND

Roosevelt I.

SOUTHERN OCEAN

Ross Sea

International Date Line

VICTORIA LAND

South Magnetic Pole

0   400   800 mi
0   400   800 km

KEY

Elevation

Feet		Meters
14,000		4,270
7,000		2,135
1,500		457
700		213
(sea level) 0		0 (sea level)

Ice pack

Ice shelf

Orthographic Projection

Glossary of Geographic Terms

basin
a depression in the surface of the land; some basins are filled with water

bay
a part of a sea or lake that extends into the land

butte
a small raised area of land with steep sides

▲ butte

canyon
a deep, narrow valley with steep sides; often has a stream flowing through it

cataract
a large waterfall; any strong flood or rush of water

◀ cataract

delta
a triangular-shaped plain at the mouth of a river, formed when sediment is deposited by flowing water

flood plain
a broad plain on either side of a river, formed when sediment settles on the riverbanks

glacier
a huge, slow-moving mass of snow and ice

hill
an area that rises above surrounding land and has a rounded top; lower and usually less steep than a mountain

island
an area of land completely surrounded by water

isthmus
a narrow strip of land that connects two larger areas of land

mesa
a high, flat-topped landform with cliff-like sides; larger than a butte

mountain
an area that rises steeply at least 2,000 feet (610 m) above surrounding land; usually wide at the bottom and rising to a narrow peak or ridge

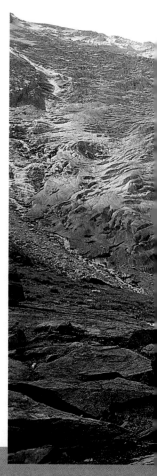

▶ glacier

◀ delta

mountain pass
a gap between mountains

peninsula
an area of land almost completely surrounded by water and connected to the mainland by an isthmus

plain
a large area of flat or gently rolling land

plateau
a large, flat area that rises above the surrounding land; at least one side has a steep slope

river mouth
the point where a river enters a lake or sea

strait
a narrow stretch of water that connects two larger bodies of water

tributary
a river or stream that flows into a larger river

volcano
an opening in the Earth's surface through which molten rock, ashes, and gasses from the Earth's interior escape

▶ volcano

Gazetteer

A

Alice Springs (23°S, 133°E) a town in Northern Territory, Australia, p. 180

Almaty (43°N, 77°E) the largest city of Kazakstan, a country in Central Asia, p. 125

Angkor Wat (13°N, 103°E) an archaeological site in present-day Angkor, in northwest Cambodia; the world's largest religious temple complex, p. 87

Aral Sea (45°N, 60°E), an inland saltwater sea in Kazakstan and Uzbekistan, p. 127

Auckland (36°S, 174°E) the largest city in New Zealand, located on North Island, p. 176

B

Bangladesh (24°N, 90°E) a coastal country in South Asia, officially the People's Republic of Bangladesh, p. 68

C

Canterbury Plain the lowland area of east-central South Island, New Zealand, p. 167

Central Asia a region in Asia including Kazakstan, Kyrgystan, Tajikistan, Turkmenistan, Uzbekistan, and others, p. 138

D

demilitarized zone (DMZ) a 150-mile-long strip separating North Korea and South Korea, p. 50

E

East Asia a region of Asia including China, Japan, Mongolia, North Korea, South Korea, and Taiwan, p. 32

Easter Island (26°S, 109°W) an island in the eastern Pacific Ocean, part of Polynesia; known for its giant human head statues, p. 172

Euphrates River a river that flows south from Turkey through Syria and Iraq; the ancient civilizations of Babylon and Ur were situated near its banks, p. 117

G

Galilee the northernmost region of ancient Palestine and present-day Israel, p. 146

Ganges River a river in India and Bangladesh flowing from the Himalaya Mountains to the Bay of Bengal; considered by Hindus to be the most holy river in India, p. 63

Ghat Mountains two mountain ranges forming the eastern and western edges of the Deccan Plateau in India, p. 67

Great Dividing Range a series of plateaus and mountain ranges in eastern Australia, p. 165

Great Wall of China a fortification wall which, with all its extensions, stretched 4,000 miles (6,400 km) through China; under construction from about 600 B.C. to A.D. 1600, p. 30

H

Himalaya Mountains the Central Asian mountain range extending along the India–Tibet border, through Pakistan, Nepal, and Bhutan, and containing the world's highest peaks, p. 10

Hindu Kush a mountain range in Central Asia, p. 117

Ho Chi Minh City (10°N, 106°E) the largest city in Vietnam, named for the President of North Vietnam; formerly Saigon, p. 104

Huang He the second-longest river in China; it flows across northern China to the Yellow Sea; also known as the Yellow River, p. 11

I

Indus River a river rising in Tibet and flowing through India and Pakistan into the Arabian Sea, p. 63

Iraq (32°N, 42°E) a country in Southwest Asia, officially the Republic of Iraq, p. 136

J

Java (8°S, 111°E) the fourth-largest island in the Republic of Indonesia, an archipelago in the Indian and Pacific oceans, p. 74

Jordan River a river in Southwest Asia flowing from Syria to the Dead Sea; Muslims, Jews, and Christians revere the Jordan, in whose waters Jesus was baptized, p. 146

K

Kashmir (39°N, 75°E) a disputed territory in northwest India, parts of which have been claimed by India, Pakistan, and China since 1947, p. 96

Kazakstan (48°N, 59°E) a country in Central Asia, officially the Republic of Kazakstan, p. 138

Kuwait (29°N, 48°E) a country in Southwest Asia, officially the Republic of Kuwait, p. 123

M

Mecca (21°N, 39°E) a city in western Saudi Arabia; birthplace of the prophet Muhammad and most holy city for Islamic people, p. 148

Mediterranean Sea the large sea that separates Europe and Africa, p. 117

Melanesia (13°S, 164°E) the most populous of the three groups of Pacific islands; includes Fiji, Papua New Guinea, and others, p. 168

Mesopotamia a historic region in western Asia between the Tigris and Euphrates rivers; one of the cradles of civilization, p. 133

Micronesia one of the three groups of Pacific islands; includes Guam, the Marshall Islands, and others, p. 168

Middle Kingdom the name given to China by its Chinese leaders, p. 30

Mount Everest (28°N, 86°E) the world's highest mountain peak, located in the Himalaya range in South Central Asia, p. 9

Mount Fuji (35°N, 138°E) the highest mountain in Japan; a dormant volcano and sacred symbol of Japan, p. 8

N

Negev Desert a triangular, arid region in southwest Israel, touching the Gulf of Aquaba, p. 143

North China Plain a large, fertile plain in northeastern China, p. 15

North Island (37°S, 173°E) the smaller and more northern of the two islands composing New Zealand, p. 166

O

Outback in general, a remote area with few people; specifically, the arid inland region of Australia, p. 165

P

Palestine (31°N, 35°E) a historical region at the east end of the Mediterranean Sea, now divided between Israel and Jordan, p. 137

Pamirs a mountain range in Central Asia, p. 117

Papua New Guinea (7°S, 142°E) an island country in the southwest Pacific; the eastern half of New Guinea, officially the Independent State of Papua New Guinea, p. 170

Philippines (14°N, 125°E) an island country in Southeast Asia, officially the Republic of the Philippines, p. 88

Polynesia largest of the three groups of Pacific islands, includes New Zealand, Hawaii, Easter, and Tahiti islands, p. 168

R

Ring of Fire the circle of volcanic activity surrounding the Pacific Ocean, includes North and South America, Japan, and Indonesia, p. 23

Riyadh (24°N, 46°E) the capital of Saudi Arabia, p. 149

Rub al-Khali the largest all-sand desert in the world, located on the Arabian peninsula; the "Empty Quarter," p. 115

S

Samarkand (39°N, 67°E) a city in Uzbekistan, p. 139

Semey (50°N, 80°E) a city in Kazakstan, p. 156

Seoul (37°N, 127°E) the capital of South Korea, p. 50

Silk Road a 4,000-mile-long ancient trade route linking China to the Mediterranean area in the west, p. 139

South Asia a region of Asia that includes Afghanistan, Bangladesh, Bhutan, India, Maldives, Nepal, Pakistan, and Sri Lanka, p. 61

Southeast Asia a region of Asia including Brunei, Cambodia, Indonesia, Laos, Malaysia, Myanmar (Burma), Philippines, Singapore, Thailand, Timor, and Vietnam, p. 64

South Island (42°S, 169°E) the larger and more southern of the two islands composing New Zealand, p. 166

Southwest Asia a region of Asia including Iran, Iraq, Israel, Jordan, Kuwait, Lebanon, Saudi Arabia, Syria, Turkey, and others, p. 134

Sydney (33°S, 151°E) the capital of New South Wales, on the southeastern coast of Australia, p. 178

T

Taiwan (23°N, 122°E) a large island country off the southeast coast of mainland China, formerly Formosa; since 1949, the Nationalist Republic of China, p. 43

Thailand (16°N, 101°E) a country in Southeast Asia, officially the Kingdom of Thailand, p. 72

Tigris River a river that flows through Turkey, Iraq, and Iran to the Persian Gulf; the ancient civilizations of Nineveh and Ur were situated near its banks, p. 117

V

Vietnam (18°N, 107°E) a country in Southeast Asia, officially the Socialist Republic of Vietnam, p. 68

Y

Yangzi the longest river in Asia, flowing through China to the East China Sea, p. 11

Glossary

This glossary lists key terms and other useful terms from the book.

A

ally a country joined with another for a special reason such as defense, p. 101

ancestor a parent of one's grandparents, great-grandparents, and so on, p. 31

aquaculture a cultivation of the sea; common crops are shrimp and oysters, p. 19

arable land land that can produce crops, p. 122

archipelago a group of islands, p. 11

artesian well a deep well drilled into the Earth to tap groundwater in porous rock, p. 180

artisan a highly trained or skilled worker, p. 105

atoll an island made of coral and shaped like a ring, p. 169

automotive industry an industry that puts together vehicles, such as cars, vans, pickup trucks, tractors, and motorcycles, p. 99

B

boycott a refusal to buy or use goods and services, p. 85

C

caravan a group of traders or others traveling together, p. 139

cash crop a crop raised to be sold for money on the world market, p. 73

caste a class of people in India, p. 82

civilization a society with cities, a central government, social classes, and, usually, writing, art, and architecture, p. 30

clan a group of families who claim a common ancestor, p. 31

collective a large farm created and owned by a national government, p. 140

colony a territory ruled by another nation, usually one far away, p. 85

commune a community in which land is held in common and where members live and work together, p. 35

communist of or relating to a government that owns a country's large industries, businesses, and most of the land, p. 34

coral a rocklike material made up of the skeletons of tiny sea creatures, p. 169

cultural diffusion a spreading of ideas and culture through the movement of people, p. 32

D

deciduous leaf-shedding; referring to trees that lose their leaves each year, such as maples and birches, p. 15

deity a god, p. 135

desalination the removal of salt from water, p. 144

desert a dry region that has extreme temperatures and little vegetation, p. 10

devastated destroyed; ruined, p. 103

developed country a country that has many industries and a well-developed economy, p. 18

developing country a country that has low industrial production and little modern technology, p. 18

dialect a version of a language found only in certain regions, p. 38

dictator a leader who has absolute power, p. 91

discrimination unfair treatment, often based on race or gender, p. 49

diversify in business, to extend activities into different areas, p. 53, 149

double-cropping growing two crops on the same land in a single year, p. 20

drought a long period without rain, p. 96

dynasty a series of rulers from the same family; Chinese history is described by dynasties, p. 30

E

emperor a ruler of widespread lands, p. 30

erosion a process by which water, wind, or ice wears away landforms and carries the material to another place, p. 145

ethnic group a group of people who share the same ancestors, culture, language, or religion, p. 39

export something sold to one country by another in trade, p. 18

F

famine a huge food shortage, p. 53

fertile containing substances that plants need in order to grow well; productive, p. 11

fiord a narrow bay or inlet from the sea bordered by steep cliffs, p. 167

free enterprise an economic system in which people are allowed to choose their own jobs, start private businesses, and make a profit, p. 43

G

geyser a hot spring that shoots scalding water into the air, p. 166

H

hajj the pilgrimage made by Muslims to Mecca, p. 148

high island a Pacific island that has been formed by a volcano and is usually mountainous, p. 169

homogeneous having similar members, in reference to a group, p. 39

hydroelectricity electric power that is produced by running water, usually with dams, p. 19

I

import something bought by one country from another in trade, p. 17

irrigate to supply dry land with water by using ditches or canals, p. 30

K

kibbutz a cooperative settlement found in Israel, p. 145

L

loess a brownish-yellow fertile soil found on the North China Plain, p. 11

low island a Pacific island that is a reef or small coral island in the shape of a ring, p. 169

M

marsupial an animal, such as the kangaroo or the koala, that carries its young in a body pouch, p. 164

migration a movement of people from one country or region to another, p. 31

monsoons the winds that blow across East Asia at certain times of the year; in summer, they are very wet; in winter, they are generally dry unless they have crossed warm ocean currents, p. 14

moshavim small farming villages in Israel, p. 145

mosque a Muslim place of worship, p. 155

muezzin a leader who summons Muslims to pray by chanting, p. 135

N

nationalist a person who is devoted to the interests of his or her country, p. 90

nomad a person who has no settled home; nomads move from place to place in search of water and grazing land for their animals, p. 38

nonrenewable resource a resource that cannot be replaced once it is used, p. 123

O

oasis a fertile place in a desert where water is available from an underground spring, p. 116

outlaw to make something illegal, p. 141

P

parliament a lawmaking body, p. 95

partition a division, p. 86

penal colony a place settled by convicts or prisoners; the British founded the first colony in Australia as a penal colony, p. 174

peninsula a body of land nearly surrounded by water, p. 12

petroleum an oily substance found under the Earth's crust; the source of gasoline and other fuels, p. 123

pilgrimage a trip to visit a special place, p. 148

plateau a raised area of mostly level land, p. 9

population density the average number of people living in an area, p. 12

purdah the practice of secluding women by covering their heads and faces with veils, especially in Islamic and some Hindu countries, p. 95

Q

quota a certain portion of something, such as jobs, set aside for a group, p. 94

R

radiation poisoning a sickness caused by exposure to radiation as a result of nuclear explosions, nuclear reactor accidents, or other causes, p. 156

radical extreme, p. 42

rain forest a thick forest that receives at least 60 inches (152 cm) of rain a year, p. 68

recession a period of time when an economy and the businesses that support it slow down, p. 48

refugee a person who flees his or her country because of war or armed conflict, p. 105

republic a type of government run by officials who represent the people being governed, p. 34

robot a computer-driven machine that does tasks once done by humans, p. 45

rural having to do with country areas as opposed to cities, p. 12

S

standard of living the material quality of life, p. 124

station in Australia, a very large sheep or cattle ranch, p. 175

steppe a treeless plain, p. 139

subcontinent a large landmass that is a major part of a continent; for example, the Indian subcontinent, p. 61

subsidize to economically support; some governments subsidize certain industries, p. 47

summit the very top, p. 9

surplus more than is needed, p. 72

T

technology the practical use of scientific principles, p. 122

tectonic plate a large piece of the Earth's crust, p. 164

terrace a level ledge cut into a steep hillside in order to grow crops, p. 20

textile cloth, p. 99

treaty a formal, legal agreement between countries, p. 103

typhoons violent storms that develop over the Pacific Ocean, p. 14

U

unified made into one; united, p. 31

W

wadi a waterway that fills up in the rainy season but is dry the rest of the year, p. 120

Index

Acknowledgments

Cover Design
Bruce Bond, Suzanne Schineller, and Olena Serbyn

Cover Photo
Jon Chomitz

Maps
MapQuest.com, Inc.
Map information sources: Columbia Encyclopedia, Encyclopaedia Britannica, Microsoft® Encarta®, National Geographic Atlas of the World, Rand McNally Commercial Atlas, The Times Atlas of the World.

Staff Credits
The people who made up the **World Explorer** team—representing editorial, editorial services, design services, on-line services/multimedia development, product marketing, production services, project office, and publishing processes—are listed below. Bold type denotes core team members.

Joyce Barisano, Margaret Broucek, **Paul Gagnon, Mary Hanisco, Dotti Marshall,** Kirsten Richert, Susan Swan, and Carol Signorino.

Additional Credits
Art and Design: Emily Soltanoff. Editorial: Debra Reardon, Nancy Rogier. Market Research: Marilyn Leitao. Publishing Processes: Wendy Bohannan.

Program Development and Production
Editorial and Project Management: Summer Street Press
Production: Pronk&Associates

Text
8, From *Living Japan* by Donald Keene. Copyright © 1959, published by Doubleday & Company, Inc. 50, From "South Korea: A Time of Testing," by Kevin Buckley, *Geo* magazine, April 1980. 58, From *An Introduction to Haiku* by Harold G. Henderson. Copyright © 1958 by Harold G. Henderson. Used by permission of Doubleday, a division of Bantam Doubleday Dell Publishing Group, Inc. 59, "The Birth of a Stone," by Kwang-kyu Kim, from *Faint Shadows of Love*, translated by Brother Anthony, of Taizé (London: Forest Books, 1991). Original poem copyright © by Kwang-kyu Kim 1983, translation copyright © by Brother Anthony 1991. 102, From "Vietnam Now," by Stanley Karnow, *Smithsonian Magazine*, January 1996. 110, Excerpt from *The Clay Marble* by Minfong Ho. Copyright © 1991 by Minfong Ho. Reprinted by permission of Farrar, Straus & Giroux, Inc. 136, From *Voices from Kurdistan*, edited by Rachel Warner. Copyright © 1991 by the Minority Rights Group. Reprinted with permission of the Minority Rights Group. 151, 152, From *We Live in Saudi Arabia* by Abdul Latif Al Hoad. Copyright © 1986 by Wayland Publishers, Ltd. Reprinted with permission of Wayland Publishers Ltd. 154, 155, From "Kazakhstan: Facing the Nightmare," by Mike Edwards, *National Geographic*, March 1993. Copyright © 1993 by the National Geographic Society. Reprinted by permission of the National Geographic Society.

Photo Research
Feldman & Associates, Inc.

Photos
iv bottom left, © Matthew Neal McVay/Tony Stone Images, iv center left, © Cary Wolinsky/Tony Stone Images, v top right, Erich Lessing/Art Resource, v center left, Zigy Kaluzny/Tony Stone Images, v bottom, © Jerry Alexander/ Tony Stone Images, 1 background, © Artbase Inc., 1 center Andrea Booher/Tony Stone Images 5 top right, © Mark Thayer, Boston, 6 bottom, © Art Wolfe/Tony Stone Images, 8 center right, © Wendy Chan/The Image Bank, 9 bottom right, © Scott Fisher/Woodfin Camp & Associates, 12 top right, © Deke Erh/Woodfin Camp & Associates, 13 bottom right, © Dave Bartruff/Artistry International, 15 top right, © Musee Guimet, Paris, France/Lauros-Giraudon, 16 top right, © Reuters/ Will Burgess/Archive Photos, 17 bottom right, © D. E. Cox/Tony Stone Images, 19 bottom left, © Ettagale Blauer/Woodfin Camp & Associates, 19 bottom right, © Mark Lewis/Tony Stone Images, 20 center right, © Karen Kasmauski/Woodfin Camp & Associates, 20 bottom, © Wolfgang Kaehler/ Wolfgang Kaehler Photography, 21 top left, © Baldev/SYGMA, 22 bottom, © Michael Newman/PhotoEdit, 23 bottom right, © Greg Vaughn/ Tony Stone Images, 26 bottom, © Howard Sochurek/Woodfin Camp & Associates, 28 center right, © Mike Surowiak/Tony Stone Images, 29 bottom right, © Vanni/Art Resource, 31 center right, © Lee Boltin/Boltin Picture Library, 35 bottom right, © Cary Wolinsky/Tony Stone Images, 36 top right, © A. Ramey/Woodfin Camp & Associates, 37 bottom, © Matthew Neal McVay/Tony Stone Images, 39 top left, Untitled, by Chen Di, age 12, China. Courtesy of the International Children's Art Museum, 40 bottom left, © D. E. Cox/Tony Stone Images, 41 center left, Ric Ergenbright/CORBIS/MAGMA, 42 bottom right, © William Sewell/E.T. Archive, 45 bottom right, © Karen Kasmauski/Woodfin Camp & Associates, 46 center left, Michael S. Yamashita/CORBIS/MAGMA, 47 top left, © AP/Wide World Photos, 48 bottom, © Ettagale Blauer/Laure' Communications, 49 center, © Cameramann International, Ltd., 50 bottom left, © SuperStock International, 52 top, © Kim Newton/Woodfin Camp & Associates, 54 center right, © Philadelphia Free Library/SuperStock International, 58 bottom right, © Janette Ostier Gallery, Paris France/ SuperStock International, 59 top left, © Corbis-Bettman, 60 center right, © Photri, 61 bottom right, © D. Jenkin/Tropix Photographic Library, 64 center left, © Chuck O'Rear/Woodfin Camp & Associates, 65 bottom right, © Jason Laure'/Laure' Communications, 68 top, In the Park, by Atima, age 11, India. Courtesy of the International Children's Art Museum, 69 top left, © Wolfgang Kaehler/Wolfgang Kaehler Photography, 69 top right, © M. Aukland/Tropix Photographic Library, 70 bottom, © Wolfgang Kaehler/Wolfgang Kaehler Photography, 71 bottom left, © Charles Preitner/Visuals Unlimited, 71 bottom right, © Christopher Arnesen/Tony Stone Images, 72 bottom, © Robert Frerck/Woodfin Camp & Associates, 73 top right, © Robert Frerck/Woodfin Camp & Associates, 75 top left, © Mickey Gibson/Animals Animals, 80 center right, © Brian Vikander/CORBIS/MAGMA, 81 bottom right, © Dilip Mehta/Woodfin Camp & Associates, 84 bottom right, © M.M.N./Dinodia Picture Agency, 84 bottom left, © Cameramann International, 85 top, © Wolfgang Kaehler/Wolfgang Kaehler Photography, 86 top right, © SuperStock International, 87 bottom, © Jerry Alexander/Tony Stone Images, 88 top, © Mike Yamashita/Woodfin Camp & Associates, 88 bottom, © Steve Vidler/Tony Stone Images, 90 bottom right, © UPI/Corbis-Bettman, 91 top, © AP/Wide World Photos, 92 bottom left, © Ann & Bury Peerless/Ann & Bury Peerless, 93 center right, © Eye Ubiqitous/ CORBIS/MAGMA, 94 bottom right, © Steve Vidler/Tony Stone Images, 94 bottom left, © Joel Simon/Tony Stone Images, 95 top center, © Jason Laure'/Laure' Communications, 96 bottom left, © SuperStock International, 97 bottom right, Roger Wood/CORBIS/MAGMA, 98 bottom right, © Charles Preitner/Visuals Unlimited, 99 top left, © D Forbert/ Photri, 100 top right, © Photri, 101 bottom right, © Natalie Fobes/ Tony Stone Images, 102 center, Bohemian Nomad Picturemakers/ CORBIS/MAGMA, 103 top left, © Arthur R. Hill/Visuals Unlimited, 104 bottom left, © Radhika Chalasani/Gamma Liaison International, 105 top left, © Wolfgang Kaehler/Wolfgang Kaehler Photography, 111 top left, © Leah Melnick/Impact Visuals, 112 top right, © SuperStock International, 114 center left, © Tom Till/Tony Stone Images, 115 bottom right, © Tony Howarth/Woodfin Camp & Associates, 117 bottom left, © Buddy Mays/Travel Stock, 117 center right, © Cameramann International, Ltd., 118 top right, © Zeynep Sumen/Tony Stone Images, 119 bottom right, © D. Jenkin/Tropix Photographic Library, 121 top left, © Wayland